Mark Challenges
the *Aeneid*

Mark Challenges the *Aeneid*

∾

Floyd E. Schneider

WIPF & STOCK · Eugene, Oregon

MARK CHALLENGES THE *AENEID*

Wipf & Stock
An Imprint of Wipf and Stock Publishers
199 W. 8th Ave., Suite 3
Eugene, OR 97401

www.wipfandstock.com

PAPERBACK ISBN: 978-1-5326-9063-1
HARDCOVER ISBN: 978-1-5326-9064-8
EBOOK ISBN: 978-1-5326-9065-5

Manufactured in the U.S.A.   DECEMBER 11, 2019

Dedications

To Christine, the best friend and wife God could have ever given me, for her discovering the topic and tolerating everything that followed. Are we done yet?

To Jennifer, for her never-ending exuberance during the entire journey.

Epigraph

"This man really was God's Son!" –Roman centurion

CONTENTS

Acknowledgments

David Sanford, for encouraging me to seek out a publisher for this book.

1

Read This!

It Will Make Sense of Everything Else

THIS BOOK WILL MAKE no sense to the reader unless the reader knows something about the Roman emperor, Augustus, his famous poet, Virgil, and Virgil's famous poem, the *Aeneid*. So, I'm taking the liberty of giving you a very short overview.

Have you ever watched the movie, *Troy*? The plot is simple, at least to the Greeks and Romans. The Greeks were upset that the goddess, Aphrodite (Greek name)/Venus (Roman name), had given Helen to Paris, a Trojan prince. Helen was the wife of Greek King Menelaos of Sparta. Menelaos asked his brother, King Agamemnon of Mycenae, for help. Agamemnon laid siege to Troy for ten years, but finally sent in a wooden horse full of Greek warriors who killed lots of Trojans, took the city, and recovered Helen.

Why did Venus give Helen to Paris? That's a bit complicated. A wedding was taking place, and an uninvited witch showed up to present a golden apple to the most beautiful goddess in the world. The Trojan prince, Paris, had to decide which of three goddesses was the most beautiful and would get the apple. He should have turned down the offer, but he was young. The three goddesses were Aphrodite, Athena, and Hera. The Romans renamed them Venus, Minerva, and Juno. Since our story ends up in the Roman world, we'll use their Latin names.

Paris viewed each one, but couldn't decide, so all three goddesses stripped nude to give him a better view of their beauty. He still couldn't decide, so each goddess offered to bribe Paris with what each goddess knew best. Juno offered to make him king of Europe and Asia. Minerva offered him wisdom and skill in war. She was never considered sexy. Venus, the goddess of sexuality, offered him the world's most beautiful woman, who was Helen, the forenamed wife of Menelaos. Paris chose Helen. Juno and Minerva went ballistic and sided with the Greeks to help them destroy the Trojans at Troy.

Have you ever heard of the Trojan, Aeneas? His mother was the goddess, Venus. His father, Anchises, was human. Her son, Aeneas, was a warrior when the Greeks attacked Troy, but he escaped with a handful of men, along with his father and son, Ascanius. He lost his wife, Creusa, in the battle.

Ever heard of Virgil? He was a Roman poet (70–19 BC). He wrote a twelve-chapter mythical poem about Augustus (63 BC–19 AD), Rome's most important and powerful emperor.

What was the *Aeneid* about? Here's the storyline.

The Trojan Aeneas escapes from Troy by ship. Remember Juno, the goddess who wanted the golden apple, didn't get it, and hates Trojans? As Aeneas is escaping, she attempts to sink his ships. She fails because Venus pulls in Jupiter's help to save Aeneas. At that point Jupiter, the highest god (though not super intelligent since he married Juno) prophesies that Aeneas will reach Italy, found an empire, and that a future emperor, Augustus, will bring peace to the world (*Aeneid*, Book 1, line 288).

Aeneas does sail for Rome, but they get sidetracked in Carthage, North Africa, where Dido, the queen and founder of Carthage welcomes them. Aeneas tells her his tragic story. He had lost his father along the way.

Dido is a Phoenician princess who escaped a similar situation. She and Aeneas fall in love with each other. Dido sleeps with Aeneas and believes that sex is equal to marriage. She wants to keep Aeneas in Carthage. The god, Mercury, shows up and reminds Aeneas of his destiny to found Rome. Aeneas flees with his ships. Dido commits suicide. That's the first half of Virgil's poem.

Juno continually tries to destroy Aeneas, or at least keep him waylaid, but Anchises, Aeneas's father, appears to him in a dream to encourage him to reach Italy. Aeneas finally reaches Italy, and then takes a side trip down into the underworld to visit his father. The sibyl of Cumae guides him, and he sees the future history and heroes of Rome. Romulus, the eventual founder of Rome, and Augustus appear in that line of future Roman heroes. Aeneas is informed that Augustus is the promised son of the deified who will make a Golden Age again and extend the empire far beyond Italy (*Aeneid*, Book 6, line 792). Remember that Aeneas himself is the son of a goddess, Venus.

Aeneas says goodbye to his father and returns to his men and ships. They sail to the coastal region of Latium. King Latinus, the Italian ruler, welcomes them. Latinus had received a prophecy that his daughter, Latinia, was supposed to marry a foreigner, and Aeneas fits the bill. Latinus's wife, Amata, disagrees. She wants Latinis to marry Turnus, a local warrior. Juno opens the Gates of Wars.

The most important events during this war center on Venus providing Aeneas with some special weapons, especially the shield, which was obviously magical. The pictures on the shield portrayed scenes of early Rome, which included Romulus, the Battle of Actium, and Augustus, who won that famous and decisive battle to bring all of Rome under his control. The shield put Augustus in the center of the senate, the people, the household gods and the great gods of the Roman Empire (*Aeneid*, Book 8, line 678).

By now, it has become obvious to Aeneas, that he will be the forerunner of Augustus, the future emperor of Rome, who will bring peace to the world, who will be the son of god, and whose image captures the middle of the magic shield provided to Aeneas by his mother, Venus.

Aeneas seeks help from the neighboring tribes further north up the coast. During this trip, Venus, his mother, gives him some powerful new weapons, one being that special shield made by Vulcan.

When Aeneas returns to Latium, Turnus's army is winning the battle. Pallas, the son of Aeneas's newest ally Evander, is killed by Turnus. Lots of people die. A truce is called so they can bury the dead, and most of the Latins want the war to stop. They suggest a hand-to-hand combat between Aeneas and Turnus. That doesn't work out right away, and the war starts up again. Aeneas is wounded in the leg, but he is miraculously healed (Venus, his mother helped), and his troops eventually threaten the enemy's capital city.

News gets back to Amata, Latinus's wife and Latinia's mother, that Turnus has been killed, and Amata hangs herself.

Turnus wasn't dead yet after all, and he and Aeneas finally meet in one-on-one combat. Aeneas, with his special weapons, wounds Turnus. Aeneas almost decides to spare Turnus's life, but Aeneas thinks of Palas and kills Turnus instead. The end.

With that background in view, I've chosen to write Mark's response to the *Aeneid* before presenting all the evidence that supports that response. I will present Mark's direct challenge to *Aeneid*'s message and Mark's contextualization of the gospel for his Roman readers.

I believe that Mark's challenge to the *Aeneid* is more important for the general reader, including pastors and professors than the research details supporting it. If you are a fanatic for research details and want to read everything that led me to my conclusions, please read the rest of the book, which lays out the background for Mark's challenge. In this background I have included chapters that cover Greek and Roman mythology, Virgil, and Augustus. If you know all about Roman history, Augustus, and Virgil, then skip these chapters. The supporting evidence for 1) the *Aeneid*'s importance as seen by its width and depth of dissemination throughout the Roman Empire and beyond, 2) the fourteen pieces of cumulative evidence that support the undeniable conclusion that Mark had access to and knowledge of the *Aeneid*, and 3) the flow of Mark's text, along with ten theological themes, bring the reader back around to the conclusion that Mark wrote his Gospel to challenge the *Aeneid*.

The brief bibliography at the end should guide the reader toward the key supporting materials for this study.

Virgil wrote the *Aeneid* as Rome's preeminent piece of propaganda that Augustus was a son of god, and that Rome was superior to all other empires. The *Aeneid* had become so prominent throughout the entire Roman Empire, from northern Britain to southern Israel, and so entrenched in Roman culture, that it became a foundation stone for the education of Roman children. This dissemination and depth of the *Aeneid* surpassed anyone's expectations.

Every Roman and many non-Romans knew every line in the *Aeneid*. Mark wrote his Gospel for the purpose of intertextuality. This is just a long word for connections. One sees connections between two texts and interprets one in light of the other. Literary techniques used allusion, quotations, plagiarism, and parody.

Mark wanted the Romans (and anyone else) to connect his gospel with the *Aeneid*. He wanted them to "see" the allusions and contrasts between Aeneas and John the Baptist, but especially between Augustus and Jesus. Mark contextualized his gospel for the Romans.

The apostles in the New Testament had a similar experience after the resurrection of Jesus when they began to see all the intertextual allusions and typology in the Old Testament as these played out in the events and teachings they had experienced during their three years with Jesus.

Chapter 3 will compare the text of Mark's Gospel with the text of the *Aeneid*. The contrasts between the texts will show how Mark connected his Gospel with the *Aeneid*, challenged the *Aeneid*'s propaganda that Augustus was the son of god, and sought to replace the worship of Augustus with the worship of Jesus.

The rest of the book supports the conclusions that, before Mark's time, the *Aeneid* had spread throughout the Roman world, and that Mark had knowledge of and access to the *Aeneid*.

Some scholars will read my dissertation and disagree with my conclusions. I openly admit that I may have drawn some wrong conclusions. I welcome any feedback, negative or positive, on my research, the flow of my argument, my use of what evidence I believe to have discovered, and my conclusions. If the reader finds a passage in this book that appears to be overly dogmatic, please make a note at that point and refer back to this paragraph. Be kind.

Almost every name or object in this book can be discovered by Googling it. The internet has changed how scholars do research and report their research. Many scholars and universities have resorted to putting their research on websites due to the high cost of publishing books and journals. I have taken the liberty of including very few footnotes in this book, but at the end of this book, I have included the sources that influenced my conclusions the most.

Almost every assertion in this book was supported by a footnote in my dissertation. My first reader on my dissertation committee commented that I had certainly used enough footnotes. I have spared you the tediousness of feeling guilty that you don't want to read three lines of text and sixty lines of font-10 footnotes, but I want you to know that the facts are, indeed, facts.

If a reader desires to find any sources I have not included in this book, the reader will need to find that author in the bibliography of my dissertation and read that author's book or journal article.

If anyone wants to read my dissertation, *Mark's Gospel Compared with Virgil's Aeneid*, here's the link: https://digitalcommons.liberty.edu/doctoral/1641/.

Did Mark write his Gospel to challenge the *Aeneid*? This book presents the author's view of how the evidence gives a resounding "yes!" to that question. Part of the answer begins in chapter seven and shows the contrasts between the theology of the *Aeneid* and Mark's Gospel.

Mark's theological engagement and challenge of the *Aeneid* presents a very profound contextualization of the gospel. The Gospel of Mark, experienced through the mind of the Romans, challenged their culture, their philosophies, their religions, and ultimately, Augustus himself, as their supreme savior, and by extension, all the Caesars. Mark wrote for the Romans, and he did it well.

Most Romans had read and studied the *Aeneid* long before they were confronted with Mark's Gospel. They experienced the gospel through the *Aeneid*. Missionaries today would do well to study the literature of their target peoples before presenting the gospel through their own culture.

Readers today have not been immersed in the *Aeneid*, and certainly not in the myriad of gods and goddess of the Greeks and the Romans. If you know nothing of those worlds, then you will struggle to understand some of the references to those worlds. What makes this mind-boggling is the affirmation that the Holy Spirit through Mark used the premier Roman propaganda to teach the gospel of Jesus Christ.

2

What and Why

I NEVER INTENDED TO write on this subject, since I knew absolutely nothing about it until my wife, Christine, asked me if I had ever heard of the *Aeneid*. She had been leading one of her on-going Bible studies in Mark's Gospel and was always looking for new information and new approaches to teaching her Bible studies.

"Have you ever read the *Aeneid*?" Christine was leafing through a book she had pulled off the bookshelf in the bookstore we had invaded during lunch time at Cannon Beach, OR.

"The what?"

"The *Aeneid*. Virgil's epic poem during the Roman Empire."

"Who's Virgil?"

She rolled her eyes. "Have you ever wondered what the Roman *believers* were reading at the time Mark wrote his Gospel?

"Uh, no."

Her mind left me and wandered further into the world of Rome. "What if they were reading the *Aeneid*?" she mumbled. She returned to my world. "Maybe you should write about Mark's connection to Virgil."

"How could that be important?"

"Well, if they were reading the *Aeneid*, then the Roman worldview would have influenced how they would have digested Mark's Gospel. And Mark could have written his gospel to counteract the Roman view of reality."

When I raised the question to my advisor, she handed me three books as my starting point and told me to research the universe to see what had already been published on the possible connection between the *Aeneid* and Mark's Gospel. I had to answer two questions: 1) how broad and deeply the *Aeneid* had been assimilated into the Roman Empire and beyond, and 2) how much access and knowledge Mark had of the *Aeneid*.

Working thirty-six hours a day for two months I discovered that I knew next to nothing of serious importance about the Roman Empire, its prolific poets, or the vast amount of Latin literature that permeated it. More importantly, no one had written on any connection between the Gospel of Mark and the *Aeneid*.

My advisor was dumbfounded. She informed me that I had probably discovered a "hole in the literature."

Like a black hole, I wondered. I doubted seriously that my PhD chair at Liberty University would accept a dissertation based on science fiction. My advisor told me to guard my topic closely until I had either failed or succeeded in producing a final dissertation on the subject. A "hole in the literature" is a gold mine for aspiring scholars. People steal gold.

Eight months later I had read so much about the Roman Empire that I began to forget things as they got pushed out by more incoming information. Edward Gibbon's six volumes on the *Rise and Fall of the Roman Empire* launched me into a world that I barely remember hearing about in undergraduate and graduate school. Then I read Mary Beard's book, *SPQR: A History of Ancient Rome*, and discovered that a lot of what Gibbon had presented as historical fact fell short of real evidence. Her book sparked a desire in me to know everything about Roman history. Failure comes from setting one's goals too high.

I began to realize that the oral and written history of the Roman Empire had been built on a mixture of fact and myth, and one was less certain about the facts than the myths.

I also discovered that a large portion of Roman history and literature has fallen out of common knowledge. Very few people even knew who I was talking about when they asked me what my dissertation topic was about. I felt that I had to keep it a secret, but soon discovered that most people wouldn't have understood anything I was reading anyway. So instead of trying to educate them in some lost history, I kept it secret and allowed them to think that I was doing research for the CIA.

After flooding my mind with the breadth of the Roman Empire, I began to dig deep into Virgil's world and his writings. (Who is Virgil? We'll get there.) The breadth of Roman literature overwhelmed me. I had not been raised on Greek and Latin books. Even Hebrew and Greek classes in seminary had not prepared me for the wealth and beauty of the classics. I found it difficult to stay focused on just the *Aeneid* and not get sidetracked chasing down a Sybil[1] who could tell me if this dissertation was worth pursuing or fighting off a Roman goddess who simply changed her name after stealing her identity from the Greeks.

My original two questions morphed into four questions:

1) How widely had the *Aeneid* been disseminated? Italy alone? Great Britain? Saudi Arabia?

2) How deeply into society had the *Aeneid* been embedded? Just the upper-class elite? The common Roman soldier? Roman children?

3) Did Mark have knowledge of and access to the *Aeneid*? None? A passing knowledge? Did he encounter it in the local church in Rome?

4) If Mark did have access to the *Aeneid*, how did he respond to it? Dismissed it with a wave of his hand? Taught it in Sunday School class as a fairy tale? Challenged it?

I found the answers to these questions.

The *Aeneid* has been *the* classic of European poetry for a millennium and a half since its unprecedented fame during the first century BC. It has soaked the English-speaking world in the thought that Virgil, the author of the *Aeneid*, was a natural Christian, and we rewrote his history and our theology to believe that was true.

We've lost it. If you read literature written before 1900, you can find many allusions and mentions of the *Aeneid*. But few people today have ever heard of Virgil and his famous poem. Common knowledge of nineteen hundred years of Virgil's influence has evaporated into the mists of lost literature. Only a few diehards in the Latin departments of dusty professors' offices still struggle to inform and inspire students who need an extra elective to graduate in chemistry or finance. So, it would be good to review what escaped: the world of Rome, Virgil, Augustus, and the *Aeneid*.

Roman religion, Augustus, and Virgil weave a tapestry of relationships that produced the most significant piece of propaganda, the *Aeneid*, in written history. Virgil could never have planned the breadth and depth that his most famous poem reached throughout the Roman Empire and how it influenced the rest of the world through the next twenty centuries. Almost immediately after its publication, the *Aeneid* permeated the

1. https://www.britannica.com/topic/Sibyl-Greek-legendary-figure.

entire Roman Empire from Masada to Hadrian's northern Britain and penetrated Roman society down into the everyday children's school lessons. The perfect timing of the life of Jesus during this era and Mark's access and knowledge of the *Aeneid* created the perfect environment for writing the first rebuttal of the world-dominating pagan religion of the Romans.

Then, we will piece together a tapestry of diverse but necessary artifacts in order to reconstruct the Roman world and Mark's connection with it.

The dating of Mark's Gospel has been thoroughly researched elsewhere. Although determining the reliability and early date for the Gospel of Mark would be valuable, that topic is not a vital part of the evidence. The theology of the *Aeneid* was fixed in time when it was published. Although the emperors came and went with the normal flow of despots replacing despots, the concepts, categories, and theology of the *Aeneid* remained unchanged. If Mark addressed the theology of the *Aeneid* early or late, that would make no difference in his comparisons between the message of the *Aeneid* and the message of the gospel. This book will accept the highly probable position that John Mark, who traveled with Paul and Barnabas, and later with Peter in Rome, wrote the Gospel of Mark.

The apostle Peter may or may not have had access to the *Aeneid*, but that has no crucial bearing on Mark's ability to interact with the theology of the *Aeneid*. If Peter had had access to the *Aeneid*, certainly he and Mark would have discussed it, but the emphasis of this book is the connection between the theology of Mark's Gospel and the *Aeneid*, regardless of Peter's involvement.

As stated above, nothing until now has been written connecting the *Aeneid* with the Gospel of Mark. New Testament scholarship has revealed that both the Jewish and the Roman worlds were the two major audiences of Mark's Gospel. Much has been written about the Jewish world connection to Mark's Gospel, some of which is directly relevant to the audience of the Roman world. Many scholars have written about every aspect found in this book, however, neither New Testament nor classical humanities scholarship has adequately researched Mark's connection with the Roman world as seen through the eyes of Virgil's *Aeneid*. It's like a dart board. All the darts hit the big target, but none of them ever hit the bullseye.

3

The Gospel of Mark

His Challenge to the Aeneid

MARK WROTE HIS GOSPEL to challenge Virgil's message that Augustus would fulfill Rome's destiny and Augustus would eventually take his place among the other emperors as a son of god. Mark presents and compares the message of Jesus Christ as he announces the kingdom of God to Jews and Romans alike.

Mark's Gospel reveals God's King, God's own Son, Jesus, as a humble servant who came to serve humanity by dying for their sins and offers the proof of his kingship by performing miracles normal human kings could not carry out. Whereas Augustus received vindication for his kingship by winning wars, Jesus intentionally allowed himself to be crucified by the Romans and postponed his vindication as king until after his death by rising from the dead. Augustus's attempt to further his kingship by establishing an heir eventually failed. Augustus had no control over the future of the Roman Empire after he died. Jesus's resurrection nullified the necessity of seeking a successor. The King had died but had risen from the dead. No one would have to replace him for all of eternity.

As we compare Mark with the *Aeneid*, we need to ask ourselves: Why would Mark *not* aggressively evangelize against the most important piece of contemporary Roman propaganda? Believers in every age have refuted false teaching of other religions and heresy within the church, especially within one's own country. Every generation has one or more prominent religious or philosophical ideas that contradict the Bible, and everyone knows those ideas. It can be taken as a fact that every Roman and non-Roman was well-acquainted with the *Aeneid*, therefore it can also be taken as a fact that Mark knew everybody was well-acquainted with the *Aeneid*, especially since every good Roman was expected to know about it, to believe it, to follow it, and to worship the Roman gods, especially Julius and Augustus.

In this section, we will demonstrate from Mark's Gospel further evidence that one of the reasons he wrote it was to be a blatant challenge to the *Aeneid*. The reader will discover how Mark did that throughout his text, with his style of indirect insinuations, mysteries, and direct challenges to the theology of the *Aeneid* without having to name the poem directly.

Following the *Aeneid's* extensive and deep distribution, and Mark's knowledge and access to the *Aeneid*, how did Mark address the theology of the *Aeneid*? Virgil, who wrote the *Aeneid*, presented Augustus as the pious son, priestly son and founding son of god. In direct contrast to the *Aeneid*, the book of Hebrews gives Jesus those three distinctions. The writer of Hebrews challenged the theology of the *Aeneid* by direct comparison with Jesus.

Mark used the same approach to challenge the *Aeneid*. He attacked the *Aeneid's* statements and theology. The wide span and deep penetration of the *Aeneid* in all areas of Roman life, culture, education, and religion had embedded the wording, concepts, and religious ideas of the *Aeneid* in the minds of the Romans. When a Roman read the *Aeneid* and then read Mark's Gospel, that Roman could not have missed the similarities and contrasts between the theologies of those two pieces of literature.

This occurs all the time. We hear a word or phrase that reminds us of something completely different. When Jesus said that the meek will inherit the earth, the church fathers immediately thought about Moses.

The Greeks studied Homer's works of the *Iliad* and the *Odyssey*, the backbone of the Greek-speaking world. The church fathers were equally steeped in Greek cultures, and what they were taught in Homer and Virgil affected how they read Scripture. When the Scriptures were read to them, Homer's harmonies, melodies, narrative connections, and allusions instantly jumped off the page to the listener to present comparisons and an alternative belief system.

We listen to a song on iTunes and later a short phrase from a completely different context brings that song back to mind. The same thing happened when people read Mark's Gospel. Their thoughts were steered toward the *Aeneid*.

In order to determine how well a reader of the *Aeneid* would recognize the similarities and contrasts between the *Aeneid* and Mark's Gospel, we need to make direct comparisons of the two texts. The church today is no longer familiar with the *Aeneid* as the Romans were during the first two centuries. Some may think, "I don't see the comparisons," but the more one reads and re-reads the *Aeneid*, the more and more contrasts materialize as obvious. And because the *Aeneid* was Rome's most important piece of propaganda, the Gospel of Mark became a major attack on the divinity of Augustus and all following Caesars.

Virgil and Mark stand opposite one another. Virgil presents the mythical Aeneas as the forerunner of Augustus, a human son of God. Mark addresses the same theme of a forerunner and a human son of God, but Mark directs the reader's attention to a different kind of forerunner in the historical John the Baptist and the historical Jesus, the Son of God.

Both the *Aeneid* and Mark's Gospel open with a forerunner. Aeneas, the mythical founder of the Roman race, will precede Augustus. They are connected by lineage. John the Baptist will establish no race or kingdom. His lineage is irrelevant in comparison to the lineage of the coming King. He will do no more than announce the coming King. Both forerunners will attempt to convince the readers of the deity of their respective Kings, Augustus having been deified, while Jesus came as the eternal King.

Augustus and Jesus, the most important performers on the stage of history, stand opposite one another. Augustus will use human wisdom and power to make Rome's destiny a political reality, while Jesus will use the weakness of the cross to save the world from their sins. Augustus will reform the realm through deceit and war, but Jesus will transform souls through truth and peace with God. Augustus will display outward strength but inward evil and sinfulness. Jesus will stand up to and confront his enemies by demanding that they show him where he has sinned, which they cannot do. Augustus will establish his temporal kingdom and die. Jesus will die, rise from the dead, and begin establishing the first part of his eternal kingdom during this age.

Ultimately Jesus will outshine Augustus. Jesus died. So did Augustus. Jesus rose from the dead. Augustus did not. Mark will address the issues that will compare the answers to two decisive questions. His Gospel will ask: "Who is Jesus, and what is his agenda?" The *Aeneid* asks: "Who is Augustus, and what is his agenda?"

These questions require scrutinizing both texts for similarities and contrasts. I will use two approaches to develop what the texts reveal. I will first compare the *flow of the text* of the *Aeneid* with the *flow of the text* of Mark's Gospel at the beginning of Mark, as well as noting the middle point and end point of each text.

The *Aeneid* was divided into twelve distinct chapters. Mark wrote no such clear chapters into his text. Chapters and verses were not part of the original manuscripts. Therefore, I will lay out a comparison of the content and concepts between the two texts in a linear fashion of what came first, then second, etc.

Dozens of comparisons exist between these two pieces of literature. I see more every time I read both texts. I cannot address every comparison. I continue to see more comparisons, and I have to stop somewhere. Once the reader catches on to seeing the connections, others will begin to appear.

The second approach will take longer. I will compare a select number of different themes and theologies of the two texts. As I have continued to research this subject, I have realized that it will be impossible to uncover all the connections between the *Aeneid* and Mark's Gospel in this one book.

Let's do this!

4

The Flow of the Texts

The Beginning of Mark's Gospel

THE BEGINNING OF MARK offers the first and direct engagement with the *Aeneid*. The very first verse, "The beginning of the gospel of Jesus Christ, the Son of God," connects directly with the opening verse to Augustus Priene Calendar Inscription[1], around 9 BC. (Read the article in the footnote.)

The epithet "son of god" had other definitions in addition to deity. Augustus's Golden Age (14 AD) was over by the time Mark wrote his Gospel (mid-sixties). Mark could have been comparing his Gospel with all the emperors who followed Augustus, since they all became more and more decadent and violent, even though each one had been given the title, "son of God."

However, none of that negates Mark's purpose of writing a text that challenged the *Aeneid*, which was still impacting the Roman world as its main piece of propaganda. In addition, the Romans always worshipped their past Caesars who had been deified. The divine Augustus was still worshipped by every Roman while Mark was writing his Gospel.

The opening line of Mark 1 contains no verb: "The beginning of the Gospel of Jesus Christ Son of God." Thus, this first line is a title and also a summary of the entire book. Mark now has to prove that there are two points of the good news: Jesus is the promised Messiah, the Christ, and Jesus is the Son of God. Mark fulfills both assignments.

---

1. http://earlywritings.com/forum/viewtopic.php?t=3255.

In Mark 8:29 Peter, the prominent Jewish member of the disciples, had his eyes opened: "But you," Jesus asked them again, "who do you say that I am?" Peter answered him, "You are the Messiah." In Mark 15:39, as Jesus finished his sacrifice, the Roman centurion, who probably directed the crucifixion of Jesus, had been stunned by "the way He breathed His last."

Mark always comes right to the point, never adding what he considers unnecessary to make his point. John 19:30 reveals that Jesus's last utterance was a victory cry: "It is finished!" That centurion heard that victory cry. Romans yelled victory when they had won a battle. A crucified criminal was the least likely person to be celebrating anything. Obviously, the entire crucifixion, and especially his exit, made the opposite impression on that centurion. "This man really was God's Son." Not Augustus of the *Aeneid*.

The opening line of the *Aeneid* begins with the description of a warrior who has lost a battle because the gods were against him.

> I sing of arms and the man, he who, exiled by fate,
> first came from the coast of Troy to Italy, and to
> Lavinian shores—hurled about endlessly by land and sea, by the
> will of the gods, by cruel Juno's remorseless anger.[2]

The contrast is extreme between "Jesus the Messiah and Son of God" and an exile chased off by the gods. Aeneas had been rejected and exiled by the Greeks, his enemies. Jesus would be portrayed as a voluntary exile from his homeland who asked why he was being forsaken by God when Jesus took the sins of the world onto himself (Mark 15:34).

Following the title, the reader is invited to view Mark's message about the actions of John the Baptist and the message of Jesus's baptism and temptation, through the lens of Rome's Aeneas and the *Aeneid*. Mark's first point in his introduction connects Isaiah's prophecy with its intended fulfillment, John the Baptist, as the herald of the Messiah and Son of God, Jesus of Nazareth. Mark veiled much of his deeper message behind the obvious, but Mark was speaking to a dual audience: the Romans and the Jews. Because of the extensive promotion and proliferation of the *Aeneid*, many people in both groups had read both texts. The connection between Aeneas and John the Baptist was unmistakable.

Mark reminds the people that Aeneas, the forerunner of Augustus, has been superseded by another. Aeneas came to establish the Roman

2. Virgil, *Aeneid*, 1.1–4.

destiny. His heritage supported his mission. His father was a prince (Anchises) and his mother a goddess (Venus). King Priam of Troy, the cousin of his father and the grandson of Ilus, was the founder of Troy. His second cousins, sons of Priam, Hector and Paris, were Trojan heroes.

Although John had a priestly background, Mark mentions nothing of John's importance. Mark focuses on comparing John with Jesus as extreme opposites. "After me comes he who is mightier than I, the strap of whose sandals I am not worthy to stoop down and untie" (Mark 1:7). John was not in the line of David. Aeneas's lineage was foundational to his mission.

John's message asked people to make a choice: with whom to identify. Baptism was a ritual of identification that resulted from a person changing his mind ("repentance") about his sins and about God's promise of a savior, whom John would identify shortly. The Roman state religion required absolute obedience to Caesar. Intentionally or unintentionally, John was preaching against the message of Aeneas.

John was also preaching about power. John's power consisted of challenging people's minds and persuading them to re-think their allegiances, because someone more powerful than himself was entering the world. Even modern-day readers will hear Propertius exclaim about the *Aeneid*: "Make way, you Roman writers, make way, Greeks! Something greater than the *Iliad* is born."[3]

The power of Mark's Messiah would surpass anything Rome had ever experienced, a power that emanated directly from *the* Holy Spirit, not from any mythical Roman harmful spirits. In addition, the position of this person would be such that John was not worthy to untie his sandals, an indication that this coming Messiah would be above humans. He would not be a weak human who needed to be deified. The implication is there for those who would read and compare both texts.

Mark shows the coming Messiah as identifying himself with the Jewish people as a peasant from a small village, Nazareth, in Galilee, the lower class of the Jewish nation. Rome already had its savior(s), and it could never imagine a savior of the world originating from such an unknown location in one of its conquered cultures.

Mark's evidence of this identification is that the heavens were torn open, a display of power in the realm above humans, and something like a dove, a symbol of peace, coming from *the* Spirit onto Jesus, and a voice

3. Heslin, *Propertius, Greek Myth*, 219.

from heaven: God's statement of Jesus's being, "*my* beloved *Son*," and God's attachment to him, "I delight in You!" (Mark 1:11).

The rumbling of the Roman gods usually indicated they were upset, and they seldom brought peace. Although the gods and goddesses occasionally bequeathed a glowing aura on a person who pleased them, or a goddess might appear to that person in a material form when that person needed help, God the Father never stated that his Son needed his help, nor did any of the gods or goddesses express such explicit love for Aeneas as the Father expressed for his Son ("beloved").

Mark in his introduction relates the Messiah's testing in the wilderness by the devil. Every person who read the *Aeneid* would think of the suffering of Aeneas at the hands of the gods and goddesses, Juno, etc., and the trials and tribulations Aeneas went through in order to reach and conquer Italy. They would see Venus, his goddess mother, helping him survive Juno's attacks. When Aeneas met Dido, the queen of Carthage, they fell in love with one another. Mark's readers would think of Dido's attempt to use her feminine wiles to tempt Aeneas to give up his divine destiny and remain with her in Carthage. The readers would not miss Aeneas placing honor and duty above personal love.

His audience would be surprised, however, to read that Jesus was attacked by the most powerful evil among the gods, the devil himself, something Aeneas never faced. Jesus faced his temptations alone, with no help from any of the mythical gods. The angels only appeared to "serve" him after the most grueling torture ever experienced by a human being was over. Mark only reveals the bare facts. God, the Spirit, wanted Jesus to be tempted continuously by the devil for forty days. Jesus endured wild animals and was then given help by the angels.

The signature verses of Jesus's mission are 1:14–15: "After John was arrested, Jesus went to Galilee, preaching the good news of God: 'The time is fulfilled, and the kingdom of God has come near. Repent and believe in the good news.'" In these verses, Jesus himself will challenge the *Aeneid*'s premise that Rome is the right kingdom, and that the deified Caesars are those to be worshipped.

Aeneas, the *Aeneid*'s hero, established Rome. In fact, the death of his father precedes and prefigures his own rise to power and authority. If his father had continued to live, Aeneas would not have been able to shine in his own right. The Father of Jesus could not die, and there was no hindrance for his son to die in order to complete his mission. John the Baptist was arrested, his mission accomplished. He is removed by execution by a ruler from Rome. Now the real King will step up and make his entrance.

Mark is not writing in a vacuum, and the good news (1:15) is only the beginning of what the real King will bring to the world. The good news brings together the language of both Isaiah and the Roman imperial worship. Most Romans understood "good news" to refer to announcements of a male child being born to a king and the future results for the kingdom.

Although Paul used the Greek word "gospel" sixty times in his letter to the Romans, he never defined it in Romans, as he did in 1 Corinthians 15:3–5. It can be assumed that Paul's readers in Rome understood what he was writing about, a concept that had already permeated the Roman world. The best good news from imperial Rome's viewpoint was the emerging of an empire of peace because the gods had sent Rome a savior: Augustus.

Even though Augustus had died by the time Mark used the word "good news," every Roman understood the meaning, and they would be surprised to see Jesus's name replace the name of the Caesar. Exaggerated praise often accompanied such "good news" announcements in the Roman world, as exhibited on a calendrical inscription from Priene about Augustus's birthday:

> It is a day which we may justly count as equivalent to the beginning of everything (. . .) it has restored the shape of everything that was failing and turning into misfortune, and has given a new look to the Universe at a time when it would gladly have welcomed destruction if Caesar had not been born to be the common blessing of all men.[4]

The Romans understood the "good news" to mean immediate salvation by the appearance of a new emperor and the accompanying sacrifices to the gods. Salvation was defined as no more civil wars, to be replaced by a restored and growing economy and social order.

Political power was viewed as worthy of divine worship. The ingrained understanding in the Roman mind of Mark 1:1, immediately connected with the deliberate language used in reference to the Roman emperors.

Mark clearly challenges the *Aeneid*'s assertion that Augustus was the son of god. Mark connected Jesus with the emperors and proclaimed an

4. Barker, *From Alexander*, 211–12.

alternative kingdom of God, an alternative view of reality and alternative hopes for the future.

Mark's Gospel clearly subverted and undermined the claims of Rome for their Caesars, which were supported by Virgil's epic poem, the *Aeneid*. Mark's "good news" differs from Rome's propaganda by using historical facts to tell the truth about Jesus, God's true Son.

The "good news" will include not only the ontology of Jesus as the Son of God, but also his death as a propitiatory sacrifice, and his resurrection to directly challenge the deification of Augustus who did not rise from the dead. Although Aeneas entered the *Dis*, the underworld (which Dante interpreted as hell), and re-emerged from it, he did not physically die in order to do so. Therefore, Aeneas's resurrection was not the equivalent of Jesus's physical resurrection from the grave.

Following these signature verses of Jesus's mission in 1:14–15, many more comparisons overwhelm the reader or listener of the text. Some commentators treat Mark as a bunch of disjointed pieces thrown together haphazardly. The truth is that Mark is one long story about Jesus. When a person reads and rereads Mark 1:16–8:38 over and over, the reader's eyes notice how the individual words and phrases begin to twinkle and dim, jolting the mind into seeing connections previously missed by a cursory reading.

5

The Flow of the Texts

The Middle of Mark's Gospel

WHEN ONE REACHES THE middle of both texts, one discovers a strong contrast between Aeneas, who represents Augustus, and Jesus. In Book Six of the *Aeneid*, Aeneas finally reaches Italy. He obeys his father by reaching the Temple of Apollo, where he has to get permission from the sibyl, a priestess, to enter the *Dis* where he can speak with his father about the future.

The sibyl informs Aeneas that he first has to find a golden bough in the forest so that fate will allow him to enter the underworld. Two doves guide Aeneas to this bough, which he uses to obtain passage into the Blessed Groves where the good exist in peace and comfort.

His father, Anchises, greets him and congratulates him on having made it thus far. Anchises then assures Aeneas that Aeneas will found a race and Rome, and that a Caesar will eventually establish a Golden Age of rule over the world. Then Aeneas returns to Italy to face more attacks from Juno, the goddess who hates him and fights him every step of the way, even though she knows that Jupiter has informed everyone that fate has determined that Aeneas will fulfill his prophecies.

This trip to the underworld allows Virgil to promote Rome's future glory, and especially the glorification of the Caesars, with Augustus being the epitome of the Roman Empire, the promised ruler over the Golden Age. One of the most important statements made by Anchises, Aeneas's father, is the command to Aeneas as to how he is to rule.

> Roman, remember by your strength to rule Earth's peoples—for
> your arts are to be these: To pacify, to impose the rule of law, to
> spare the conquered, battle down the proud.[1]

Virgil justifies the conquering of other nations by being merciful to
them and bringing justice, law, and warfare to pacify the conquered.

Mark's clear and stunning contrast of this myth with Jesus's transfiguration in 9:1–10 overshadows Augustus.

> And he said to them, "Truly, I say to you, there are some stand-
> ing here who will not taste death until they see the kingdom of
> God after it has come with power."
>
> After six days Jesus took with him Peter and James and
> John and led them up a high mountain by themselves. And he
> was transfigured before them, and his clothes became radiant,
> intensely white, as no one on earth could bleach them.
>
> And there appeared to them Elijah with Moses, and they
> were talking with Jesus.
>
> And Peter said to Jesus, "Rabbi, it is good that we are here.
> Let us make three tents, one for you and one for Moses and
> one for Elijah." For he did not know what to say, for they were
> terrified.
>
> And a cloud overshadowed them, and a voice came out of
> the cloud, "This is my beloved Son; listen to him." And suddenly,
> looking around, they no longer saw anyone with them but Jesus
> only.
>
> And as they were coming down the mountain, he charged
> them to tell no one what they had seen, until the Son of Man had
> risen from the dead.
>
> So, they kept the matter to themselves, questioning what
> this rising from the dead might mean.

When Jesus ascended the mountain on which he was transfigured,
he did not descend into hell. God, the Father, came down to Jesus on that
mountain. Jesus took three disciples with him. He needed no mythical
sibyl to guide him to a magic artifact to open the door of hell. Aeneas
needed constant guidance through the *Dis*. Jesus was in complete control
of his journey.

Nothing new was revealed about Aeneas through his experience in
hell. Jesus began walking up that mountain as what appeared to be just a
human being, but when he arrived, he was transfigured into a whiteness
that revealed something completely supernatural about his very being.

1. Virgil, *Aeneid*, 6.1151–1154.

In hell, Aeneas was assured that fate would direct him to found Rome, and that Augustus would eventually establish a rule of peace. Jesus received the declaration directly from the Father, "This is my beloved Son; listen to him," not from other future rulers.

6

The Flow of the Texts

The End of Mark's Gospel

FINALLY, WHEN ONE REACHES the end of both texts, another vivid contrast between Aeneas/Augustus and Jesus stuns the reader. Aeneas kills Turnus out of extreme anger and revenge. Mark ends his Gospel with the death of Jesus at the hands of the Romans but follows that with Jesus's resurrection. Both Aeneas and Augustus died, and it is assumed that they both entered the Blessed Groves of the *Dis*, but neither rose from the dead to re-enter the world of the living.

The similarities and contrasts between the message of the *Aeneid* and Mark's Gospel are clear to all who read both texts. Many, many more such contrasts permeate the rest of Mark's Gospel between the beginning (1:1–15), the middle (9:1–10), and the end (16:1–9).

We will now shift our comparisons between specific texts to the themes and theologies of these two books.

7

Themes and Theologies Compared
God's Control of History

THERE HAS BEEN NO end to the publishing of information about the gods of Rome. Many texts combine the subject of the Greek gods with the Roman gods. Within the world of classical studies, the knowledge of the gods has been placed under the concept of common knowledge as a backdrop of deeper studies on Roman history and culture. This book will confine itself to consulting the common knowledge of the Roman gods.

No omniscient and omnipotent God existed within the Roman religion. No god with those attributes surfaces in the *Aeneid*. Therefore, the Roman gods had no foundation of absolute truth. No god has ever been infallible. No god was eternal past. No god was omniscient nor omnipotent nor omnipresent. Whenever Jupiter proclaimed the fate of something or someone, it could not be changed. Jupiter did not control fate. He was semi-bound by it.

In demonstrating that Mark is responding to the *Aeneid* one needs to stay within the boundaries of Mark's Gospel. It is tempting to make use of cross-references from the other Gospels, but since Mark wrote for the Romans to address the *Aeneid*, he chose his material quite selectively to make his points. He did not need to present every facet of the life of Jesus. He only needed to lay out the essentials.

Mark never focuses on God's attributes. Instead, Mark pictures God as invading history to direct and push history in his own predetermined direction with the purpose of beginning something entirely new that will save humanity from itself. Mark reveals Isaiah's prophecy of God directing the historical events that would send a forerunner ahead of his Messiah in Mark 1:2–3:

> As it is written in Isaiah the prophet,
>
> "Behold, I send my messenger before your face,
>
> who will prepare your way
>
> the voice of one crying in the wilderness:
>
> 'Prepare the way of the Lord,
>
> make his paths straight.'"

John the Baptist's arrival challenges the character, nature, and mission of Aeneas, the forerunner of Augustus.

God does not place himself front and center throughout Mark. God makes his first entrance at Jesus's baptism to introduce the first eight chapters of Mark: "You are my Son, whom I love; with you I am well pleased" (1:9–11). By the quote from Isaiah, God challenges Jupiter's nebulous and indeterminate control of the future. Jupiter had trouble controlling the goddesses, Venus and Juno, as they wanted different futures for Aeneas. God, the Father, had only one Son, whom he praises and whom he does not have to control. God has never had a counterpart, male or female, whom he fought to control.

The Romans should note that Augustus's father, Gaius Octavius, died when Augustus was four years old. It can be assumed that Gaius was proud of his son, Octavian (who was renamed Augustus), though that praise was never recorded.

Mark, however, does not present Joseph, the husband of Mary, as the one praising the true Savior. God, the Father, praises his Son. Jupiter never expressed love for Augustus. Mark begins his Gospel with the personal relationship between God, the Father, who controls history, and his Son, who will offer a personal relationship to those who choose to follow him.

God remains in the shadows until the middle of Mark (9:3–7), where Jesus is revealed in his true divine glory. God, the Father, again praises the Son: "This is my Son, whom I love. Listen to him!" Once Jesus has been shown to be the true Son of the real God, he will begin revealing his mission to those who choose to follow him.

Therefore, God issues his injunction to listen to the true Son of God. The real Savior's mission was to place Mark's Gospel into the hands of every Roman willing to listen. God appears one last time at the end of

Mark when God rips the veil from top to bottom (15:38), as his Son dies on the cross. God has opened the door of access to himself to everyone.

Jesus, filled with the Spirit (as opposed to the magic of Roman religion), announced that the time had been fulfilled (1:15) for a new stage in God's determination to save humanity. God's Son had arrived. When the Son is executed, mourning will follow (2:19–20), along with persecution (13:5–13).

Mark does not give a detailed chronology of this new age that has just been ushered in, nor how it will play out in detail, but Mark reveals that God will in some aspect protect "the elect, whom he has chosen" from the tribulation (13:20). God is in ultimate control of man's entire history, including the end, and only God knows the time of the coming of the Son of Man, "not even the angels in heaven, nor the Son" (13:32). God's final confirmation that his kingdom is the only kingdom will occur when his Son returns in glory as the final victor (13:24–27).

8

Themes and Theologies Compared

God as Father

JUPITER'S ORIGINAL NAME, *DYEUS-PATER*, means "Father Sky—god." The closest he came to being a father figure was a higher-distant being in the sky. He never reached out to every Roman, inviting them into a personal relationship with himself. He remained a distant "parent." Mark reveals the true God as first having a loving relationship with his own Son (1:11), who has come with the same glory that the Father has (8:38). The Son reveals his close emotional relationship with the Father when the Son requests of the Father that the cup of the cross be circumvented (14:36), but the Son will still obey (14:36).

Jesus addresses God as "Abba" (14:36). It would never have entered Aeneas's mind to address Jupiter with such an intimate term, even though Aeneas addresses Venus as his mother.

Jesus informed his disciples that he considered them his brothers. Their life—both biological and spiritual—originates with the Father, who is "in heaven" above all.

9

Themes and Theologies Compared
God as All-Powerful

NONE OF THE ROMAN gods were omnipotent, not even Jupiter. Virgil never even attempts to invent this myth among the gods in the *Aeneid*. The omnipotence of God is undisputed in Mark's Gospel. Jesus, as God's representative, uses his power to heal the sick (1:34 et al.), bind Satan (3:23–27), cast out demons (1:21–26 et al.), and raise the dead (5:41–42). Augustus was incapable of doing any miracles.

When Mark claims for God that "all things are possible" (9:23; 11:23), Mark is not making reference in those contexts to the miracles of Jesus, but to the miracle that occurred on the cross (14:36). The Romans were powerful enough to have crucified thousands of people for the purpose of putting down insurrection and subjecting other cultures to the Roman Empire. God is all powerful and can therefore do all things to do just the opposite: putting down evil and saving humanity from their sins. Virgil attempted in the *Aeneid* to cover up the evil carried out by Augustus. Mark reveals that Jesus was powerful enough to give himself as a paid ransom for the evil (10:45), and still rise from the dead.

Themes and Theologies Compared

God as the One Who Breaks Down Barriers

THE *AENEID* PRESENTS AENEAS and Augustus as religious and political protectors of the realm. Jupiter sent Aeneas (both mythical creations), who represented Augustus, a mere mortal, to fulfill the destiny of one specific culture, the Romans, and force everyone to submit to the Roman state religion. Jesus made no distinction between cultures. He rejected any religious traditions that functioned as fences to keep people away from his Father (9:13).

Jesus came to heal the sick, not those who considered themselves healthy. Rome despised the sick and weak. A strong Roman soldier was Rome's model of a perfect citizen. Augustus was determined to guard and protect the empire with the use of force. The only force that Jesus used was the power to heal people and cast out demons. The only force the Father used was to tear open the veil at the baptism of Jesus.

Normally when the heavens open, they close again. The action of forcefully ripping them open indicates that the heavens are no longer intended to close again. Access to God directly has been performed by God himself. God removed the protective barriers. He no longer required humans to meet him only in sacred spaces.

Jesus is going to break down all barriers for humanity to directly connect with the omnipotent God, his Father, anywhere, anytime, and anyplace. Jesus is going to do so from a position of weakness: becoming human and dying on the cross. His display of power will be revealed through the resurrection and the final barrier of death will be overcome.

Themes and Theologies Compared

God as the Justified and Justifier

JUPITER DESTINED AENEAS TO succeed and to not die. Aeneas has to justify himself and his actions by achieving the victory that fate has already
willed for him. He cannot die until that is accomplished. Mark makes it
clear that God intended for Jesus, his Son, to die (14:21, 49) in order to
succeed in his mission.

Aeneas is advised to pray to the gods for victory and for protection against the other gods. Jesus predicts three times in Mark that Jesus
"must" suffer many things and be killed (8:31). When Jesus prayed in
the garden that the Father find another way other than the cross to accomplish salvation for mankind (14:36), Jesus acknowledged that God
was not going to provide another method or a different sacrifice. Jesus
was the centerpiece of human history at that moment on Calvary, and
with the heavens opened and all of creation watching, God, the Father,
had destined his Son to die on the cross. Jesus is actually "handed over"
to Pilate in 15:1.

God is in charge of this entire operation. Evil humans were nothing
more than tools that God used to carry out his predetermined plan to put
his Son on the cross. God does not distance himself from the destiny of
his own son. God is not a remote, impersonal, aloof divinity.

At the Last Supper, Jesus quotes Zech 13:7 referring to God striking
the shepherd (14:27). Mark does not state clearly that God's active execution of his own Son is carried out for the purpose of satisfying (justify-
ing) God's righteousness. The fact, however, that God is the driving force

behind the cross, and that Jesus is going to die in order to save people from their sins, points toward God being the one who justifies the sinner who repents. The apostle Paul will flesh out God as justified and justifier in Romans 3:26, but Mark, the earliest announcer of God's salvation for mankind, reveals indirectly that the Father is going to be justified (his Law satisfied) by paying the price he himself demanded by the Law for the sin of mankind.

Themes and Theologies Compared

The Humanity of Jesus vs. Aeneas/Augustus

As a young person, Augustus (Octavian) overcame some tremendous obstacles in his life. His father died when Octavian was four years old. He was plagued by frequent sicknesses. Having been raised by two women, he had little military experience as a boy. His age was a brutal one, and feeble young men did not survive long.

At sixteen, however, in spite of being seriously ill, he traveled through enemy territory with just a few companions and suffered a shipwreck before arriving on the battlefield to join Julius Caesar and take part in the battle against the Spanish. This event endeared him to Caesar, who began to treat him as his own son, praising him for his tenacity and ingenuity.

When news arrived that Caesar had been assassinated, history records Augustus's revenge and the five civil wars he waged. His public morals were impeccable and strict. He became a pontifex (priest) at the age of sixteen and, later in life, he exiled his daughter and his granddaughter for lax morals.

He almost died in 23 BC from illness and his faith in spiritual forces re-exerted itself. He began consulting spiritists for their interpretations of omens and dreams to discern the best course of action to take in order to maintain an appropriate relationship with spiritual forces and spiritual beings, so he could continue climbing in power. He despised the less fortunate (e.g., those disfigured and crippled) as a bad premonition. He even considered some days as unlucky to his own personal well-being.

He was petrified of lightning and thunder, thinking that the god Jupiter was upset. In direct contrast to Augustus's relationship to the gods, and especially Jupiter, Mark reveals a relationship of love and trust between Jesus and the Father (14:36).

Destiny (*Fortuna*) played a vital role in the Greek and Roman worldview. Livy wrote about this common attitude in his Roman history. He attributed equal power over human destiny to fortune, military courage, and the general's ingenuity in war.

Octavian was brutal with his enemies, even Roman ones, but overly generous with his trusted friends. He always exhibited outward humility by rejection of flattering titles and by melting down gold and silver statues that had been raised in his honor and dedicating the money to statues that had been raised to the gods, like the golden tripods to Apollo.

His lifestyle was modest (clothing, food, sleeping quarters), but he gladly accepted praise from others who believed that he had divine powers. In 12 BC, Augustus assumed the religious title of *pontifex maximus*, "greatest priest," thus giving himself the highest religious position in the empire. The pinnacle of his successful grab for power came in 2 BC when the senate gave him the title of *pater patriae*, "the father of the country."

The significance of this for Mark's Gospel must not be overlooked. In the Roman worldview, the family god and the national gods were strongly connected. Everything was protected by the gods, and the "Father" presided over them all. Roman worship elevated the Roman home, and the Roman city functioned as a religious center above all other functions. The *pomerium* was home to the local gods that protected the sacred land around the city. The home, the city, and the administration were all centers of worship, and the temples served as government buildings.

Once Augustus received the title of *pontifex maximus*, all the gods supposedly brought their successes together for the Roman state, under their "Father," who had become their "Savior." As a gracious benefactor, he alone received glory and he alone bestowed glory. In 29 BC, the provinces honored him as a savior who stopped war and brought order out of chaos. Consequently, they proclaimed him to be the "son of god."

Augustus had reorganized the politics and the military of the Roman Empire. These functions were permeated with a religious nature of full dedication to Augustus. Soldiers swore an oath calling down the vengeance of Jupiter on themselves for perjury if they ever spoke negatively about Augustus. He had created a realm ruled by peace and unprecedented prosperity. He won far-reaching support by hosting games, building new buildings, updating the city's water system, building two new aqueducts, and restoring eighty-two temples in one year, one of those temples being the huge Mausoleum of Augustus. He built himself a palace on the Palatine Hill, yet outwardly avoiding any signs or symbols of monarchy. In 27 BC, he even gave the right of coinage, a symbol of sovereignty, back to the senate.

He allowed the senate to believe that they ran the country, while styling himself "*divi filius*," son of the deified Caesar. He avoided any form of worship directed at himself, even though this was normal procedure for the kings in the world at that time. He was a master of delegation. He allowed Agrippa to carry out most of Augustus's plans, as well as serve as his brilliant military general.

The images and symbols of Rome functioned to bring all glory to Rome through Augustus. He designed the image of his own seal as a sphinx for passports, formal documents, and personal letters. Later he changed it into an image of Alexander the Great. Eventually he made it into an image of himself. In 27 BC he was given three items of religious significance: a sacred laurel tree that represented Roman religion, an oak wreath represented victory, and a Greek shield represented virtuous rule.

Mark's detailed knowledge of Rome's religion allowed him to challenge even the coinage that drew worship to Augustus. In Mark 12:14, the Pharisees attempted to trap Jesus by asking him a question about paying taxes. He ordered them to bring him a denarius.

The Greek drachma and the Roman denarius were basic money units. Mark wrote in Greek, but he didn't use the Greek word, "drachma," because he was writing for the Romans. He used the Latin word, "denarius."

Jesus looked at the coin and told them to give it back to Caesar, since Caesar had put his face on it. Taxes paid to a pagan Caesar who wanted to be worshipped by putting his image on coins were completely irrelevant and not even worth discussing compared to giving God what God deserves. The Romans would have seen this connection immediately.

The message from Augustus was clear: his victory at Actium restored Rome to its deserved glory. The assimilation of this message filtered into the entire realm, including the private sphere. Augustus manipulated the official imagery embedded in memorials, statues, and decorative detail that skillfully portrayed the glorious past. He channeled the symbols to all the buildings that drew the people's attention to him.

Every monument and building included religious themes: skulls of sacrificial animals, priestly tokens, and offering bowls. There was no such thing as a secular building.

Aeneas and Romulus played a prominent role in gracing the architecture as their imagery portrayed the Roman virtues of *pietas* and *virtus*. Their actions as heroes were displayed and linked with the living *Princeps* (the noble man). This generated an emotional and spiritual connection between the present and the mythological past. Virgil's *Aeneid* became the centerpiece of all such images. It stood prominently in the Forum of Augustus to celebrate Augustus's revenge over Julius Caesar's murderers.

The mythological symbolism of Aeneas and his family served as a token of loyalty. These images have been found on finger rings, lamps, and terracotta statuettes. Wall paintings in a house from Pompei reflect the imagery of Aeneas and Romulus depicted in the Forum of Augustus. Furthermore, sculptors and patterns use the scene of Aeneas and his family on grave monuments as a symbol of personal piety and devotion.

After a person had lived under this extensive visible propaganda for a time, he absorbed the message subliminally. Political symbolism was found everywhere. No object escaped the emperor's stamp: utensils, textiles, ceilings, roof tiles, ash urns, jewelry, furniture, walls, clay facings, tombs. No one in the entire world that was controlled by Rome could have missed the *Aeneid*.

Augustus's success was unprecedented. No one had seen it coming. He lived a long life, but he produced no personal dynasty. He died at Nola in 14 AD. His ashes were placed in his Mausoleum.

Creating a kingship and building a dynasty requires an intricate weaving together of personalities who all eventually find their place in the power structure of the kingdom. Augustus navigated that process in the usual manner by killing his enemies and rewarding his supporters. Virgil presents Aeneas in the *Aeneid* as Augustus's forerunner who preceded Augustus in establishing Aeneas's kingdom in the same fashion. Virgil used every tactic to convince the Romans of the deification of Augustus.

In stark contrast to Virgil's presentation of the personage of Augustus, Mark's Gospel reveals Jesus first as human. Mark described Jesus as a frail human who gets tired and hungry, while casting out demons. Jesus sleeps through a storm (4:38); he cares for children (10:14–16); he loves those who reject him (10:21); he complains about people's unbelief (9:19); he gets angry at the Pharisees (3:5); and yet, in that same verse, Mark shows Jesus's divinity in that Jesus can read the hardness of their hearts.

Jesus even gets upset at his own disciples when they attempt to chase away parents who have brought their children to Jesus for a blessing.

His most intense emotion ("deeply distressed and troubled") surfaces (14:33) in the garden before the cross when he knows what he is going to go through within the next twenty-four hours. Jesus is fully human with parents and siblings and enemies. He was a humble servant who came to serve humanity by living a simple life while healing people and teaching them. He used no deception, no propaganda. He often told his followers to *not* tell others about his miracles.

Mark presents Jesus as God's king, God's own Son, who offered the proof of his kingship by performing miracles that normal human kings could not carry out. Whereas Augustus received vindication for his achieving kingship by winning wars, Jesus, on the other hand, never practiced revenge. In fact, Jesus commands his followers to love their neighbors as they love themselves (12:31). Mark does not go further, as does Matthew, that Jesus's followers should love their enemies (Matt 5:44)—but neighbors could include enemies.

Immediately after Jesus had taught in his hometown synagogue, the people who knew him best were astonished at his teaching and rejected him because they could not believe that one of their own, who had not been raised as a rabbi, could have acquired such a splendid education as was evident by Jesus's teaching. Nor could they accept the implications that came with acknowledging his miracles. A carpenter's son never received the necessary training that led to such wisdom.

In addition, his mother, Mary, and Jesus's brothers were used as evidence that Jesus could not have been anything other than a normal human being, raised in semi-poverty in a small village that would never have a reputation for anything more than a bumper crop of grapes during the harvest season. His humanness revealed itself in his amazement at the unbelief of his own people. They referred to him as the "son of Mary" (6:3), indicating that Jesus probably lost his earthly father before Jesus entered his ministry at the age of thirty. Jesus would have been the oldest son and would have taken on the responsibility for the family. He was fully human.

Both Augustus and Jesus were human, but the similarities stop there. Augustus came from human royalty; Jesus was raised in obscurity (even though he was in the line of David). Mark does not even mention the name of the village Jesus was raised in (6:1). Augustus was placed in high society for his own advancement; Jesus was raised as a carpenter, around common people, who seldom left their village. Augustus grew in favor with Julius Caesar because of Augustus's persistence, precision, and discernment in the face of weakness, sickness, and struggles.

Mark does not even mention Jesus's reputation in the temple at twelve years old (Luke 2:41–50), nor that he obeyed his parents for the next eighteen years before beginning his ministry (Luke 2:51–52).

Mark contrasts the position and prominence of Augustus with the obscurity of Jesus. Mark does not mention the birth of Jesus and the attending shepherds and angels. Mark says nothing about the date of Joseph's death, nor the line of David that preceded the Messiah.

How can Mark ever hope to convince his readers that Jesus will replace Augustus as the Savior of the world? The only incident that Mark mentions in just these two verses (1:12–13) is the temptation of Jesus in the desert. The major comparison with Augustus is obvious to anyone who had been steeped in the *Aeneid* and then heard someone reading (let alone teaching) the Gospel of Mark.

Combining all the struggles of Augustus into one vision produces a terribly weak and shallow comparison with the suffering and torture of Jesus that permeated the forty days of direct and unceasing and relentless temptation by the most powerful evil force in the universe. With Aeneas, Augustus's prototype, Venus fought against Juno to help Aeneas. With Jesus, the Spirit drove him into the arms of God's biggest enemy to endure that enemy alone.

The only animals Augustus encountered during his lifetime were his horses. It can be assumed that the wild animals in the desert with Jesus were not looking to be petted but hoping to have lunch. This negative relationship of wild animals with Jesus would have been understood by the Romans as painting a picture of the torture of humans in the coliseum among the lions. A Roman steeped in the *Aeneid* would probably ask why those animals were there, and why Jesus survived their arrival. Only after the period of torture, does Jesus, very much human, receive service from angels.

The vague nebulous sacrificial offerings of Augustus to the gods for victory, safety, and a more comfortable lifestyle could not compete with God's angels serving Jesus after that forty days. Virgil would have the readers believe that Aeneas suffered significantly but managed to overcome adversity with the help of Venus. Mark tells his readers that God sent Jesus directly into the devil's persecution, alone, to make the point that Jesus needed no help and was therefore clearly superior to Aeneas/Augustus.

In the end, Jesus intentionally allowed himself to be crucified by the Romans and postponed his vindication as King until after his death by rising from the dead. Augustus's attempt to further his kingship by establishing an heir failed miserably. Augustus had no control over the future of the Roman Empire after he died. Jesus's resurrection nullified the necessity of seeking a successor. The King had died but had risen from the dead. No one would have to replace him for all of eternity.

13

Themes and Theologies Compared

The Deity of Jesus vs. Aeneas/Augustus

THE GREEKS CONTRIBUTED CONSIDERABLY to helping the Romans accept the idea that man could become a god. Virgil made good use of deified humanity in the *Aeneid*. Jupiter had been elevated to the highest position among the gods. Evidence of the deification of man is overwhelming in Roman religious thought, and Julius Caesar wanted that status. He did not receive that title until immediately after his death. Virgil had gained fame for himself as promoting Caesar worship long before he wrote the *Aeneid*. He openly presented himself as deifying the young Augustus.

Virgil endows the *Georgics*, one of his three major works, with an authority that places Caesar as the climax of Virgil's catalog of deities. Virgil advocated more than private worship toward Caesar. Caesar will become a god. This is not simply an altar sacrifice to honor Caesar, but a temple to be built and garnished with tokens of the most important successes and achievements by Caesar abroad and at home.

Virgil's last *Georgic* comes full circle to assert that Caesar is more than a mortal victor; he is moving into the heavens. Julius Caesar's official and popular deification was Virgil's launching pad for Augustus to follow suit. Augustus would be compared to none other than Jupiter himself.

Virgil had already deified Augustus as his personal god, but now he had to insert Augustus's divinity into the life of Aeneas through a national epic poem. However, the chronology of turning Augustus into a god plagued him. Many gods already existed, but Augustus could not simply replace one of them. He had to be a new god, not an old, inactive one.

Therefore, Virgil had to resort to prophecy, as demonstrated throughout the *Aeneid*. Virgil's short revelation of Jupiter's communication to Venus, the divine mother, is intentionally placed in the first prophecy of the poem. Virgil needed to begin the deification process of Augustus early in the poem. And Venus makes no objections. Caesar worship will enter human history at the proper time.

Deification seemed to assault the Roman mind with revulsion, and Virgil produced no simplistic theory to be presented for blind acceptance, nor did he present an explanation of how what he wanted everyone to believe could actually happen—a man becoming a god. Virgil presents a human who had already achieved deification: Anchises, the father of Aeneas. Anchises's first appearance presents him as fully human, when Dido asks Aeneas if the Trojan Anchises was his father. In Book 2, Anchises is described as "worn-out with age." And since normal humans die, even Dido considered Anchises to be dead and buried ("the ashes and ghost of his father Anchises").[1]

Yet Aeneas views Anchises as his divine parent, and after Aeneas establishes Rome, he goes beyond honoring his father by simply writing something in remembrance of him; Aeneas dedicates temples to his father, an act carried out, not for humans, but for the gods. Although no longer among the living, prayers are offered to Anchises.

When Aeneas appears at the tomb of his father to pay tribute to his father, a snake slithers out of the tomb. Aeneas has to decide if the snake is simply guarding the place, or guarding his father. He concludes the latter and proceeds to make an offering to his father as having achieved divinity. Aeneas calls on the spirit and shadow of Anchises to accept his gift. Aeneas's companions join in by bringing gifts gladly and sacrificing animals on high altars. If Aeneas was only honoring his dead parent, Aeneas's friends, who had no obligation to honor someone outside of their own family, would not have made offerings that were fitting for the gods. Upon their departure, the entire company sets up a sacred grove for the divine Anchises.

Virgil uses both the humanity among the dead and the divinity among the gods to place Anchises in the perfect position to reveal to Aeneas the future and greatness of the Roman race. Toward the end of the sixth book, Anchises is partially separated from the dead and is met by Jupiter and Venus, in the context of receiving prayers, making him

---

1. Virgil, *Aeneid*, 2.597, 4.427.

their equal in nature (which does not contradict the various stations and power positions among the gods).

Thus, Virgil had circumvented any logical explanation of how humans can become divine and presented Anchises as an example (not explanation) of the deified Julius Caesar. Aeneas and his struggles to establish Rome and bring his gods to Rome would be a palatable parallel to Augustus, who had just spent twelve years keeping Rome on the foundations set by Aeneas and restoring the prestige and dignity of Aeneas's gods to Rome. Aeneas is obviously human, as was his father, but his divine mother has destined him for divinity.

Jupiter, who was the son of Saturn, had somehow become the high king of the Roman Pantheon of the gods. He ruled from a distance, treating the affairs of humans in an arbitrary manner. He spent much of his time mediating squabbles among the lesser gods. He had the power to deify humans after their death. After Aeneas died, Venus, his mother, asked Jupiter to make her son immortal, to which Jupiter agreed. The river god Numicus was called in to cleanse Aeneas, and Venus anointed him with nectar and ambrosia, thus turning him into a god.

Just before the last drama in the *Aeneid* closes, Jupiter announces Rome's future fame and prominence, and adds that Augustus is both a divine race and mortal. Augustus has not yet arrived at a state of complete divinity, but he will, just like the experiences of Aeneas. Virgil has succeeded in revealing resemblances between these two loyal human Romans who are dedicated to sacrificing their own agendas and embracing their fate from the gods, and who will be honored with divinity for their efforts. Both men will be worshipped. Deification has firmly embedded itself inside the Roman state religion. All Roman citizens will eventually bow to divine kingship.

Emperor worship during the Roman age blurred the particular distinctions between the gods and men. In the *Aeneid* Virgil was able to convince the Romans that Augustus was the son of a god, thus making him a god, whom Virgil promised would establish a golden age:

> Now direct your eyes here, gaze at this people, your own Romans. Here is Caesar, and all the offspring of Julius destined to live under the pole of heaven. This is the man, this is him, whom you so often hear promised you, Augustus Caesar, son of the Deified, who will make a Golden Age again in the fields where Saturn once reigned, and extend the empire beyond the Libyans and the Indians (to a land that lies outside the zodiac's belt,

beyond the sun's ecliptic and the year's, where sky-carrying Atlas turns the sphere, inset with gleaming stars, on his shoulders.[2]

Virgil mentions Augustus as one of the "gods among us," leaving
the impression that Augustus was exceptional enough to have inherited
divine qualities. Since the lineage was so nebulous, the adherents to these
religions habitually honored their rulers by giving them mementos of
devotion worthy only of the gods, thus elevating those humans to the
heavenly realm, those who had chosen to appear on the earth. If the rulers found themselves no longer in power, and maybe even dead, they
were deified.

The imperial cult permeated the Roman era during Mark's day. The
Roman rituals supported and promoted the power of the state foisted
on the conquered world. Barrett unveils how Caesar used this tradition
politically. He publicly rejected any desire for divinity, but he put his face
on his coins and on his inscriptions, thus insinuating that he was the son
of a god.

The Romans had not gone so far as to worship the person of the
emperor. They supposedly worshipped the emperor's mental capacity,
which guided his leadership, but Philo's *On the Embassy to Gaius* shows
the emperor actually expecting divine accolades while he was still alive,
and he was upset that the Jews offered no sacrifices to him. An angel
killed Herod with stomach worms because he accepted such praise (Acts
12:23). A person usually lasted a few days before expiring from this sickness, a very humiliating disease. God is going to humble Augustus by
comparing him to Jesus.

Jesus is labeled as the "Son of God" in Mark 1:1. Only a deaf and
stupid Roman would have missed the direct challenge of Jesus to the Roman emperor. Considering the drive of the Romans to force their religion
onto all other cultures, Mark was putting himself in the dangerous position of writing his own piece of propaganda that was clearly intended
to directly challenge the Roman piece of propaganda, the *Aeneid*, and
Augustus who was presented to the world as a god.

In the first half of his Gospel, Mark veiled Jesus's identity by showing what Jesus was doing, and along the way asked the question: Who is
Jesus? Once the disciples recognized that Jesus was Messiah, Mark began
communicating what was going to happen to Jesus, as the Messiah.

---

2. Virgil, *Aeneid* 6, 789–98.

The second half of Mark presents a Son of God who is intentionally heading toward persecution and crucifixion, not the expected path of victory over the world, as would have been presumed by the Roman perception of success. Augustus came to serve by ruling, whereas Jesus came to rule by serving through his perfect life and death on the cross. Obviously, this made no sense to anyone, not even to the disciples who had recognized Jesus as the Messiah. If Jesus was intentionally going to die, then he was no threat to Augustus or the Roman Empire. But Jesus came to win the Romans over to his message in Mark's Gospel, and as he died on the cross, he succeeded in convincing his first convert: a Roman. "When the centurion who was standing opposite him saw the way He breathed His last, he said, 'This man was really God's Son'" (15:39).

The centurion's declaration leaves no doubt as to what that Roman understood. He did not say, "This man has become a son of a god, like Augustus." Jesus had not started out as a human who was to be deified by other humans because of his military and political prowess, as had occurred with the Caesars.

Mark is not mocking Augustus. The Romans themselves did that. The satire by Seneca, *Apocolyntesis (The Pumpkinification of [the Divine] Claudius)*,[3] made a farce out of the ceremony of deification of the Emperor Claudius when he died. Even the Emperor Vespasian was reported on his deathbed to have said, "Oh, I think I'm becoming a god!"[4]

Mark made it clear: that centurion understood the ontology of Jesus by stating that Jesus "was" the Son of God. Mark's quote was intended to challenge Augustus in the most unique way possible. The death of Jesus was a victory. Jesus had conquered, not killed, a Roman centurion.

Some scholars believe that centurion's statement in 15:39 was not made sincerely, but it was nothing more than a cynical statement that rejected the idea that Jesus was the Son of God.

Nothing in the text indicates sarcasm, but they support this claim with three reasons: the lack of a definite article ("the") before "son," the use of the Greek imperfect of "was" (not "is"), and the centurion's status as a defender of the Roman Caesar as a son of god.

Even taken together these three arguments are weak. The lack of a definite article often shows the quality of the person: "*Son* of God," not just any ordinary crucified human criminal. The imperfect of "was" fits

3. Seneca, (*Pumpkinification*).

4. Cassius Dio, *Rom. Hist.* 66.3.

who Jesus "was" before he died. And third, centurions were as supersti-
tious as any other Roman. The manner in which Jesus died and the three
hours of black darkness made an immediate impression on this human
soldier. His military career had not turned him into a Roman robot. His
mind could be influenced and changed.

Those scholars also miss the fact that the centurion used a word for
truly that is never used in the New Testament to express sarcasm.

Mark focuses the reader's (and listener's) attention on Jesus, not on
the centurion. Mark uses the centurion to show that anyone can recognize truth when they see it, and that Jesus is more than a small-town
messiah for a conquered people. He is someone that even the Romans
realize is not a criminal, but just the opposite, the Son of God. Once a
Roman recognizes this then the crucifixion of the Son of God becomes
another proof that the *Aeneid* is a myth.

Rome, through Augustus and all the emperors who follow him, will
not rule the world through war and terror. The splitting of the heavens at
the beginning of Mark (1:10) and the ripping of the veil at the end (15:38)
also bracket Mark's Gospel, not just for his Jewish audience, but for the
Romans as well.

Virgil wrote the *Aeneid* to demonstrate the connection between
Jupiter's heaven and Aeneis's earth. Mark wrote his Gospel to reveal the
true connection between those realities. The rending of the veil would
have been viewed by the Romans, as well as the Jews, as having revelatory
consequences. The glorious expanse of the heavens forced the centurion
to recognize that Jesus was more than just another criminal murdered by
the Romans. The Romans had crucified the Son of God.

The rending of the veil demonstrates that God transcends the limi-
tation of the Roman gods because the real God is not confined to some
holy place on the earth or to the heavens. The secret is out: Jesus is God's
Son. The first proclamation that Jesus is the Messiah came from a Jew:
Peter (8:29). The first proclamation of Jesus's deity came from a Roman
(15:39).

The centurion had not come to that crucifixion expecting any supernatural revelation, but a miracle happened. He saw the truth about the
person of Jesus. Since Jesus is the center of attention, Mark does not comment further on the possibility of that centurion comparing Jesus with
Augustus and possibly becoming a martyr himself. Listening to Mark's
Gospel challenged other Romans to look up and scrutinize Jesus with the
same perspective as that centurion.

Jupiter never spoke directly to Aeneas or Augustus. Aeneas and Augustus always had to guess what the gods were up to, and they were always offering sacrifices to please the gods in hopes that the gods would look favorably on them. Mark reveals God speaking directly to humanity about his Son who is the bridge between heaven and Earth.

At the beginning of Jesus's ministry, the Father spoke to Jesus: "You are my beloved Son, I take delight in You" (1:11). Halfway through Jesus's ministry, the Jewish disciples recognized that Jesus was the Messiah (8:29), and the Father confirmed this immediately thereafter: "This is my beloved Son, listen to Him!" When Jesus collided with demons, even they knew who he was, "the Son of God" (3:11), where Mark includes the definite article, "the" Son of God, and "Son of the Most High God" (5:7). From the perfect good Creator who is above all of creation to the lowest most evil beings within creation, Mark leaves no doubt that everyone knows who Jesus is, except the Jews and Romans who rejected the truth.

God is affirmative to Jesus, and the demons are hostile. The high priest is hostile (14:61) and the centurion is affirmative (15:39). This interesting arrangement places the high priest in league with Satan, but the Roman agreeing with God. Is Mark unveiling a shadowy allusion? Mark is famous for concealing a deeper meaning with veiled allusions. Since allusions speak to those seeking more than the obvious meaning of the text, Mark may be describing the rise of the gentiles who had already populated the church (Cornelius, Acts 10) by the time of Mark's composition of his Gospel.

In any case, Mark's placing the revelation of the Son's ontology in four locations arranges his narrative within two sets of brackets: the "Son of God" at the beginning (1:1) and the end (15:39), and "My Son" at the start of the question phase (1:11) and after the arrival of the correct answer in the middle of the book (9:7). This bracketing demonstrates that Mark did not simply throw a pile of isolated events together in a weak attempt to promote a failed messiah concocted by the early church. Mark's structure reveals a piece of literature equal to the best in the Roman world, including Virgil's epic poem, the *Aeneid*, but Mark based his Gospel on historical fact not made-up myth.

Another aspect of the deity of Jesus that Mark compares with Augustus is their respective residences. Augustus began in wealth and ended in deification, but he was not assigned any special place in the heavens. Apparently, he moved in among all the other nebulous half-human and half-gods who would eventually be forgotten as they were replaced by new generations of humanly fabricated mythical beings who would push them out of the memories of the latest worshippers.

Mark leaves no doubt of Jesus's residence and the accompanying permanent position of power by quoting Jesus himself: "I am, and all of you will see the Son of Man seated at the right hand of the Power and coming with the clouds of heaven" (14:62). Jesus was not politically correct. With the wave of a hand, he obliterated the boundary between humanity and divinity by claiming his place of power and authority on God's throne. He announced that he was coming back. Considering that he was speaking to those who wanted to kill him, his return would not be one of reconciliation.

The possibility that Jesus could be the Jewish Messiah would not have disturbed the Roman mind, since Rome had experienced a number of Jewish messiahs during the Jew's conquered history. However, sitting at the right hand of God in heaven raises the status of his claims beyond any self-asserted, elevated position of the Roman gods. The position of power next to God will find Jesus returning to judge everyone, Jews and Romans alike, for their rejection of his deeds and works, and especially his sacrificial payment for their sins. He will return to carry out divine vengeance. This declaration places Jesus far beyond a temporal messiah, but equal with God himself. Virgil would never have ventured to make that claim for Augustus. Nothing in the *Aeneid* even approaches such an inconceivable, but unashamed, declaration by Jesus himself.

14

Themes and Theologies Compared

The Power and Authority of Jesus vs. Aeneas/ Augustus

POWER AND AUTHORITY, EVEN when connected, are separate entities. A free system will be based on authority, backed up by power. A tyrannical system will reverse these two. A free system only needs to use its power when its authority is spurned. A tyrannical system will use power first to force its people to submit to its authority. In the *Aeneid*, Aeneas and Augustus, his prophesied reality, had to use power to force the submission of its conquered peoples. The Romans were tired of the civil wars, five of which Augustus took part in. Without those wars Augustus could never have gained the authority that allowed him to rule the empire.

Mark's Gospel, bypassing myth, reveals the reality of the mature Jesus entering the empire with authority. John the Baptist stated at the outset of Jesus's ministry that "someone more powerful than I will come after me," referring to Jesus. Yet, the temptation by the devil is barely mentioned, with the devil having failed to entice Jesus to sin. John is arrested and Jesus uses no power to free him. Somehow Jesus motivates his first disciples to follow him, although Mark gives no reason for their decision. Such unmotivated calls fail to appear in any other ancient literature. It is almost as if God had called them to follow Jesus.

As opposed to Augustus's use of power, followed by self-proclaimed authority, Jesus begins with teaching which the people recognize as authoritative (1:22, 27). Jesus used the power of miracles to convince the people to listen to his teaching, but he never coerced them into following him. Mark wants his listeners to recognize the authority of God in Jesus's teaching, which motivates the minds and hearts of people to follow him, as opposed to the external force exercised by the Romans to submit.

When Jesus called Levi, Levi responded as quickly as the earlier disciples, and his submission to the authority of Jesus was an even more radical break from his previous worldview. Fishermen could always fish, but tax collectors could only move forward. Mark is discussing discipleship here. He is focusing on Jesus calling with (divine) authority to follow him.

Fishermen and tax collectors were not ignorant people with little education. Fishermen faced death every time they left port. They were (and still are) extremely skeptical people. Tax collectors were always looking over their shoulders. These two would have been the most difficult to convince that they needed to follow Jesus on the basis of nothing more than his word.

The miracles pushed them to ask the question: "Who is this person?" When they recognized God's authority in the miracles, they listened to his message and discovered God's authority in his teaching. "They were all amazed, so that they debated among themselves, saying 'What is this? A new *teaching with authority*! He commands even the unclean spirits, and they obey him'" (Mark 1:27, emphasis added). Jesus never commanded humans in the same way. He allowed human free will to make its own decision. He had the power to force submission, but he never used it on humans, in contrast with Augustus.

Some clearly followed Jesus before he demonstrated his power over nature and sickness. With his word alone, he calmed the storms (4:39), raised a dead girl (5:41–42), opened a deaf man's ears (7:34–35), and withered a fig tree (11:14, 20). Yet, when he calls men to follow him, Jesus never used his authority (1:22). Augustus never dreamed of gaining adherents with authority alone. He needed his civil wars to force his will on the people. They were forced to recognize his authority because of his power.

Jesus begins his challenge toward the power of Rome by demonstrating his power when he drives out demons (1:21–28). Jesus does not begin his challenge with an insignificant display of power. The war with the devil immediately after his baptism will continue, but Jesus is attacking the devil's own stronghold, the demons themselves.

Augustus needed to be protected from the gods who would do him harm. The contrast is blatant. Humanity needs divine power to overcome the satanic world. Further, Augustus forced people under his control, whereas Jesus uses his power to help people. With every occurrence noted by Mark of Jesus's contact with demons, Jesus wins every time (1:21–28, 32–34, 39; 3:22–30; 5:1–20; 7:24–30; 9:14:29). Even further, Jesus gives his authority to his disciples to cast out demons (3:15; 6:7, 12–13). Augustus had no authority over the demonic realm, nor could he help his people fight that world, nor could he delegate any authority or power to his followers to do what he could not do.

Mark also emphasizes that the demonic world clearly knows who Jesus is: the Son of God. Only spirit beings recognized Jesus's true identity. They were not concerned with the Roman Empire. Ancient literature contains very few exorcism narratives or stories about any specific exorcist. Jesus was not one of many exorcists in the region, and few would have expected a self-proclaimed religious leader, who was only a carpenter's son, to have such authority and power. His authority was viewed as "a new teaching" (1:22). The demons knew they had met the ultimate enemy, the one who had come to destroy them and their master (1:24; 5:7). In 1:24, they call Jesus "the Holy One of God," but in 5:7, "Son of the Most High God."

The demons made one mistake. They came in contact with Jesus, who is both the Holy One of God and the Son of the Most High God. They met the one who had come to destroy them, and he was more than capable of doing so. It was only a matter of time. They were petrified of him. They were not afraid of Augustus.

Jesus had come to free the human race from demonic power. He needed no special magic chants or objects or incantations. Jesus doesn't make an elaborate statement. Jesus needs no sacred name or mysterious formula or special knowledge. His supernatural word ("rebuke") alone seizes the power from the demons, and they are left powerless. Mark challenges Augustus by comparing his power over the Roman Empire with Jesus's power over the demons.

Jesus's authority and power coexist because of his divinity, but he exhibits his authority first. This word "authority" refers to supernatural powers and usually comes from supernatural authority. Mark uses the word ten times, seven in connection with Jesus (1:22, 27; 2:10; 11:28, 29, 33). Twice Jesus gives authority to his disciples (3:15; 6:7). Mark shows the difference between Jesus's authority and that of the scribes, who never claimed direct revelation from God. The impact on those who viewed his encounter with demons was dramatic. Mark records three things that occurred simultaneously: God's powerful deed, human response of shock, and their statement of amazement.

The people, Jews and Romans alike, viewed the miracles as clear presentations of God's power to bring in his kingdom, and he was doing it through Jesus, not Augustus. Something far greater than the Roman Empire is being presented to everyone. Only God could have cast out demons. Mark is showing Augustus to be merely a pawn compared to the Jesus, to whom God has given his authority for the purpose of bringing down the demonic world and bringing real peace to the world.

The crowd did not initially ask, "Who is this?" but "What is this?" The people believed that these miracles against the demonic world were publicly revealing a struggle within the realm of apocalyptic power. Something supernatural was going on. This struggle was God's kingdom attacking the kingdom of Satan, and this assault was probably just the beginning of the end.

The scream of the demon before the holy presence of the Son of God was followed by the man being freed from, and left unharmed by, the demons (Mark 5:1–17). Jesus was delivering a premonition to all who would believe Mark's Gospel and "follow Jesus," leaving the myth of the *Aeneid* and its weak hero sitting on a useless throne in Rome.

Jesus's authority extends to every aspect and relationship of life. He healed Peter's mother-in-law of fever (1:29–31). Fever was regarded as punishment from God for violating the covenant in Lev 26:16 and Deut 28:22. Jesus in no way reprimanded this woman. He simply took her hand and raised her up. Since a fever is not always a result of sin of some kind, this first healing miracle performed by Jesus in Mark's Gospel reveals that he will heal people who are suffering under wrong theology. The second healing dealt with leprosy. Scholars have written extensively about this disease in its context of the Bible and the affect it had on the Jewish people.

The leper was considered a dead person. Curing a leper was equivalent to raising the dead. The Greeks and Romans associated leprosy with death. Aeneas in the *Aeneid* never encountered leprosy, nor did Augustus ever heal anyone—especially not someone with leprosy. The government required lepers to remain apart from society. No Roman would have ever expected Augustus to violate those norms by crossing over into a leper colony and hugging a leprous person, let alone curing him. The Romans may or may not have been familiar with the Torah that stated that only God could cure leprosy (Deut 32:39).

Although leprosy was thought to have been God's punishment for sins, Jesus never claimed that sin caused leprosy. Jesus focused on the forgiveness of sins, not the cause of the disease. When he heals the lame man (2:1–12), Jesus states clearly that he has forgiven the man's sins. This miracle is described in detail, illustrating the depth of faith on the part of the man wanting to be healed that led him and his friends to so doggedly pursue their course to reach Jesus inside that house.

Instead of healing the man first, and then telling him that his sins were forgiven, Jesus did the reverse. In numerous passages the Old Testament connected forgiveness as a requirement for physical healing to take place. "If my people who are called by my name will humble themselves, and pray and seek my face, and turn from their wicked ways, then I will hear from heaven, and will forgive their sin and heal their land" (2 Chr 7:14). The disciples held this view: "And his disciples asked him, saying, 'Rabbi, who sinned, this man or his parents, that he was born blind?'" (John 9:2).

Since Jesus forgave the man's sins before healing him, the Jewish leaders stopped the sequence by asking a very valid question, "Who can forgive sins but God alone?" (Mark 2:7). These leaders had the Old Testament to support their question (Exod 34:6–7; Isa 43:25; 44:22; Micah 7:18). This was a question of authority and power combined. Anyone could claim to have the authority to forgive someone's sins, but a display of power was needed to verify that claim.

Jesus accommodated them by stating: "That you may know that the Son of Man has power on earth to forgive sins," and he healed the man (Mark 2:10). The healing was a clear indication that Jesus had forgiven the man's sins. Jesus used this healing to draw attention to his claim that he has the same authority and power that God has.

Neither Jewish leaders nor Roman emperors would ever claim to be able to forgive sins. There is no incident in the *Aeneid* where Aeneas forgives someone's sins, and then verifies that claim by a display of power. Even when Aeneas has an opportunity to show mercy and forgiveness, he kills instead. During the last battle, Turnus realizes that he has lost the battle with Aeneas. At that point he begs Aeneas to have pity for Turnus's father and for Aeneas to end his hatred. Aeneas hesitates to kill Turnus, "his eyes flickered, and he held back his hand: and even now, as he paused, the words began to move him more deeply,"[1] but then Aeneas remembered the death of Pallas, caused by Turnus. Aeneas's emotions took over and Virgil writes:

> a memory of cruel grief, Aeneas, blazing with fury, and terrible in his anger, cried: 'Shall you be snatched from my grasp (. . .) Pallas it is, Pallas, who sacrifices you with this stroke, and exacts retribution from your guilty blood.' So, saying, burning with rage, he buried his sword deep in Turnus's breast.[2]

Instead of loving forgiveness, Aeneas chose rage and death. He did not have power over his own emotions. Although Turnus had sinned against Aeneas by killing his friend, and Turnus had been severely wounded, he begged for help. Aeneas killed him.

When Mark records Jesus healing the man on the stretcher, Mark is drawing the listener's attention to the contrast of a mere human ruler (whether Aeneas or Augustus), who himself is no different from any other human being, and Jesus. When confronted with a sinful human being whom he is going to heal, Jesus is in complete control of his emotions. He forgives the man's sins, which were ultimately against God—and therefore against Jesus—and heals him to prove that the forgiveness, which can only come from God, is real. The human emperors who became deified gods never made such claims because they did not love people or desire to forgive their sins; they knew that they could not prove their claims by healing people.

In Mark 5, Jairus begs Jesus to come and save his daughter from dying. Jesus goes with Jairus, but on the way to see the daughter, an older woman, who had had uterine bleeding for twelve years, managed to get close enough to Jesus to merely touch Jesus's garment (mentioned four times) and was immediately healed. Mark reveals that the power that healed her "had gone out of him" (Mark 5:30). When Jesus finally arrived at Jairus's house, Jairus's daughter had already died. Jesus raised the daughter from the dead.

There was no loss of power from healing the woman, and the source of power did not originate outside of Jesus, with him acting simply as the channel. Mark makes it clear that the power is inexhaustible and that it is sourced in Jesus. Since God is the source of all power and all-powerful, these two events demonstrate that Jesus is equal with God.

---

1. Virgil, *Aeneid*, 12.939–42.
2. Virgil, The *Aeneid*, Book 12, 31–52.

The woman was afraid when she was discovered to have touched Jesus. A number of commentators believe that the woman feared destruction because her impurity had come in contact with holiness, which should have resulted in her destruction. Contact with the Roman gods was not fearful because of their holiness, but because of their emotional arbitrary use of their power.

Mark presents Jesus as the holy one, and Jesus is redefining the relationship between impurity and holiness. The woman could not contaminate Jesus, but his holiness could heal her sickness. When Jesus raises Jairus's daughter, Jesus simply grasps her hand and commands the girl to get up. Mark makes it clear that Jesus is not using any type of magic or incantations, but simple language, indicating the power of his spoken word. Only God can speak and something happens immediately thereafter. Augustus needed his army to force humans to obey. Jesus speaks, and the dead arise.

When Jesus feeds thousands of people in Mark 6:30–44 and 8:1–10, Mark is saying one thing to the Jews and another thing to the Romans. The Jews would have understood the connection with Ezek 34:14–15 because of the reference to the lost sheep. The Romans, however, were the conquerors, not the lost sheep, at least from their perspective. They did not need a shepherd; they needed a strong king. And their strong king needed to feed his army. Many a battle has been lost due to poor supply lines. Jesus used no supply lines. Whereas *Aeneas* needed to constantly connect with locations that would provide him and his men with food, Jesus went into the desert to perform this miracle. Jesus provided the food directly from heaven, not from Rome.

In two miracles, Jesus walked on the water and calmed a storm. When Jesus calmed the storm (Mark 4:35–51), he had fallen asleep in the stern of the boat. The storm was vicious. The wind was so strong that the waves were breaking over the sides of the boat and the boat was filling with water. The severity of the storm raises the question as to how Jesus managed to stay asleep in the boat, even if he was strapped in. The disciples woke him up, their politeness of addressing him as teacher ceasing after they accused him of not caring that they were going to die. He made no response to the disciples. He simply gave an order: "Peace! Be still!"

The *Aeneid* contains a couple of storms caused by the gods for the purpose of hindering Aeneas from arriving in Italy and fulfilling his destiny. Virgil placed Aeneas and his crew at the mercy of the gods, whom Aeneas could not control. The uncertainty and fear caused by those storms was well-known throughout the Roman world. Every time Aeneas landed on a strange shore, he never knew if that was where he was supposed to be. Jupiter had not communicated the final outcome of Aeneas' destiny to Aeneas.

Virgil wrote the *Aeneid* to assure the Romans that Aeneas's fate was firmly established even if Aeneas did not have any emotional certainty through those challenges. The real story in the *Aeneid* is the battle between the gods, with Aeneas as their pawn. In one storm incident, Juno persuades Aeolus to throw a storm at Aeneas to slow him down and Neptune intervenes and calms the storm.

Mark does not portray Jesus as causing the storm, but as someone who is so calm in the middle of it that his disciples wonder if Jesus even cares about dying. When Jesus rebukes such a severe storm by simply speaking, the Roman mind would not connect that event with Neptune but with Jupiter, the highest god among the Romans. Jupiter, however, did not have absolute power to control nature. In fact, he had to control the damage caused by the lesser gods, especially Juno, in order to assure that Jupiter's declaration of fate would come to fruition. Even after it became clear to Juno that Aeneas would reach Italy, establish his kingdom, and destroy Carthage, and even after Juno acquiesces, Jupiter has to negotiate with her by agreeing to force the victorious Trojans to take on the name and language of the Latins.

Mark portrays Jesus as making no concessions with any lesser gods. With his word alone, he stills the storm. He does not find a safe harbor to save the disciples from Juno. He does not call on Neptune for help. He does not make the storm less severe. He speaks and stops the wind and flattens the sea, instantaneously. Then Jesus asks about their faith in him (not in the Roman gods). Jesus had just performed every kind of miracle possible that demonstrated his authority and power over every aspect of creation: the demonic world, fever, leprosy, forgiveness of sins as proven by a healing, curing an impurity and not becoming contaminated, raising the dead, and feeding an army of hungry people. If Jesus could stay asleep in that kind of storm, why would they believe that he thought they were going to die? Did they not believe that he was the Messiah? Had he not done enough thus far to demonstrate his own innate divinity—a divinity that far exceeded all of the self-proclaimed divinity of the entire mythical Roman Pantheon?

When Jesus walked on the water the significance for the Romans had more to do with Mark's comment that Jesus was "meant to pass them by" (6:48). Romans understood epiphanies. Aeneas needed an explanation for the fact that he had to flee from burning Troy. He found his excuse in an epiphany of Hector appearing to him in a dream and telling him to leave. The majority of ancient epiphany dreams in literary texts attempt to give prestige or explain action. Such dreams revealed the inner thoughts of a mind that needed to make a decision. Aeneas was always hesitant in major decisions, therefore most of the dreams in the *Aeneid* are epiphanies. Mark wants the Romans to view this vision of Jesus walking on the water as an epiphany of Jesus demonstrating his unwavering resolve that resided in his transcendent and divine majesty to the men in the boat.

The first question about the identity of Jesus was "What is this?" (1:27). The second question appears when Jesus calms the storm, "Who is this?" (4:41). The third question comes as an exclamation of fear when Jesus walks on the water. Their reaction to this epiphany was typical and Jesus answered, "Have courage, I am, do not be afraid" (6:50). "Have courage" is appropriate as a first response to their fear; "I am" signals that they are not seeing a ghost; "Do not be afraid" wraps up the Lord's response to their fear. When he enters the boat, the storm ceases, again. Mark's message to the Romans: this transcendent and divine human being need not be feared because of who he is.

The major epiphany in Mark is clearly the transfiguration (9:2–13). When an epiphany occurred, the Romans thought they were viewing a god. The character of the Roman gods was scarcely revealed or discussed. They came to cause fear or to give guidance or assurance. Mark places the transfiguration at the turning point of his Gospel. Two questions have been directly stated with the same answer: What is this? (1:27); Who is this? (4:41); It is I (6:50). It is now time to open the heavens and let the disciples, and the Romans through Mark's Gospel, see the Son of God for themselves.

At Jesus's baptism, God said, "You are my beloved Son; with you I am well-pleased," *spoken to Jesus* (Mark 1:11). At the transfiguration, God will say, "This is my beloved Son; listen to him!" *spoken to humanity* (Mark 9:7). This event is absolutely unique. There is no comparison in ancient literature with this transfiguration. No analogy in the Bible or extrabiblical Apocrypha, rabbinic literature, Qumran, pseudepigrapha, Nag Hammadi, or any Hellenistic literature.

The Greco-Roman world understood metamorphosis, as seen in Ovid's *Metamorphoses*, fifteen books of myths about the history of the world from creation to the deification of Julius Caesar. Mark uses that word, metamorphous, as a starting point to contextualize his message to the Romans, although the Greek and Roman concept of Ovid's mythical metamorphoses cannot be compared with the physical, historical transformation of Jesus.

Jesus is revealing to everyone that his humanity does not negate his inherent divine essence. Jesus is not just a backwoods self-proclaimed Messiah, but the actual Son of God. The simple clothing of a peasant from Galilee is transformed before their very eyes into clothing that only the gods could wear. What had appeared to be a normal human teacher from Nazareth turned out to be the actual Son of God.

The spiritual and material world meet in reality, not in myth. The mystery of the divinity of Jesus, veiled by his incarnation, is revealed to three men who will eventually tell others, and Mark will write it down for all of Rome to ponder. Jesus will not be deified as was the mythical Aeneas or the historical Augustus because Jesus had no need to be deified. Human deification is a myth, while Jesus's divinity is reality. Jesus's divine preexistence enters the Roman world to show mankind what humanity was really meant to be like—not a myth or a tyrant who hopes that his followers will believe that he was pushed by humans and pulled by the gods into divinity. Thus, the transformation of Jesus culminates in God's pronouncement to Rome: your myths are false and your emperors are temporary. Real authority and power have arrived because the preexistent Son of God is inherently divine.

15

Themes and Theologies Compared

The Salvation of Jesus vs. Aeneas/Augustus

A DEAD MESSIAH CANNOT logically save anybody from anything. The Roman understanding of the purpose of a Roman savior was to kill the enemies of Rome and stop the civil wars. No savior could do that from the grave. When Mark states the key to his Gospel, that the Son of Man came to give his life a ransom for many (10:45), Mark did not clarify, except to write that it would be for "many."

Mark begins his Gospel with the words of Jesus that people need to "believe in the gospel" (1:15), and he ends his Gospel with the words of Jesus that "he who believes . . . will be saved" (16:16).[1] Neither verse clarifies the "gospel." In the middle of Mark, Jesus says, "Whoever wants to save his life will lose it, but whoever loses his life because of me and the gospel will save it" (8:35).

The content of the gospel is not spelled out as a theological statement, nor does Mark present any standard creed that contained "the gospel," as Paul did later in 1 Timothy 3:16. Mark's emphasis was not on the theological content of the gospel, but on the person of Jesus. Mark did not compare Roman theology with the Bible; he compared Jesus with Aeneas and Augustus, who were both kings. Jesus, as the Messiah, had to

---

1. Mark 16:9–20 is disputed as having been part of Mark's Gospel because these verses do not appear in the Sinaiticus and Vaticanus, two of the oldest Greek manuscripts of Mark's Gospel. The bracket of 1:15 with 16:16 supports the view that these verses were part of the original manuscript, but somehow came up missing in those two manuscripts. They were found in later manuscripts from which Irenaeus and Hippolytus quoted in the second and third centuries.

die as a king. Neither Aeneas nor Augustus died to save their people. The mythical Aeneas died after he had fulfilled his destiny of establishing the Roman race. Augustus died after he had made Rome the world power in the Middle East and Europe. Neither Aeneas nor Augustus died to "save" their people from sins. Neither died to offer a personal relationship to the gods. Jesus's death was his destiny. How did their journeys and lives compare with one another?

When Aeneas is compared with Jesus, Aeneas had no idea how much he was going to have to suffer on his journey to fulfill his destiny to establish the Roman people. The gods helped or hindered him, depending on their emotional investment in their chosen human objects of affection, Venus for Aeneas, Juno for Dido and anti-Aeneas. Aeneas knew none of this along the way. The gods had not revealed anything to him, until he was informed that he had to leave Dido behind because his fate was calling him to fidelity to and honor for his destiny.

Jesus, on the other hand, spent the first half of Mark demonstrating his authority and power over every aspect of creation, and when he reached the midpoint of his ministry in Mark he announced that the Son of Man *must* suffer many things, be rejected by the elders, the chief priests, the teachers of the law (scribes), and be killed (8:31). Mark is challenging the *Aeneid*'s presentation of a savior who is destined to establish a people (Romans), but who is clueless as to that destiny or, once he leaves Dido, clueless as to how fate is going to work out the details.

Jesus was not an indecisive ignorant loser who had to flee from the Greeks in Troy and then who needed help from the arbitrary gods of Jupiter, Venus, Juno, Neptune, *et al.* Jesus needed no help for anything during his time on this earth. Jesus's death was not an accident because Jesus misjudged the level of rejection his message would encounter or simply an unexpected twist of fate, as was Julius Caesar's end, whose death saved no one. Jesus knew his "destiny" before he arrived. Jesus foretold his death three times in Mark (8:31; 9:31; 10:33–34), and each time echoed an underlying theology of providence. His death on the cross was the payment for human sin, but the Father was the one who demanded the payment. The Father laid this plan down before the foundation of the world, as opposed to Jupiter's weak attempts to fight off Juno's endeavors to sidetrack Jupiter's declaration of Aeneas's fate.

When Pilate asked Jesus if he was a king, Jesus answered in the affirmative (15:2). This confession could have been enough to crucify any criminal in the Roman Empire. Pilate, however, recognized no threat from this King of the Jews. It seemed as if Jesus wanted to die. From Rome's perspective, that would be the end of this messiah's kingdom, having not even saved himself. Mark does not elaborate on Jesus as a savior. Mark focuses on establishing the deity of Jesus in the minds of the Romans. The high point of success for Mark was the Roman centurion's declaration, "Truly this Man was the Son of God" (15:39). Only the Son of God could somehow save people.

How did Mark define and describe this salvation offered by a king who would die to save the people? When Jesus announced his death in 8:27, he culminated this announcement with his statement about paying a ransom. Toward the end of Mark's Gospel at the high point of the Last Supper (14:24), Jesus adds more information about his ransom when he states that the cup is his blood, which is poured out for many—a ransom for many (8:27) and his blood for many (14:24). As his life was sacrificial, his death would facilitate some type of salvation for mankind (many) that had nothing to do with economics or the military or politics.

The Romans understood paying a ransom for the release of prisoners. Jesus had identified himself with sinners who needed a physician (2:14–17) and then states that they need to be ransomed (10:45). His death would pay their debt for their sins. Jesus was not an unwilling scapegoat, but an active volunteer giving his life to pay a debt to God. Even more bizarre, Jesus paid their debt by actually taking their place and took their punishment of divine wrath to make propitiation with the Father.

Drinking blood would have been abhorrent to the Jews, but the Romans would have connected Jewish sacrifices with the temple, not with a hill outside of Jerusalem. Jesus's blood was shed for "many" at Golgotha, the place of the skull, a symbol of death. Death resulted from sin, and Jesus had identified himself with sinners very early in Mark's Gospel. Sinners were never considered a part of any Jewish in-group, thus the "many" included the Romans.

When Jesus rode into Jerusalem on a donkey (11:1–11), the Romans would have wondered how weakness could save people, and when Jesus attacked the money-changers and turned over their tables in the temple (11:15–19), the Romans would have viewed that as sacrilegious, but there would have been no doubt that Jesus was rejecting the Jewish worship service. In fact, it looked as if he was actually condemning it by pronouncing God's judgment on it. Jesus will ultimately prophesy the temple's destruction (13:1–2), a destruction that Mark does not record.

Any Roman who read Mark after 70 AD would note the fulfillment of Jesus's words.

Jesus's rejection of the Jewish temple as a place of ritual sacrifices for the atonement of one's sins would cause the reader to ask: How then does one get forgiveness of one's sins? The Romans were never allowed to offer sacrifices in the Jewish temple for their sins. Is Jesus offering the Romans a different way of atonement? Jesus had already made it clear that he had the authority and power to forgive sins (2:1–12). When the temple was actually destroyed in 70 AD, the point would have been blatantly clear to anyone who had read Mark's Gospel: the sacrifice on the cross had replaced the temple, and now atonement for sins was open to everyone— even the Romans who had carried out the crucifixion.

The atonement is a foundation stone for the study of salvation, but the study of salvation needs a more concrete definition. Mark 15:39, the centurion's confession, defines Mark's view of soteriology: "Truly this *man* was the *Son of God*." Mark is not simply presenting the gospel to a general audience, but he is connecting Israel's blessings to the Romans and all gentiles. Humanity is blind to itself and God, and therefore Mark opens their eyes to "see" eschatologically what God is doing in human history through Jesus. The centurion "sees," at the moment of Jesus's death, who Jesus is by how ("in what manner") Jesus died on the cross. Humanity is separated from God, but at the moment of his death, Jesus as a man is declared to be the Son of God, a clear declaration that God and humanity have joined in the same realm to remove the hostility between them.

Mark states his challenge to Rome by showing that the centurion is "standing opposite" Jesus, indicating that the Romans were not previously a part of Israel's calling but their enemy. Now they are included in Jesus's offer of salvation from their sins (not from enemies of Rome or from civil wars) through his payment on the cross for everyone. Jesus's salvation cures blindness, reconciles to God, and redeems Jews and gentiles alike. Rome wanted to assimilate all cultures and religions under Roman authority and power. Jesus wants to bring all of humanity under the love and protection of God. Augustus was connected to the Roman religion of myth. Jesus is connected to the living God who saves people's souls.

Most scholars understand soteriology to be defined as the comprehensive content of how God saves mankind through Jesus. This definition makes soteriology propositional, which it is, and therefore, scholars look primarily for these propositions, especially explicit statements, in any given text to build their theology of soteriology. This highlights Mark 10:45 as the epitome of Mark's soteriology,although Mark makes no clear propositional statement that Jesus's death is an atoning sacrifice for sin. Instead, Mark simply tells the reader how Jesus died. Mark is not filled with propositions that need to be organized theologically, but a story intended to simply proclaim "the beginning of the good news about Jesus the Messiah, the Son of God" (Mark 1:1). If the centurion in Mark 15:39 is the high point of Mark's narrative, then Mark is very interested in challenging Rome's claim to salvation.

Early on, Jesus is the target of death by enemies who had found a common enemy (3:6). The reader is reminded that this murderous atmosphere existed at the beheading of John the Baptist (6:14–29) long before Jesus fully revealed his mission. When the passion narrative begins, this hatred connects the Jewish clergy with Judas, who betrays Jesus into the hands of God's enemies (the Jews). There seems to be no good outcome to this conflict. Jesus will die, as have all other Jewish messiahs during Rome's occupation (Acts 5:33–39). Jesus did die, but "how" he died revealed to a Roman the true meaning of the ransom in 10:45 and the blood that was shed in 14:24. The Son of God died as that ransom.

Different from propositional teaching, narrative allows the reader to discover what is being said by watching events instead of listening to a lecture. This does not negate the necessity of propositional teaching but offers another door to understanding.

The narrative passion passage (14:1–15:47) details the death of Jesus which Mark makes clear that everyone wanted and that Jesus himself foretold. It culminates in the centurion's confession (15:39). The clearest focal point centers on the actual death of Jesus (15:33–39) which connects the identity of Jesus as the Son of God, not recognized by the disciples even at the transformation (9:14–29), although the demons understood. Another focal point is that the Son of God is actual deity as revealed by the three references to him at the beginning (1:11, baptism); the middle (9:7, transfiguration); and the end (15:39, death by crucifixion). The centurion is the first human to recognize that the man hanging on that cross is the actual divine Son of God, and Mark makes it clear that that first human is a Roman.

Did the centurion really believe that Jesus was the divine Son of God? Was this part of Mark's plan of reaching the Romans with the gospel? As noted earlier, numerous scholars have tackled this topic. The title

"Son of God" is the most important title for Jesus in Mark. It occurs eight times in the Gospel (1:1, 11; 3:11; 5:7; 9:7; 13:32; 14:61; 15:39). The first seven times lead up to the finale of the eighth time.

Mark calls Jesus the Son of God in 1:1; God does so in 1:11; the demons did in 3:11 and 5:7; God does in 13:32; and the Jewish high priest asked him if he was the Son of God in 14:61. For the first time in 15:39, a human being recognizes what Mark has been revealing through the text, through God, through demons, and through the question of the high priest: that Jesus is in fact God's Son.

How would Mark's readers have understood this soldier's exclamation? This was a Roman centurion. This monumental statement spontaneously emerged from someone who seldom reacted out of pity or simple credulity. Other Romans had shown the same recognition and even faith in Jesus (Matt. 18:5–13; Luke 7:1–10; and especially later, Cornelius in Acts 10). In contrast to the responses of everyone else at the cross, the centurion is not mocking or taunting Jesus, and certainly not after he died. This is this centurion's first appearance in Mark, and Mark wants his Roman readers to fully understand what this Roman centurion discovered, understood, and professed: Jesus is the (without the definite article, a character quality) Son of God.

This Roman's exclamation reveals Mark's understanding that the death of Jesus offers salvation to the world. For Mark, spiritual blindness is a condition that grips the entirety of humanity. Jesus appears preaching the good news of God's kingdom (1:15), defeating the spiritual forces oppressing humanity (1:21–28), and announcing that his coming marks the end of satanic tyranny over the world (3:23–27). Yet the world does not recognize Jesus as God's agent of deliverance but rather disowns him (6:2–3) and conspires to "destroy" him (3:6).

For Mark, however, this christological blindness is the classic kind of blindness that is inherent to the human condition as a whole. After Jesus offers his parable about the sower (4:1–9), he explains to his disciples, privately, why he speaks in parables: "for those outside everything comes in parables, in order that seeing they might see and not perceive and hearing they might hear and not understand lest they turn and it be forgiven them" (4:11–12). God, through the agency of Satan, has blinded the "outsiders" while offering insight to the privileged "insiders." Thus, the world as a whole is oblivious to the spiritual realities that govern their lives. Human beings as human beings do not know the truth about God, Jesus, or their own condition. God has to show them.

Although Jesus offers the "mystery of the kingdom of God" (4:11) to his disciples, still they do not understand. Therefore, it comes as a shock when Jesus dies and the temple veil rips and the centurion "sees." The Jewish leaders deride Jesus as the "King of Israel" and suggest that if he comes down from the cross, they will "see and believe" (15:32). Others standing around are waiting to "see" if Elijah will come (15:36). No, a Roman first "sees" who Jesus is and utters "truly" this is the Son of God.

Mark places the tearing of the veil first, just before the centurion's confession. *This is important.* The ripped veil represented to both Jews and (now through Mark's Gospel) the Romans that God is removing an obstacle that is preventing him from an apocalyptic revelation of himself to humanity. When the centurion makes his confession, he connects two opposites: "Truly, this *man* is the Son of *God*" (15:39, emphasis added).

The centurion was not claiming that Jesus had *become* a Son of God, as was claimed of the deified Aeneas and Augustus. Essence, not progression, is the issue because Jesus can do what only God can do. Humanity and deity come together on the cross, and Mark wants his readers to know that a Roman saw it first. Jesus combines God and humanity and thereby replaces the temple as the meeting place between God and man. No one needs a building to connect with God any longer. Jesus is that connection.

I don't want to use too many Greek or Latin words in this book, but this next point hinges on the differences. In Mark 15:39–45, Mark wanted to make his point very clear that he was addressing and challenging Virgil's Latin (not Greek or Hebrew) audience of the *Aeneid*. Matthew and Luke used the proper Greek terms that translate into "martyr" in English, but Mark used the transliterated Latin loanword for centurion to describe the Roman in charge of the crucifixion of Jesus on the cross.

Mark's statement that the Roman stands "opposite" of Jesus could imply initial opposition, as in "against" or "in opposition" to Jesus. Mark does not explicitly write that, but the centurion would be considered an enemy of the Jews, and especially of a criminal considered bad enough to be crucified. This was probably the only centurion present, since more than one was not needed to oversee a crucifixion. The symbolism of a centurion standing against this criminal would emphasize the surprise of that Roman representative being shocked into a confession that the Romans had just crucified the Son of God. That a Roman centurion would care is significant to Mark's argument that Jesus is speaking through his death to Augustus, whose own death opened no doors to heaven for his people.

Mark is not interested in the reader figuring out the centurion's motives for making his confession. So, what is Mark trying to tell us? A gentile Roman soldier known for oppressing Jews—an enemy overseeing this everyday crucifixion—has his eyes opened to see the reality of the person on this cross, and he spontaneously exclaims: "This was the Son of God!" (15:39). Mark's message: the first person to grasp the implication of Jesus's death was not a Jew, nor a Greek, but a Roman!

Mark's Jewish audience would most certainly remember Ps 22:27, which announces that "All the ends of the earth will remember and turn to the Lord. All the families of the nations will bow down before You." This background would not have entered the Roman centurion's mind. His response was not ignited by the Old Testament but by "how" Jesus died. Whatever that meant to the centurion, Mark uses that centurion to proclaim to Virgil's worldview that the Son of God's death will affect Romans more than anything that the mythical Aeneas or the historical Augustus did with their lives or their deaths.

Centurions, as important as they were within the Roman system, were still a dime a dozen. The insignificance of a single statement from a trained killer over the entire existence of the Roman Empire would normally never even be worth mentioning. The Jews, like Peter or James or John, should have proclaimed that God was reaching out to the nations, but Mark reaches out to quote that one insignificant centurion to make a statement so profound that the fact of that statement will assign the entire Roman Empire to the normal oblivion of every other temporary dictatorship throughout written history. The Son of God will save those who choose Jesus over Augustus. The cross does not simply "show" salvation to the world, but it "accomplishes" it (14:24) because the Son of Man, not a Roman emperor, paid mankind's debt of sin. All of humanity's destiny is fixed to the cross, and a Roman centurion has informed humanity that the man Jesus, the Son of God, used the cross to become a "ransom for many" (10:45).

16

Themes and Theologies Compared

The Afterlife of Jesus vs. Aeneas/Augustus

MARK WROTE HIS GOSPEL shrouded in just enough mystery to raise important questions. His terse style left some of these questions unanswered, forcing the reader to ask how those things were possible and why they had happened. This approach to communication makes the reader wonder if the author just wants to raise the curiosity of the reader, but has no interest in satisfying the reader's curiosity, or if the author realizes that the reader cannot comprehend well enough what is being witnessed without more information and further experiences. The resurrection of Jesus supports the second reason for Mark's unanswered questions.

The Gospel began with fulfilled prophecy (Isa 40); it seems to end with prophecy that will be fulfilled within hours of its prediction ("I will strike the shepherd, and the sheep will be scattered," Mark 14:27), and then closes with a prophecy that would be filled within three days ("But after I have been resurrected, I will go ahead of you to Galilee," Mark 14:28; "But go, tell His disciples and Peter, 'He is going ahead of you to Galilee; you will see Him there just as He told you,'" Mark 16:7). The first mention that Jesus was going to rise from the dead (Mark 8:31) occurs after Mark has been asking the question, "Who is Jesus?" through the first half of the book. Immediately after Peter answers the question correctly, Jesus reveals that he will die and three days later rise from the dead. Then Jesus reveals his true identity to three disciples.

Augustus did everything he could to promote himself as the fulfillment of Aeneas's fate for the Roman race. Virgil wrote the *Aeneid* for the main purpose of propagandizing Augustus to the people. Virgil wrote an epic poem, a form of writing that had become firmly embedded in the reading habits and theaters of the Roman people. By using the form that was familiar to everyone, Virgil's story went straight to the heart of every Roman who desperately wanted a live savior, a champion, who would grant them the comfort of a people who would rule the world.

Virgil's story was reverse history. He wrote a myth about Aeneas that rewrote history to support and elevate Augustus to his desired position of divinity. When Aeneas and Augustus died, they supposedly entered the realm of the gods, but the realm of the gods is a vague, grey, nebulous world with minimal connection to the physical world of Rome. Neither Aeneas nor Augustus ever predicted that they would rise from the dead, nor would it have even entered their minds. Not even Virgil could have imagined any of his heroes physically rising from the dead and actually returning to eat and drink with their followers.

Jesus not only predicted his resurrection, but he revealed that he was in complete control of the entire event, even to the point of predicting the time he would be absent: three days. He made that added statement three times in the Gospel. But Jesus had no aspirations of becoming immediately famous. His plans were focused on others, not himself, and those plans encompassed eternity. He charged the disciples to tell no one about his transfiguration until after the resurrection. When they discussed among themselves what he meant by rising from the dead, Jesus gave them no further clarification. His agenda went beyond the selfishness of a deceptive dictator who was intent on using people to promote himself. Jesus was intent on serving others for their sakes and rising from the dead so he could have an eternal relationship with those who chose to follow him.

The second revelation of his resurrection comes between the story of a vicious and powerful demon that Jesus casts out and the argument among the disciples as to which one of them is the greatest. Jesus's resurrection will finalize his victory over Satan, and the disciples will realize that their discussion is equivalent to Augustus's attitude about himself.

The third prediction of his resurrection precedes Jesus's central verse that he came to serve and give his life as a ransom for many, as opposed to Augustus's drive to serve himself.

Although Aeneas, Augustus's forerunner, never argued for his place as the greatest, he is clearly chosen by the gods for greatness from the beginning. Aeneas's main motivation was to serve his present and future people. He gives up almost all personal desire to accomplish this, giving of himself in a way incredibly selfless for a human (Book 4).

Initially the sacrifices he makes are intended for his own people, but the *Aeneid* implies that with the establishment of the Roman Empire, the safety and security of the world can be secured. The similarities and differences between the sacrifice of Aeneas and the sacrifice of Jesus on the cross are obvious. The main difference between Aeneas's sacrifice and Jesus's sacrifice is the lack of a personal relationship with God through the forgiveness of sins. Augustus, on the other hand, did not sacrifice himself for his people, as did Aeneas. It could be contended that Aeneas, the forerunner, was a better man than the person he represented. In any case, with these three predictions of his resurrection, Jesus is not putting his hope in a general resurrection at the end of the age, but his own, specific physical resurrection.

The idea of a physical resurrection was believed by many, as evidenced by those few who openly rejected the idea. When the Sadducees tried to mock Jesus and the resurrection, he uses the physical resurrection as the main presupposition for his argument when he replies, "For when they rise from the dead" (12:25). Only a few people doubted that a physical resurrection was a real phenomenon. Yet, no one believed that any Roman emperor would ever experience such an event.

When Jesus rose from the dead, no one saw it coming. Some women had come to anoint his dead body, but when they went to the grave, the last thing they expected to experience was an angel telling and showing them that they had the right tomb but that Jesus, the Nazarene, who was still very much human, was "not here," i.e., physically alive and in a different physical location (16:6).

John the Baptist had been a camel-skin clad messenger when Jesus began his servant ministry, and now the opposite appears: a live angel, a messenger, dressed in radiant white clothing, informs the ladies that Jesus is risen, and then that angel makes them messengers to tell the disciples. Jesus had come from Nazareth in Galilee (1:9), and after the resurrection he is returning to Galilee (16:7), returning to his starting point.

One might expect Jesus or the angels to have instructed the women, or at least some of the more important men in Israel, to immediately communicate to Pilate that Jesus had risen from the dead and suggest that he inform the Caesar. Mark records that the women "said nothing to anyone, since they were afraid" (16:8). This response plays a major part in the discussion about which ending of Mark is the most probable:

the shorter one that ends at 16:8, or the longer one that continues on to 16:20. Neither ending clouds Mark's message. The fear of the women could have been an initial normal response to the resurrection of Jesus. As the other gospel writers tell us, the women did not stay silent. They told the disciples.

Of all the accomplishments completed by Aeneas and Augustus, they never had to rise from the dead in order to make sense of their lives or to fulfill their agenda and destiny. Only God could have done what Jesus did, and the resurrection proved that. Aeneas's and Augustus's essences were not ontologically divine but declared divine by humans who followed them. There is no competition possible between what they did and what Jesus did.

When Augustus died, Rome moved on to the next emperor. When Jesus rose from the dead, the empty tomb became the beginning of a new era. Before the cross Jesus had gathered no army, attacked no enemy, won no battle, bypassed an earthly throne, received the death sentence from a confused Roman ruler, and died a horrible death at the hands of a Roman centurion. What appeared to be a failed attempt by an idealistic would-be Messiah turned out to be the necessary prerequisites for the central event in human history: God's predetermined and decisive act of saving humanity from their sins by the death of his Son on the cross. And the proof of this assertion? The resurrection of the eternal emperor.

When Jesus prophesied his coming in glory in 8:38, he brought the shame into the discussion. "For whoever is ashamed of me and of my words in this adulterous and sinful generation, of him will the Son of Man also be ashamed when he comes in the glory of his Father with the holy angels." No Roman wanted to be shamed. Nationalism and loyalty to Augustus controlled and directed the Roman mind. Jesus boldly claimed that he would return in the glory of the Father, not Jupiter, and with the holy angels, not the apparitions and ghosts of the *Dis*, the underworld, of Virgil's *Aeneid*. If a person chose the Roman savior over Jesus, he would experience God's shame instead of the expected Roman honor. Those who chose to follow Jesus now will be gathered by the angels from anywhere on the earth (13:26–27). When Jesus returns, everyone will experience his power as they view him seated at the right hand of God (14:62).

The resurrection becomes the ultimate foundation that verifies the reason for his death and teaching about his second coming. As he would return to Galilee before them and "see" them after his resurrection, so would he return to take them with him into his eternal kingdom.

His coming kingdom will not be limited to the conquered territories of the Roman armies. Reading and listening to Mark's Gospel allows one to "see" Augustus and Jesus from God's (not the Roman gods's) eternal perspective.

17

Themes and Theologies Compared

The Kingdom of Jesus vs. Aeneas/Augustus

THE FIRST MESSAGE JESUS begins with in Mark is that "the kingdom of God has come near" (1:15). The Roman kingdom had already arrived, begun by Aeneas and brought to its pinnacle by Augustus. For Jesus to claim that the kingdom "has come near" reveals that God's kingdom is different than Rome's kingdom. As the people watched Jesus edge closer and closer to the cross, he continually presented different aspects of God's kingdom with his teachings and miracles. Later in the Gospel Jesus will reveal that the kingdom of God has a facet of power that some of his disciples would see come in the future (9:1).

The entrance requirement to become a member of Rome's kingdom was to accept and support Rome's state religion, which included recognizing Aeneas and Augustus as deified. The entrance requirement to become a member of God's kingdom was a two-sided coin. Repentance (a "change of mind," "a conversion from one system to another") meant turning away from other religious systems and believing (place one's trust in/on) the good news, as will be expressed and explained by Jesus through Mark.

The kingdom of Rome contained all the normal human aspects of land and cities, citizens and non-citizens, economics and taxes, laws and government structure, kings and vassals, soldiers, merchants and peasants, priests and laymen. It was founded on the myths of Virgil and the blind obedience of the people. The required religion permeated every aspect of life, but no Roman or foreign god had conquered the hearts and minds of the people.

The kingdom of God consists of God creating humanity and being actively and directly involved in directing human affairs to accomplish his ultimate purposes. When Jesus says, "The time is fulfilled," he is claiming that God's plans are absolute, as opposed to Jupiter's arbitrary "fate" that was continually challenged by the other gods (Juno). God placed his divine Son, the human Jesus, at the center of his reign and focused everything on who Jesus is, what Jesus does, and why Jesus does it. God's kingdom is effectively the kingdom of Jesus. The followers of Jesus have entered his kingdom, but because Jesus's kingdom is directly connected to the supernatural spiritual world, everyone is directly affected by his kingdom.

God's kingdom has been in existence for eternity. The revelation of his kingdom during the Roman era appeared deceptively small and temporary. Jesus had no army and no support system to support an army. No one believed that his kingdom would last long. Then he began to feed thousands of people, and he had no discernable food source from which he received his supplies. Jesus compared his kingdom to a mustard seed, the smallest, most insignificant seed among seeds, but regardless of human response to this small seed, the kingdom's future growth was as certain as the growth of that mustard seed—and that growth will surpass any human kingdom, since God's visible kingdom will become "the largest of all garden plants, with such big branches that the birds can perch in its shade" (4:32).

Jesus had no intention of storming Rome with an army of fishermen to free the Jewish people from Roman oppression. Had he done so, his kingdom would have been no different than any other human-led kingdom based solely on human power that could not have overcome the death of its king.

If King Jesus had not risen from the dead, his perfect life would not have paid for all of humanity's sins. God's kingdom did not focus on the disciples achieving success in society (9:33–35), nor Jesus final step up to sit on the throne in glory (10:35–45). Earthly triumph would come soon enough.

First the inexplicable suffering, and then the growth of the kingdom through the spreading of the gospel, followed by the return of the equally inexplicably resurrected King. During and after the suffering, the kingdom of God will experience cosmic opposition. Augustus's kingdom had to defend itself against other human kingdoms, and it survived because God allowed it to do so. God's kingdom coexists with Satan's kingdom, and God allows that to exist as well, but Satan's kingdom is coming to an end (Mark 3:26).

Augustus's kingdom was not in opposition to Satan's kingdom, and it could be argued that Satan supported Augustus through the false worship of the gods, from Jupiter on down. Satan removes the seed from the Romans (4:15) in order to keep them from being drawn to God's kingdom. Augustus has a powerful ally, but both kingdoms—the evil spiritual one and the puppet one, with Augustus playing the role of a marionette without knowing that he was that insignificant—would be destroyed. Augustus's kingdom would disappear into the pages of history while Satan would move on to find another minion to continue his losing battle against the true King: Jesus.

Satan lost the battle in the desert (Mark 1:12–13), and the victor has arrived to destroy him (1:24; 3:11; 5:7–8). The King will come as someone who is stronger (1:7), and he will bind the strong man (3:22–30) and free the captives. Mark illustrates the helplessness of human effort to fight satanic power in the story of the demon-possessed Gerasene (5:3–4). If the people choose Augustus as their king, then they will face the demonic world armed with only human power. Augustus will be of no help since he had to ask the gods for help to ward off the evil spirits. Romans were helpless in the real spiritual war, but salvation is available if a Roman would return to the words of Jesus in Mark 1:15—repent and believe.

18

Themes and Theologies Compared

Discipleship with Jesus vs. Citizenship with Augustus

A ROMAN CITIZEN HAD privileges beyond anyone else in the realm.[1] Protection, wealth, and prestige topped the list of benefits enjoyed by a Roman citizen. A person was not "called" to be a Roman citizen. One was born with that position or one earned it, or one bought it. From a comfort-level perspective, it was highly recommended that a person be a Roman citizen. Such citizenship was obtained at birth if both parents were Roman citizens themselves, even if the mother had been an alien with the right to marry a Roman man. Citizenship could be granted by generals and emperors to people for any number of reasons.

Voting rights usually came with citizenship, but the Roman society was organized around property ownership, thus voting rights were normally channeled toward the wealthy landowners. Public office was available to citizens, as well as the right to serve in the military if the person owned enough land or was connected with a wealthy relative. Inhabitants of communities and towns came to govern their local affairs while remaining loyal citizens.

Some members of non-Roman communities were given Latin rights but were not allowed to vote in any national politics. If they moved to and lived in Rome, they received full citizenship with all the ensuing rights. The non-Roman allies connected to Rome by treaty had no

1. Beard, *History of Rome*, 66–69, 137, 254. See also Gardner, *Being a Roman*.

Roman citizenship rights but still had to fight for Rome and pay taxes. These allies revolted in 90–88 BC and were granted full citizenship at the end of the war.

Under Julius Caesar, citizenship to soldiers and aristocrats was extended outside of Italy, not everywhere, but the move quickened Romanization among the conquered cultures around Rome. By 212 AD Roman citizenship was no longer of great importance.

In Acts 16 Paul mentioned his Roman citizenship. That information caused a stir among the officials in Philippi, who had instigated the beating of Paul without a trial. Rome had strict laws against treating Roman citizens in such a way. In Acts 22:28 a Roman commander told Paul that he had bought his Roman citizenship. Paul informed him that he, Paul, had been born a Roman citizen.

In Mark, Jesus never spoke about citizenship in the kingdom of heaven, but he did speak extensively about being a disciple. Jesus immediately begins Mark's Gospel with a call to discipleship (1:16–20). (Luke does not get around to doing that until Luke 5.) During this time period, the aspiring young men chose the rabbis they wanted to follow. The rabbis could reject a request, but rabbis seemed to rarely request a specific disciple. Rabbinic literature reveals no rabbis officially calling pupils to follow them. The young not-yet-rabbis realized that their main loyalty was to the Law, not to a rabbi.

Jesus never said that he was a rabbi, which would have been presumptuous since he had been raised as the son of a carpenter and never studied under a rabbi. He simply called people to follow *him*, not to get a degree in the study of law, but to be his disciple. Jesus's call did not focus on a proven academic record. He chose men who lived in the real world, with real professions, with the responsibilities of having families and neighbors and problems—not educated Roman poets or highly intelligent political advisors.

The call to discipleship came with different benefits and with lots of problems. The benefits included a personal relationship with Jesus, much closer friendships than in normal Roman society, a different kind of life on this earth that transformed the person into the image of the one being followed, and the promise of eternal life.

The problems consisted of suffering and being misunderstood by almost everyone along the way. The disciples would learn to compare the challenges and benefits between the kingdom of Rome and the kingdom of God. Only Judas chose Rome over Jesus. Commitment to Rome entailed moral duty and ritual worship. Discipleship under Jesus required the complete person: body, mind, soul, and heart.

Augustus wanted loyalty. Jesus wanted unwavering love. Augustus commanded his people to kill Roman enemies. Jesus commanded his followers to love the Romans. Augustus promised a comfortable life on this earth. Jesus promised suffering now with comfort to follow in the next life. A person could earn Augustus's respect. The eternal life promised by Jesus could only be accepted as a gift of grace.

The Roman people were to avoid being negative about Rome in any way. Jesus sent his followers out to actively and intentionally preach the good news to everyone. Augustus had little patience with those who were slow to understand. Jesus gave the disciples the same lessons over and over. Augustus always attempted to motivate the people to be proud of the Roman Empire. Jesus replaced pride with humility and servanthood. Augustus considered desertion to be treason. Jesus forgave Peter for denying him three times. Augustus treated women well but considered them less qualified than men for the more important things in life. Jesus put women in the position of being his first messengers to proclaim that he had risen from the dead. Augustus did everything to promote himself. Jesus healed people. Augustus allowed no competition, no other kingdom, during his reign.

When the Herodians attempted to trick Jesus into either heresy or treason (Mark 12:13–17), they asked him about paying taxes. He responded that they should give the coins back to Caesar whose face was on them. They were amazed. It is possible that their amazement was based on Jesus's requirement of denying oneself in order to follow Jesus. That type of commitment did not usually acknowledge another kingdom that might have some authority over the followers. The disciples would eventually recognize that Jesus had introduced a different type of kingdom to them, but not only to them—a kingdom that a Roman centurion "saw" when Jesus died on the cross (15:39).

19

Themes and Theologies Compared

The Secrets of Jesus vs. Aeneas/Augustus

BECAUSE JESUS DID NOT clearly state that he was the Messiah, some scholars teach that he did not know he was the Messiah. These scholars claim that Jesus's disciples invented his messiahship after he died. That would have come as a surprise to Jesus.

Jesus was the master teacher. These scholars are not. Jesus always chose the best time to reveal things about himself, so the people could discover what they were looking for. If they were truly seeking the Messiah, they found him in Jesus through his actions and words throughout his three years of proclaiming the kingdom of God. If they were not truly seeking the Messiah, they saw Jesus as deluded and a threat.

A good piece of literature always keeps the reader looking for more. Mark was a master of holding the interest of even those who reject the claims of Jesus.

Empty speculation contributes very little to serious biblical scholarship, but such speculation has plagued serious research throughout the history of the church. In light of Virgil's success at spreading the blatant message of the *Aeneid* across the known world, Mark chose tantalizing secrecy to reveal the God's ruler of his kingdom.

Virgil used an epic poem, a commonly understood form of communication, to convince the people that his myth was true. Mark used parables. Parables were not stories used to simply explain or compare ideas, nor to spice up a boring conversation. Parables spark one's curiosity to force a person to evaluate, decide if he wants to know more (Mark

4:9–12). Those who were truly seeking truth were given an explanation of the parables. The others were left to believe that Jesus was a nutcase.

Parables also allow the inherently paradoxical to find clarity. How can a messiah die and still save his people? How can humility and service overcome pride and the regime of dictators? The parable of the vineyard owner answers both questions. The Messiah will rise from the dead (12:10). Parables also reveal new panoramas that sabotage wrong biases and assumptions by using commonly understood people and plots to paint a different view of reality.

God's kingdom exists in the present because Jesus has entered the scene with his teaching and miracles, but it will continue to exist in the future, as explained by the parable of the mustard seed (4:8, 20, 26–29, 30–32). God's kingdom, in spite of resistance, will thrive and outgrow the opposition. The kingdom of Rome came with Aeneas's and Augustus's armies; Jesus came from an obscure village among an inconspicuous, conquered people. Augustus was constantly looking over his shoulder to see who would try to topple him from power. Jesus was constantly looking at the cross, an event that would not rob him of his power: Augustus's uncertainty contrasted with Jesus's absolute certainty.

Mark does not record Jesus making the direct claim that he alone is in absolute control of his death (John 19:18), but characteristically, Mark reveals Jesus stating unequivocally that he will be killed and that "after three days he will rise" (Mark 9:31). There is no hesitancy or wavering or "if fate allows it" or "if it is written in the stars." Jesus said it; that settles it. The proof that he knew what he was saying comes with the realization of the statement when he did, indeed, rise.

The glorious kingdom of Rome has passed its pinnacle, but the visible aspect of the kingdom of God was just emerging in its eschatological glory.

The parable of the sower (4:3–8) compares Jesus to the sower of the seed, as God's representative, to draw people to himself. He sows to everyone, regardless of their attitude toward the seed. Entrance to the kingdom of God does not depend on one's relationship to the Roman gods but to the seed of God, his word, in the person of Jesus and Mark's written revelation.

The sower is the key. Mark's secret is not that the kingdom of God will surprise everyone when it suddenly appears, but that the sower has already arrived incognito and is already sowing the seed. Immediately after the parables about seed, Jesus surprises the disciples with his ability to control nature (4:35–41), which forced the disciples to ask the question, "Who is this?" Is Jesus the sower, who scatters the seed? Is Jesus the secret? The kingdom of God is so very different from the kingdoms of this world: that God sent his messenger to reveal his kingdom piece by piece, requiring those seeking his kingdom to focus on the messenger, the sower, Jesus of Nazareth, a carpenter's son who does not fit the cultural description of the Jewish messiah nor a king who could oppose Augustus.

The sower's ministry progresses like a hidden seed growing in the ground. The kingdom of God cannot be recognized and understood by looking at the surface ground before the seed has sprouted (4:27). That "revelation" will appear when the time is ready. Mark does not state directly that "unless a grain of wheat falls to the ground and dies, it remains by itself. But if it dies, it produces a large crop" (John 12:24). Mark lets the reader figure it out for himself, which the reader cannot do until after the resurrection. The real kingdom of God finds no place in the world's views of society. It's like a two-year-old looking at a bicycle and only seeing a shiny spot on the handle bars. An adult needs to slowly introduce that child's mind to a picture not possible in that child's simple mind. Only divine revelation can place the pieces of the kingdom of God into the mind of man and make it understandable. Because both the Roman and Jewish understanding of God's kingdom were alike—and wrong—both would need to wait until after the resurrection to grasp God's kingdom as revealed through the risen Son of God.

The unique feature of parables is the different effects they have on the listeners. Whether Jewish or Roman, a person could be an insider or an outsider, depending on whether that person was sincerely listening or not (4:9). Jesus was not a Jewish messiah who had come to support a Jewish rebellion against the Roman Empire. He came to challenge everyone's view of God's kingdom.

Besides that, the present hiddenness of God's kingdom was not to be permanent, as illustrated by a parable about a lamp that "comes" (active voice) to be put on a lampstand instead of being hidden under a bed (4:21). By staying close to Jesus and observing with the intention of discovering truth, one will discover that Jesus is the lamp that comes (1:38) as the materialization of God's kingdom. Looking closely at the light, one discovers that Jesus is the Son of God, not just a myth to trick people into believing in the glory of God's kingdom, as Virgil intended with the *Aeneid*. Jesus's hidden method of saving mankind will be revealed when the divine Son of God volunteers to die on the cross and then surprises the Roman world by rising from the dead. God values weakness over power and he rewarded the humility of the cross with vindication of the resurrection. Rome valued power over weakness and Augustus never rose from the dead to be vindicated for anything.

Sometimes Jesus demanded silence about his person or some event, but sometimes he ordered an announcement. The Gerasene demoniac was told to go home and tell everyone what happened (5:19–20). Jesus required no silence about his public miracles which, with so many witnesses, could not have been hushed up anyway.

After some of the healings, Jesus did not tell people to keep quiet about his person but about the miracles (1:32–34; 3:6–12; 6:54–56). Even though Jesus told Jairus's household to be quiet about raising their daughter, he openly promoted the knowledge that he had been the one who had healed the woman on the way to Jairus's home (5:22–43). The people obeyed his commands to be silent about his person, but they openly proclaimed his miracles. There is no coherent system of theology that surfaces from these instances. The three specific types of silencing commands have different things to say to Rome.

When the demons shrieked out who Jesus was (3:11–12), they were petrified. They were either hoping to ward him off by shouting his name, or more likely, fear simply exploded into screams. Speculating which is true would require interviewing the demons, but such contact is the very thing that Jesus wanted to hinder. When Jesus silenced them, he was stopping the use of their supernatural knowledge that humans did not have.

Jesus began demonstrating his power over the demonic world early, and silencing them was more proof of his superiority over them. Mark's readers would notice that almost immediately (3:11–12).

In contrast, Aeneas and Augustus ruled in a world of magic, and Jesus wanted no source of information coming from the demonic world about himself. Jesus called people to follow him long before he revealed his true identity. Being assured of Jesus's identity by demons held a person in the Roman world of animism and precluded trusting Jesus before knowing all that he was going to reveal through the cross and the resurrection. In addition, Jesus did not want the people to become enamored with demons and be drawn away from his message of repentance (1:15, 38).

Mark wrote his Gospel to point out to future readers that Jesus did not want his identity to be revealed by the demonic world. The power of his word silences the demons and this allows people to "see" Jesus through the event without being hindered or deceived or misguided by demonic messengers. Jesus was not hiding his divinity by silencing the demons. He was demonstrating his power over them and hindering the people from looking to demons instead of directly at Jesus to answer their questions about him when they asked, "Who is this?"

Augustus did everything he could to promote his power and authority through Virgil's propaganda of the *Aeneid*. Augustus attempted to squash any mention of his part in the civil wars so the Roman people would believe that fate had brought him to Rome to solidify what the mythical Aeneas had begun when he established Rome. All other actions by Augustus were promoted by every means possible to draw attention to himself in order to gain the populace's approval and support. It was the only way that Augustus, and any other world ruler, could envision receiving the power of the people to support him.

Jesus, on the other hand, did not need the masses to support him. Although he opened the door to everyone, he only drew those who wanted to follow him before they knew all that he was going to reveal to them in the course of time. Although Augustus gave his all to a propaganda machine throughout the Roman Empire, he still could not erase entirely many of his previous cruelties, thus exposing his weaknesses to those who chose to look closely enough. Jesus chose to conceal his personal identity and his power until it became obvious that the people recognized Jesus's miraculous power, and they began to exclaim, "Who is this person who drives out demons?"; "Who is this person who rules over nature?"; Who is this person who heals the sick?" Humility in Jesus is contrasted with arrogance in Augustus. Jesus never sought fame or glory for himself, which was quite the reverse with Augustus. Maybe Jesus was just being humble and modest. Why did people want to kill him? Didn't the Romans value such things as humility and modesty?

Jesus also never took the offensive to bring in the kingdom of God, as opposed to Augustus's passion to see his Roman Empire above all other kingdoms. Jesus never raised an army nor debated the positives and negatives of myth over history. In fact, Jesus made it quite clear to Pilate that Rome had nothing to fear from him as the King of the Jews (15:2–5) because his kingdom was categorically different from the Roman Empire. This stance made Jesus a different kind of Messiah.

Maybe Jesus wanted silence so that his miracles would not rile up the Roman government, especially if they perceived that Jesus wanted to use his power to attract supporters who were willing to overthrow the government. Then why did Jesus never worry about other people's reactions causing him problems or not allowing him to fulfill his goals?

He clearly could have raised an army by demonstrating that he would have no trouble feeding them (6:30–44), raising any of his soldiers killed in action from the dead, or winning battles of power against demonic forces, something that the Romans could not do. His secrecy focused on giving people time to learn and re-learn lessons about his person (miraculously feeding the masses, 6:30–44 followed by 8:1–10) before revealing his true identity at the transfiguration (9:2–7).

Jesus forbid the disciples to reveal his identity to others in 8:30. He knew that the people would misunderstand his kingship and his presentation of the kingdom of God if they drew their conclusions about him before they had experienced all they needed to know in order to "see" him properly: his death and resurrection. Even the transfiguration would not have been enough without the cross and the resurrection (9:9).

Notice how differently demons and humans responded to Jesus's commands. When Jesus silenced demons, they always obeyed (1:25, 34; 3:11–12). Those humans who benefited from some miracle usually disobeyed Jesus. Eventually, there would be no doubt as to who Jesus was; everything will be disclosed (4:22). After the resurrection, Jesus is fully revealed to those who had chosen to follow him. Mark's "suspended ending" in 16:8 has a direct parallel to Homer's *Iliad* and *Odyssey,* and Virgil's *Aeneid.* All three end in suspense. Is Mark deliberately using the same literary device?

When Aeneas met his father in the *Dis,* his father advised Aeneas to spare the conquered. At the very end of the *Aeneid* Aeneas rejects his father's advice. Aeneas had just defeated Turnus in battle, and Turnus begs for mercy. The last three lines of the *Aeneid*: "So saying, burning with rage, he buried his sword deep in Turnus's breast: and then Turnus's limbs grew slack with death, and his life fled, with a moan, angrily, to the Shades."[1] The contrast with the last three verses of Mark 16:6–8:

> And he said to them, "Do not be alarmed. You seek Jesus of Nazareth, who was crucified. He has risen; he is not here. See the place where they laid him.
>
> But go, tell his disciples and Peter that he is going before you to Galilee. There you will see him, just as he told you."

---

1. Virgil, *Aeneid,* 12.950–52.

> And they went out and fled from the tomb, for trembling
> and astonishment had seized them, and they said nothing to
> anyone, for they were afraid.

The contrast would not be missed by anyone who had been steeped in the *Aeneid* and then read the Gospel of Mark.

Mark portrays Jesus as holding back information about his person and his mission until the disciples are presented with the transformation. Jesus had no sins which he needed to hide from his followers, so they would continue to think well of him. His secrecy was for their benefit, not for himself.

Augustus had his own secrets. He preached Roman traditional family values and virtue. He presented the Romans with a public face of a strict but noble and high-minded landowner and father-run family who treasured a simple lifestyle. He stayed married to one woman for over fifty years, and he set up morality laws to regulate sexual behavior and to punish adultery. He despised the mysterious fertility rites of foreign cults. At one point he ordered a favored ex-slave to commit suicide because the freedman had been having sex with women of Roman nobility. He banished his own daughter for adultery.

Augustus was no saint, however. He was married three times. Although his third wife, Livia, never gave him a child, he remained married to her for over fifty years. However, Tacitus called her an "easy wife" because she ignored his notorious womanizing. Many asked her how she had obtained such a commanding influence over Augustus. She answered that "it was by being scrupulously chaste herself, doing gladly whatever pleased him, not meddling with any of his affairs, and, in particular, by pretending neither to hear of nor to notice the favorites that were the objects of his passions."[2]

Augustus divorced his second wife on the day she gave birth to his daughter, Julia. He married a heavily pregnant Livia immediately. Augustus also took to bed Terentilla, wife of his best friend and closest political advisor, Maecenas. It was rumored that Livia procured young girls for Augustus's pleasure. Everyone in Augustus's household were involved in gross immorality, conspiracy and scandal, with Augustus arranging and rearranging many of their marriages.

Whenever someone suspects a secret to be discovered, one usually thinks that some immorality or crime is involved. Augustus fit that

---

2. Cassius Dio, *Dio's Roman History,* 6 vols., 54.19.3; 58.2.5.

normal human pattern well. With Jesus however, the deeper one dug into his life, the more perplexing the revelation. How does a person enter a world of evil and debauchery without being dragged down into that world and becoming like everyone else? Hypocrisy was normal life. Jesus was not a normal person. Jesus never lied, he never broke a Roman law, he never committed a crime, he never had an affair. Mark used secrets to draw the Roman mind to a man, Jesus, who would completely put Augustus to shame, simply by showing up.

20

Themes and Theologies Compared

The Mission of Jesus vs. Aeneas/Augustus

THE MISSION OF A king arises from that king's culture, his own personality, and his own dreams and goals. Although those dreams and goals vary, there are only so many options. Power, fame, and wealth, and a combination of those three, perfectly describe the history of political aspirations in every society and kingdom. Augustus wanted all three. He spent his life accumulating wealth, but not for the sake of wealth itself. He used it to bring himself power and fame. His intrigue and wars all contributed to placing him in the center of everything, even to the point of being deified. He surrounded himself with trusted people who could and would fully support him personally and support his goals. He even hired an "historian" (Virgil) to tell the story the way he wanted it told. He wanted them to focus on him and his kingdom.

At the very beginning of his ministry, Jesus called his disciples to go with him as active participants in his mission. "Let's go on to the neighboring villages so that I may preach there too. This is why I have come" (Mark 1:38). Jesus gave them training by teaching them and showing them what he was doing, then he sent them out to do the same thing (6:6b–13, 30–31). Augustus was only interested in the activity of his followers if that activity drew attention to himself. The same could be said of Jesus since he did want people focusing on him, but Jesus was also sincerely interested in helping people, not just using them as supporters. Jesus focused on freeing people from sickness, the demonic world, and their sins.

Augustus could do none of these, thus placing the two kingdoms and their missions in two different realms. Jesus gave his followers power over demons (6:7, 12–13): "They went out and preached that people should repent. They drove out demons and anointed many sick people with oil and healed them." When the disciples returned to Jesus, they "reported to him all they had done" (6:30). Furthering the kingdom of God involved more than preaching about the King, and it included no forced submission.

Augustus had to supply his followers with an array of provisions, which took empire-wide preparation, whereas Jesus told his disciples to just take a staff and sandals (6:8–9). Jesus wasn't patterning his ministry after the wandering Cynic philosophers in the ancient world. Jesus was not thinking primarily of mobility and speed. He was also teaching them that their dependence rested completely on God, who would supernaturally motivate the people they met to provide for their physical needs.

Augustus needed to motivate the citizens to support his troops by taxing and threatening them. For the disciples, self-sufficiency would not teach them to rely on God when they encountered opposition, as they would. Although Jesus called Matthew to be one of his disciples, and Matthew was obviously wealthy as indicated by his profession and his home (2:14–15), there is no mention of Jesus asking the disciples to fund their ministries out of their own pockets. Mark only mentions the woman at the house of Simon in Bethany who poured expensive oil on his head, which he accepted as worship, not support. Matthew mentions women who had "served" Jesus during his ministry (Matt 27:55), but no mention was made of his needs. Therefore, it can be assumed that Jesus accepted their help as their gift to him for his ministry to them.

Being involved in Jesus's mission did not always mean success. The disciples were warned about rejection and they were told how to respond to it. They were to shake the dust from their feet as a symbol of acknowledging that rejection (6:11). The disciples were not sent out to force everyone into the kingdom of God, nor to change the world into a Christian culture. Augustus expected the Roman army to win every battle to bring more honor to Rome and more people under Roman power. Augustus wanted the Roman culture to replace all those conquered cultures from the Middle East to Britain.

A few scholars claim that Mark never preached to the gentiles or cared about their fate in the next life. Apparently, these scholars have overlooked Mark's location in Rome with Peter and the Lord's directive to disciple all the nations. Even if the idea might be entertained that Mark focused solely on the Jewish believers in the local church in Rome, there is no way that Mark would have kept the gospel from those gentile Romans who found their way to Jesus through a number of channels (Mark 15:39; Acts 10). The apostle Paul heavily influenced Mark toward evangelizing the gentiles.

Mark shows Jesus drawing Romans into the kingdom of God in a number of ways. Whoever does God's will brings that person into a new family relationship as Jesus's "brother and sister and mother" (3:31–35). Jesus healed many gentiles: the Gerasene demoniac (5:1–20) and the Syrophoenician woman's daughter (7:24–30) being just two examples. Jesus tells Pontius Pilate, figurehead of the ruling world power, Rome, that "the gospel must first be preached to all nations" (13:10; 14:9).

Mark is directly competing with the *Aeneid*'s myth that Rome will rule the world. Jesus's mission is to rule the Romans and the rest of the world. Herod's temple will be destroyed. Jesus wants the temple to be "called a house of prayer for all nations" (11:17) so that even Romans can have a personal relationship with the Father based on forgiveness (11:25), as opposed to the non-relational god system of Rome based on myth.

The Romans relied on religious rituals to bring them contact with their gods. Roman ritual impurity was not considered to be sinful or problematic except that the offender was barred access to the temple and any approach to the gods in the sanctuary until the impurity was removed. Sexual immorality was generally assigned to the category of moral impurity, rather than ritual impurity. Even grave sins held no devastating punishment, meriting nothing more than disbarment from civic sanctuaries. Everything could be purified through ritual means because the Roman system of the gods ascribed to no close relationship between humans and the gods.

In Aeschylus's *Eumenides*, Orestes is successfully purified from matricide.[1] The law from Selinos shows the process of purification for a murder: until he was purified, he could not speak or be addressed, and he could not feed himself. After the rituals were completed, he was free from exile and carried out all the normal human functions.[2]

Jesus changes the definition of defilement. In Mark 7:1–23, he classifies the Roman external defilement as only a symptom of internal

1. Sidwell, "Purification and Pollution," 44–57.
2. Jameson, Jordan, and Kotansky, A "*lex Sacra*," 174–78.

defilement which takes place in the heart (7:6). Jesus actually vilifies those who emphasize external defilement as "hypocrites" who have no connection with God (7:6), and their worship is useless (7:7a). The Book of Jubliees 22:16–19 scornfully forbids any contact between Jews and gentiles, including simply conversing with them out of politeness. Eating with them was strictly forbidden. Jesus demolishes those cultural walls with his scathing reply to their accusations of impurity. "Nothing outside a person can defile them by going into them. Rather, it is what comes out of a person that defiles them" (7:15). Jesus declares all foods clean (7:19). This barrier had kept the Jews separated from the gentiles for centuries. Jesus wants his disciples to follow him as he reaches out to Romans with the gospel.

21

Themes and Theologies Compared

The Eschatology of Jesus vs. Aeneas/Augustus

STRONG LEADERS CHALLENGE THEIR followers to seize the day and to look to the future. Augustus convinced the Romans that utopia had arrived under his leadership and that the Roman Empire would last. He used Virgil's *Aeneid* to support his contention that the god, Jupiter, had ordained the fate of Rome to place Augustus in that position and all Romans would enjoy the fruits of their victories under Augustus. Augustus desired to be viewed as the pinnacle of Roman history. Having successfully pushed the civil wars behind him and out of sight, he tricked the Romans into believing that he had brought eternal peace into the world. If this was believed, his deification was more than justified.

Mark counters this fantasy by laying out the authentic and unquestionable eschatology that Jesus was bringing to the world. One could expect that the Son of God could and would bring eternal peace to the world, but God the Creator, superior beyond comparison to the mythical Jupiter, has already established his own fate for the world, while allowing individuals to choose their place in that fate.

Mark begins his Gospel with "The time is come!" (1:15) in the context of challenging the world's view of peace, and especially Augustus's rendition of that peace. Mark ends his Gospel with "The hour has come!" (14:41) in the context of Jesus making eternal peace possible and offering it to all of mankind by going to the cross. The gospel is not the message of Rome, and the peace of salvation comes not from the external civil wars ceasing, but from having one's sins forgiven.

As Augustus sought to establish his kingdom on the earth, Mark is proclaiming in 1:15 that God has always been active within history and he is now challenging Augustus publicly by inaugurating Jesus's kingdom on the earth, which can be experienced by following Jesus. Like Yahweh challenging Pharaoh, who claimed to be the Egyptian god, Ra, Jesus is challenging Augustus, who views his future among the Roman pantheon of the gods.

But God's kingdom is not temporal. Jesus also revealed a bigger fate than expected by any of the mythical gods of Rome. When Jesus was asked about fasting (2:18), he spoke of himself as a bridegroom and the joy of his followers as his bride in present time, but then he revealed that the bridegroom would be taken away, which will occasion fasting (2:19–20). A bridegroom only leaves under duress. Mark reveals the immediate cause of such duress: the hatred of Jewish leaders (3:6). Warnings about persecution toward Jesus's followers surface throughout Mark and then Jesus reveals even worse things for his followers: wars (13:7), persecution (13:9), betrayal (13:12–13), trials (13:19), and deception (13:21–22). His followers can expect hatred and rejection from the world.

Augustus promised his followers peace and comfort, things that every Roman longed for—a promise no human being can guarantee. Jesus promised persecution and discomfort, things that no one wants. How could Jesus ever imagine that anyone would want to follow him? His most important message to them was a warning that they not be deceived by the negative things he prophesied. One would expect a message of comfort to minimize the fear of such prophecies, but why was deception the main thing that Jesus warned them about?

Jesus's followers, which included both Jews and gentiles, were being offered two diametrically opposed kingdoms, Rome's and God's. Jesus's followers would be persecuted by the other kingdom. The *Aeneid* promised a temporal kingdom on this earth which would persecute God's kingdom. Then Jesus reveals that there is more to God's kingdom than the current visible one. The disciples need to recognize and understand both aspects of God's kingdom and not be deceived into believing that this present world is the extent of total reality. Jesus would be ushering in a future aspect of God's kingdom, "in his Father's glory with the holy angels" (8:38).

Augustus could make no such promises. Augustus knew that he would not return to the earth to continue his rule after his death, and therefore, he made no such promises. Augustus had died and there was only the common-held mythical belief that he had been deified. He would not be returning to complete the setting up of his kingdom.

Jesus warned his followers to not be deceived by the transient nature of Rome's empire. If some of his followers became "ashamed" of him and his word, in preference for "this adulterous and sinful generation," then he would be ashamed of them and they would be judged (8:38), not welcomed into God's kingdom. The Son of Man would "send his angels and gather his elect from the four winds, from the ends of the earth to the ends of the heavens" (13:27).

Jesus offered no timeline for the coming of the second part of God's kingdom. Rome claimed that the wars were over, but Jesus prophesied a future of wars beyond the Roman Empire. These wars would be accompanied by natural disasters, false prophets, and persecution. The followers of Jesus would be sorely tested to continue in believing in Jesus as God's representative for God's kingdom. In spite of the challenges promised by Jesus for his followers (13–14), Mark closes his challenge to the mythical *Aeneid* with an event that no one could have foreseen: the resurrection of the Son of God.

The debate over the authenticity of the additional endings to Mark contributes little to the fact that Mark wrote his Gospel to challenge the *Aeneid*. If the shortest ending is to be preferred, then Mark used those last verses of Mark 16:1–8 as a culmination of his nebulous predictions, three times, that he would die and rise from the dead (8:31; 9:31; 10:33–34).

Jesus knew that the disciples would not comprehend his predictions. Mark builds his case as a master literary craftsman, introducing the conflict between the two kingdoms, reaching the climax by having the earthly kingdom win the day by crucifying the king of the intruding kingdom and blindsiding the readers with the most unexpected resolution ever to have appeared in written history: the crucified victim rises from the dead.

With that resolution Mark drove a stake into the heart of the *Aeneid*'s message about a temporal kingdom founded by Aeneas and set in place by Augustus. Aeneas/Augustus were dead. They were not returning to the earth to complete anything. Their destiny was already finished. Jesus had risen from the dead. His kingdom was just beginning. Augustus's death did not redeem the Roman Empire. Jesus death offered redemption to anyone choosing to follow him. Augustus's grave still contains his corpse, or the dust that it became. Jesus's tomb is empty. The response of the women demonstrates Mark's success of grabbing the reader's complete attention: "So they went out and started running from the tomb, because trembling and astonishment overwhelmed them" (16:8).

22

Background

The Shroud of Greek and Roman Mythology

SOMETIMES HISTORY RECORDS THE factual names of the founders of empires, sometimes not. The foundation narrative of the Roman Empire is based on a myth. The Romans were not very inventive when it came to creating their gods. They were religion thieves. They actually stole them from the Greeks and simply changed their Greek names into Latin.

Let's begin with a wedding that took place among the Greek gods.[1]

Eris, the goddess of discord, was not invited. (Imagine not wanting someone to disrupt your wedding. How rude!) She showed up uninvited and threw a golden apple of discord among the other goddesses, saying that the apple was "to the Fairest." (Snow White had not arrived at the wedding on time.)

Before we witness the outcome of this wedding party, we should drag some other gods into the room. The mythical Roman gods provided an ongoing soap opera for the gullible and the cynical. Different mythical versions attribute different abilities to each god. No eternal god existed in either system, so we will choose to start with Saturn (Kronos in Greek).

1. The legend of the beginning of the Roman Empire is common knowledge to anyone who has had a smattering of Greek and Roman history. Thayer, "Cassius Dio"; Thayer, "Dionysius of Halicarnassus," http://penelope.uchicago.edu/Thayer/E/Roman/Texts/Dionysius_of_Halicarnassus/; Thayer, "Plutarch," http://penelope.uchicago.edu/Thayer/E/Roman/Texts/Plutarch/Lives/Romulus*.html; Encyclopedia Britannica, "Romulus and Remus," https://www.britannica.com/biography/Romulus-and-Remus; Electronic Text Center, University of Virginia Library, "Livius, Titus. The History of Rome, Vol. I," http://web.archive.org/web/20080926121037/http://etext.lib.virginia.edu/toc/modeng/public/Liv1His.html.

No one knows where or when the original mythical gods showed up. The Greeks stole their gods from the Babylonians (Google it), but that's not part of this story.

Saturn was Jupiter's father (Zeus in Greek). Jupiter married his sister, Juno (Hera in Greek). Venus (Aphrodite in Greek) had one of two origins. The reader gets to choose. One possibility: Saturn fought with his brother, won the battle, cut off his genitalia, threw them into the sea, and the foam created by the genitals created Venus. Another possibility: Jupiter was a typically unfaithful god who had sex with Dione, an oracle goddess, and they produced Venus. Venus was beyond gorgeous, so in order to avoid war among the gods over her beauty, Jupiter forced her to marry very ugly Hephaestus. Venus, following in her father's unfaithfulness, had sex with Ares, the god of war, and had four children, but she eventually got tired of Ares and stumbled onto Anchises.

She craved sex with a human male. Anchises was a handsome junior member of the royal family of Troy and a shepherd. Venus seduced him and they had a son, Aeneas, the hero of Virgil's *Aeneid*. The *Aeneid* opens with Aeneas being chased out of Troy with his father, Anchises, who dies along the way, but they meet again in the underworld. We are getting ahead of ourselves.

Back at the wedding three goddesses claimed the apple: Athena (love and beauty; Roman name: Minerva); Hera (supreme goddess, marriage and childbirth, protected women, or at least those women she liked; Roman name: Juno); and Aphrodite (virgin goddess of reason, intellect, arts and literature; Roman name: Venus). We'll drop the Greek names since the Greeks became servants of the Romans anyway. As other gods arise in the discussion, we'll label them appropriately. There will be a quiz at the end of the book.

Zeus, a male god, would not mediate between the three female goddesses. He exhibited some intelligence here. Mythical goddesses can be dangerous when ticked off. Zeus directed Hermes, the god of herds and flocks (among a myriad of other duties—he was overworked), to require Paris to make the decision. Paris, not a god, just a dumb human, was the son of King Priam of Troy.

Paris had been a shepherd in his youth, thus becoming a shepherd prince. Each goddess wanted the apple. They all took baths and cleaned up to impress Paris. He couldn't make up his mind, so all three goddesses stripped nude to convince him of their beauty. Enjoying the contest, Paris couldn't make up his mind. Scholars have wrestled for centuries wondering why Paris was so slow in choosing which goddess he preferred.

The nude goddesses got tired of walking around nude, so each goddess tried to bribe Paris. Juno offered him kingly power over Europe and Asia. Minerva promised to make him a warrior with wisdom and skill in battle.

Venus apparently understood men better than the other two goddesses did, so she offered Paris the most beautiful woman in the world, who happened to be Helen of Sparta, the already wife of the Greek king Menelaus.

Paris chose beauty (Helen) over power; Juno went ballistic and Menelaus launched the Trojan War to get his wife back. That took more than one thousand ships and ten years and ended with the Greek deception of Troy by using a Trojan horse that housed a hidden group of Greek warriors. They got inside the city, snuck out at night, and devastated the place. Although very few Trojans survived the battle, Aeneas, a Trojan warrior, managed to escape. Who was Aeneas and what happened to him? Virgil and the *Aeneid*.

23

Background

Virgil

VIRGIL, OR VERGIL, OR *Publius Vergilius Maro* was born on October 15, 70 BC in Andes, a small village near Mantua, Italy (Cicalpine Gaul at the time of his birth). Two myths recorded by Suetonius describe the birth of Virgil.

> While he was in his mother's womb, she dreamt that she gave birth to a laurel-branch, which on touching the earth took root and grew at once to the size of a full-grown tree, covered with fruits and flowers of various kinds; and on the following day, when she was on the way to a neighboring part of the country with her husband, she turned aside and gave birth to her child in a ditch beside the road. They say that the infant did not cry at its birth and had such a gentle expression as even then to give assurance of an unusually happy destiny. There was added another omen; for a poplar branch, which, as was usual in that region on such occasions, was at once planted where the birth occurred, grew so fast in a short time that it equaled in size poplars planted long before. It was called from him "Vergil's tree" and was besides worshipped with great veneration by pregnant and newly delivered women, who made and paid vows beneath it.[1]

His physical characteristics somewhat fashioned his lifestyle. He was tall, dark-skinned, and rustic. He suffered from stomach and throat troubles, as well as with headaches, and had frequent hemorrhages.

---

1. Thayer, "Suetonius," vv. 3–5.

Apparently, he was exceptionally shy. His poems and their presentations made him famous. When he showed up in Naples, people called him *"Parthenias,"* ("the Maiden"). Whenever he appeared in public in Rome, which was rarely, he hid in the nearest house to avoid being recognized and followed by his admirers.

He lost his parents and two brothers when he was an adult. His family was wealthy enough to have owned land and to have sent Virgil to Cremona, Mediolanum, and Rome for his education. In Rome he studied rhetoric (standard Roman education topic), medicine, astronomy, and in particular, mathematics. He made only one attempt to plead a case in court but failed miserably because he spoke so slowly that he sounded like an ignoramus with no learning whatsoever. He settled on philosophy and focused on Epicureanism (pleasure rules above all else), having studied under Siro the Epicurean.

Virgil's early poetry reflected Epicurianism but later began to morph into Stocism (don't upset the apple cart, just get the job done), which promoted active participation in human affairs and proclaimed that following the order of the universe (closely influenced by the Roman pantheon of gods) demanded order and duty, which would lead to moral conduct shown by tranquility of mind. That's a lot to expect from a philosophy, but these two outward characteristics, order and duty, fit the Roman mind perfectly.

Suetonius mentions that Virgil began his poetry career as a boy by writing about a schoolmaster called Ballista who was stoned to death for highway robbery: "Under this mountain of stones Ballista is covered and buried; Wayfarer, now night and day follow your course without fear."[2] Today he would have written zombie stories.

When he was sixteen, Virgil wrote *Catalepton, Priapea, Epigrams,* the *Dirae,* the *Ciris,* and the *Culex.* The *Culex* tells the story of a shepherd who had fallen asleep under a tree, exhausted by the heat, and a snake was creeping upon him. A gnat flew from a marsh and stung the shepherd between his two temples; he at once crushed the gnat and killed the snake. Then he made a tomb for the insect, inscribed with this couplet: "Thee, tiny gnat, well deserving, the flock's grateful keeper now offers For the gift of his life due funeral rites in requital."[3]

His last three literary endeavors made him famous.

2. Thayer, "Suetonius," v. 17.
3. Thayer, "Suetonius," v. 18.

He was twenty-six when Julius Caesar, in 44 BC, was assassinated. Octavian (who would take on the title of "Augustus") took vengeance on Caesar's enemies at the Battle of Philippi in 42 BC. Octavian took many family estates away from the nobility and gave those estates to veterans.

Virgil's family probably lost their estate near Mantua at that time. Whether Virgil's family had anything to do with the enemies of Caesar is unknown. Virgil was devastated. He wrote the *Bucolics* (also known as the "Eclogues"), which praised his friends Asinius Pollio, Alfenus Varus, and Cornelius Gallus, because they had begged Octavian to give Virgil his estate back. Octavian magnanimously agreed and gave Virgil his farm back.

During Virgil's lifetime, civil war, from at least 31 BC to 20 BC, raged throughout the Roman Empire. Fear and hatred of civil war permeates the writings of Virgil and Horace. Somehow, Virgil was not dragged into those wars, either politically or militarily. He managed to spend his life studying, writing, and performing poetry. His demeanor contradicted the idea of being involved in human affairs, except for the arts. He was a very good Stoic.

He never married, and he entered society only when his poetry made him famous. His province of Cisalpine Gaul had been taken by Hannibal, but was recovered later; it was not incorporated into Rome until 42 BC. This meant that Virgil was not originally a Roman citizen— when he and his family became Roman citizens is unknown. Virgil came to Rome from the outside. All these things sharply molded Virgil's world-view, thought patterns, and how he wrote the *Bucolics* and the *Aeneid*. His history weighed heavily on his attempt to climb out of his violent culture of six civil wars that every Roman wanted to shove under the carpet. Civil war dominated Rome as a curse and destiny from its birth.

Virgil's first *Bucolic* presents Virgil's love of Rome as he writes about the shepherd Tityrus's amazement of the beauties of Rome when he visited the capital for the first time. The *Bucolics* were a collection of ten short pastoral poems on rural topics. Theocritus had introduced this form of poetry in the third century BC.

Some of the *Bucolics* promoted escapism, running away to the countryside, the dream of all Romans who hated civil war. Virgil sang scenarios that idealized imaginary hard-working shepherds relishing the simple joys with minimal sorrows (collapsed love affairs or early deaths of friends or themselves). Roman eyes misted over and tears flowed down their cheeks as they longed for peace. They adored Virgil. Reality ripped them apart. Fiction and poetry ruled.

The allegories Virgil inserted from time to time touched the real world. The fifth *Eclogue* depicted the death of Daphnis, the shepherd king, who portrayed Julius Caesar well. The tenth *Eclogue* presents Gallus, a Roman poet and soldier, who characterized those real people of Virgil's day. The first and ninth mourned over the eviction of shepherds from their farms, which Virgil had personally experienced. He stole the hearts of the Romans as they listened to Virgil's own story. They connected. The dispossessed all wanted the same thing: a simple and good life with no civil war—lessons for today.

The fourth, sometimes called the messianic *Bucolic*, and probably the most famous in the world of Christianity, prophesizes in resounding and mystic terms the birth of a child who would bring back the Golden Age. The Romans were ready for any remedy.

This child would abolish sin and restore peace to the realm. This fourth poem is dated 40–41 BC, when the civil wars appeared to be declining. Virgil never clarified which child he meant. It could have been the expected child of Antony and Octavia, sister of Octavian, but the only child that brought harmony and peace to the Roman Empire was Augustus, the Roman savior.

Christians have believed that Virgil, being familiar with Isaiah, was writing somewhat beyond his own consciousness and predicted the birth of Jesus. This poem came as a reaction to the civil war that had devastated rural Italy by forcing the farmers to go to war, causing their farms and families to suffer greatly.

Virgil's second set of poems that followed the *Bucolics*, the *Georgics*, were composed between 37–30 BC toward the end of the civil wars. The *Georgics* are a brilliant and desperate appeal for the restoration of the traditional agricultural life of Italy. Although they were written more as a lecture to teach, Seneca categorized them not as instruction toward the farmers, but as pure entertainment for the audience. The instruction Seneca referred to (plowing, growing trees, tending cattle, keeping bees) is laid out with clear insight into nature, and the entire poems are peppered with forays into topics about the Italian countryside and the farmer's joy as he takes it all in.

When Virgil had the *Bucolics* performed on the Roman stage, their visionary politics and eroticism brought him immediate public acclaim. Gaius Maecenas, a patron of the arts, had become one of Octavian's closest and trusted acquaintances within Octavian's small circle of allies. Maecenas manipulated the social ladder connections for Virgil with the literary giants of his day, including Horace and Lucius Varius.

When Virgil wrote the *Georgics,* he dedicated each one at the beginning of each book to Maecenas. Before Virgil became famous, Maecenas had helped him against the violence of one of the veterans, from whom Vergil narrowly escaped death in a quarrel about his farm.

He finished the *"Bucolics"* in three years and the *"Georgics"* in seven years. Augustus came to adore Virgil and his writings.

When Augustus was on his way home after his famous victory at Actium, Virgil read the *Georgics* to him four days in succession. Virgil's reading was sweet, and his training in rhetoric made his presentations very effective. Seneca said that the poet Julius Montanus had wanted to steal some of Virgil's works but only if he could have stolen his voice as well. Virgil's voice expressed dramatic power, and when others read his poetry out loud, their voices fell flat and toneless.

When the *Aeneid* went public, Sextus Propertius declared: "Yield, ye Roman writers; yield, ye Greeks; A greater than the *Iliad* is born."[4]

Virgil was not a politician and he had not yet written political propaganda, but his poetry was clearly connected with the current events of political and civil war. He wrote just at the time when the wars were ending and the empire began the process of resettling the land and taking pressure off the cities. He agreed with the new direction of peace that Rome was taking.

When Virgil was thiry-eight, Octavian won the Battle of Actium (against Antony and Cleopatra), the last of the civil wars. Virgil was entering the relief of the Augustan Age, an age of peace. Virgil, a man who felt at home in the countryside, had a heart for the simple life with high morality (relative to their day) and religious traditions. Augustus's desire to preserve the traditions of the republic and to make Rome great again resonated with Virgil.

When Octavian received the honorary title of "Augustus," he commissioned Virgil to write an epic poem that would glorify Rome and the Roman people. Virgil spent the last eleven years of his life writing the twelve books of *Aeneid*. He sought to challenge the Greek poet Homer, and Homer's *Odyssey* and *Iliad*, both epic stories about the ancient

4. Thayer, "Suetonius," v. 30.

Greeks. Although Virgil modelled the *Aeneid* on these two epic stories, Virgil substituted his own Caesar mythology as his primary content.

Virgil had just finished writing the *Aeneid* and now wanted to spend three years in Greece and Asia, where he could visit the places he had written about and verify his writing. Being almost finished with his life's work, he had intended to devote the rest of his life studying philosophy.

He never made it home. In Athens he ran into Augustus, who was returning from the Orient. Virgil chose to travel and return with him. He caught a fever in Megara, which worsened when they arrived at Burndisium.

He was fifty-one and he had not completed the editing of the *Aeneid*. Realizing that he was going to die, Virgil asked Varius to burn his poem instead of publishing it. His motives for that wish went to the grave with him.

Varius emphatically refused to burn the *Aeneid*. Virgil kept requesting his book-boxes in an attempt to burn the poem himself. No one listened to him, so he gave up asking. He simply requested Varius and Tucca that they publish it exactly as he had written it. No additions, corrections or modifications.

He died on September 21, 19 BC in Brundisium, near Naples, Italy. His ashes were taken to Naples and placed in a tomb with an epitaph he had composed himself: "Mantua gave me the light, Calabria slew me; now holds me Parthenope. I have sung shepherds, the country, and wars."[5] He had written out his will and left one-fourth to Augustus.

Immediately upon Virgil's death, Augustus ordered Virgil's literary executors, Rufus and Plotius Tucca, to publish the *Aeneid* immediately with few changes. They did so, with few corrections, even leaving the incomplete lines just as they were. Incomplete or not, it became an immediate success and Virgil has been "worshipped" ever since. The writings of his predecessors and contemporaries faded into insignificance in comparison to the *Aeneid*.

5. Thayer, "Suetonius," v. 36.

24

Background

Augustus

Pre-Augustus

Flashback: You might need to Google some of these figures in Roman mythical history. Few people become as famous as Augustus, but even famous people slid away into forgotten history. Aeneas was the forerunner, like John the Baptist, but Augustus laid claim to deity. He will be Mark's main target. But we need a short preview of the "history" that Virgil had to work with before he could convince the Romans to worship Augustus.

After the mythical Aeneas fulfilled his destiny, many years and many generations later, the myths of Romulus and Remus surfaced. Numitor was a king of Alba Longa, the ancient city of Latium in central Italy. Numitor was a descendant of Aeneas. Numitor had a daughter, Rhea Silvia. Numitor's younger brother, Amulius, usurped Numitor's throne, killed his male heirs, and forced Rhea Silvia to become a Vestal Virgin.

These virgins kept the sacred fires burning so the gods would keep Rome secure from her enemies. A virgin who attempted a secret one-night stand was brutally executed. Rome's security was important.

Rhea Silvia did not remain a virgin. No surprises there. Conflicting mythological accounts present various options for her pregnancy (Mars or Hercules), but Livy, the great Roman historian during Augustus's time, blamed her pregnancy on divine conception. That was gracious of Livy since he wasn't there. He wanted Roman history to be as clean as possible. Apparently, Rhea thought that sex with a god was a higher calling than protecting Rome, or one of the gods cared more about sex than protecting Rome from interlopers.

Rhea gave birth to twin sons. Although Rhea should have been put to death, King Amulius feared the paternal god (Mars or Hercules), so he only imprisoned her. He did, however, order the twins to be killed by natural causes (drowning, etc.).

The servant tasked with the deed took pity on them (minimal originality in this myth as we note the similarity to the story of Moses) and placed them in a basket on the Tiber River. The river god Tibernus calmed the river and caused the basket to land in a fig tree at the bottom of the Palatine Hill in the Velabrum swamp. History is glad that Tibernus was observant.

A she-wolf suckled them and a woodpecker fed them. Eventually a shepherd and his wife, Faustulus and Acca Larentia, raised them as shepherds. While still young adults they met some shepherds of King Amulus, who kidnapped Remus. With a group of shepherds, Romulus rescued Remus and killed King Amulius. Shepherds against shepherds. That works. Where was King Amulius's army? The brothers reinstated Numitor as king.

A mixture of numerous myths about the founding of Rome drew plenty of skepticism from the ancient writers. The Romans desperately wanted to believe these myths about a fanciful wolf conveniently showing up to nurture two little boys (Romulus and Remus) floating down a river, thus saving their lives. Eventually Romulus and Remus began their political careers with a series of unheroic deeds, which included murder, rape, and abduction, and they founded Rome with a bunch of criminals and runaways.

After a quarrel between Romulus and Remus over the location of where to build their city, Romulus killed Remus and built the city on the Palatine Hill. The birth of a nation began with the death of a relative caused by a quarrel over a location. Rome was founded on the day of Remus's death, which is dated by Livy as April 21, 753 BC. Virgil wrote his epic poem on what the Roman people had already come to believe.

Rome's foundation story is one of the weirdest and unique "historical legends" of a city's beginnings. It becomes even more bizarre when one realizes that the Romans bought it, in the broadest of terms, as history.

Why is this background important?

Virgil wanted the people to view Augustus as an extension of Romulus's government. The partial history/partial myth of Rome, as she developed from Romulus to Augustus, will fascinate history addicts, but we only need to focus on Augustus for Mark's future comparisons with Jesus. The most significant *events* just before Augustus's arrival were five civil wars. Four hundred years before Augustus, Rome had achieved a partial democracy, unlike any previous attempt at such a thing. A senate ran the government and the Roman people (SPQR, *Senatur Populusque Romanus*) carried out the government's recommendations through committees.

Around 44 BC, things began to fall apart.

No empire has ever emerged from an era of peace. War builds empires. Rome had been at war with the surrounding peoples for most of its history during the time of the dictators. Rome became an international power after the "Punic Wars" (264–241 BC, 218–202 BC, and 151–146 BC) with Carthage. Once Carthage and Greece (Spartans) had been defeated, Rome dominated the Mediterranean. Life was good, for the Romans.

However, civil war began to rage inside the country. All the normal reasons, generated by greed for wealth, power, and sex. The senate had degenerated into total corruption, which further divided the social classes. The continual expansion of territory did nothing to relieve the internal strife.

After making himself famous in the Gallic Wars, Julius Caesar was installed as dictator for ten years in 47 BC. Hiding behind fake diplomacy, he had said that he would do whatever necessary to make the republic successful. He asked (commanded) everyone in Italy to lay down their arms, stop being afraid of more war, hold free elections, and he let the senate and the Roman people run the republic.

On February 14, 44 BC, he was installed as dictator for life. His life was short. One month later he was assassinated on March 15, 44 BC. His eternal life began two years later when he was deified in 42 BC. No one knows how he fared between death and deification.

Julius Caesar's rise and fall occurred during Virgil's lifetime. No writer of epic poetry was better prepared to connect all the past events leading up to the rise of Augustus. When Julius Caesar had become master of Rome, he governed the way all emperors had previously governed. No major changes. Taking Gaul gave Rome complete power throughout Europe. Roman rule extended from Britain to Egypt and included the entire Mediterranean. Caesar's age of culture raised Rome to the ideal. Romans were proud to be Romans.

Greek was the language of the entire empire. Greek literature and religion flourished disguised as Roman literature and religion. Virgil was a master of adaptation. He launched the *Aeneid* on the two previous Greek epics: the *Iliad* and the *Odyssey*.

However, the internal turmoil of civil wars, social class divisions, and the external wars had taken their toll. The Romans were ready for a change. Caesar had destroyed the democracy and replaced it with a civilization that wanted the old days back. Enter Augustus (Octavian renamed).

Augustus

Everyone is a product of his or her upbringing. Augustus was no different. Gaius Julius Octavius was born in Rome in 63 BC. His father was a wealthy land owner who owned lots of horses. He was the first family member to become a senator. Gaius was a normal politician. He used his wealth for political leverage toward higher positions. He was a provincial governor. He counted on diplomacy, righteous conduct, and courage to bring him a high position in the Roman government. Those weren't enough. Death is not impressed with human achievement.

He died when Octavian was four. Octavian's mother, Atai, was Julius Caesar's niece. This is going to get interesting. Octavian was raised in part by Julia Ceasaris (mother of Atai, Octavian's grandmother, and Caesar's sister).

Octavian, plagued by frequent sicknesses, was a graceful person, which caused people to think positively of him early on in his career. Raised by two women, he had little military experience as a boy. This did not bode well for becoming an emperor.

When he was twelve, he delivered an oration in honor of his grandmother Julia. Even that early in his life it was obvious that Octavian was becoming fit to rule an earthly kingdom. Out of nowhere his leadership abilities surfaced between the ages of twelve to sixteen.

His mother and stepfather made sure that Octavian spent his time learning and building relationships with people in power. They kept him away from one of the civil wars in Italy. At fourteen, he carried out all the sacrificial rites required for manhood, but his mother forced him to stay home. Grounded.

So, he sat in the tribunal in the forum, and that gained him the reputation as an honorable young man. Seneca added a bit of dirt, however, by pointing out that Octavian had a bad temper, which Octavian regretted later in life. No emperor ever remained placid. A perfect leader could never succeed in leading a kingdom of imperfect people. They would kill him.

As a young teenager Octavian was cruel, but he managed to control it and mellowed as he grew older. His age was a brutal one and weak young men did not survive long. He acquired the ability to request favors at the right moment, which brought him more respect.

When leaders in Carthago Nova, Spain, had been charged with crimes, they pleaded with Octavian to represent them. He did, and Julius Caesar was so impressed with Octavian and his defense, that Caesar dropped the charges. This gained Octavian the reputation of "savior," and others began to seek his friendship.

At sixteen, Octavian followed Caesar to Spain to take part in the war. History does not record if his mother tried to stop him. In spite of being seriously ill, he traveled through enemy territory with just a few companions and suffered a shipwreck before arriving on the battlefield and taking part in the battle against the Spanish. Caesar won that battle, and Octavian's tenaciousness, courage, and ingenuity endeared him to Caesar, who began to treat him as his own son.

As Octavian grew into manhood, his upbringing and character became evident. He tolerated criticism, had a sense of humor, loved playing dice even to the point of loaning his friends money to play the game. Later in life, although unfaithful to his wife, Livia Drusilla, he did not leave her, and she remained his faithful wife. She recognized that she couldn't change him, and she would never find a more secure position in society.

His public morals were impeccable and strict. He became a pontifex (priest) at the age of sixteen and, later in life, he exiled his daughter and his granddaughter for lax morals. Few spoke of his private morals. Image was everything. Even to the gods.

At eighteen, he took a senior military command in the Parthian expedition of 44 BC. Then the world changed.

Julius Caesar was assassinated that year. Some in the senate realized that Caesar had wanted to become the king of the Roman Empire with sole power and authority. No surprise there, either. Few emperors escaped the desire for more power.

When Octavian returned home, he was informed that Caesar had adopted him in his will. Octavian began systematically killing Caesar's murderers.

Over the next few years, Octavian had to navigate the intrigues and politics that threatened to destroy him. He developed the clever ability to attract people to himself. In a very short time Octavian won the support of Caesar's supporters and much of the army. He used his own resources to pay Caesar's debtors.

A stroke of genius. This endeared him to the Roman people significantly. Mark Antony focused his generosity on those in power, but Octavian gave generously to the soldiers and the people. Brilliant move.

Octavian pretended to side with opposing sides—the senate and Antony—and eventually got the senate to declare Antony an enemy of the state. Then Octavian made a secret truce with Antony, marched on Rome and forced the senate to "elect" Octavian as consul—at eighteen.

Octavian had become a general by then. He purged Rome of Caesar's enemies—three hundred senators and two thousand knights were sentenced to death.

At the battle of Philippi in 43 BC Octavian and Antony defeated Brutus and Cassius, who had assassinated Caesar. Octavian bloodied the entire Roman Empire with his extermination of Caesar's murderers, but Octavian put a spin on his part of the killing by taking all the lands from the accomplices and giving that land to more than forty thousand veterans. At the same time, he placed the blame for the atrocities on Antony.

The people praised Octavian as an honorable man, even though the monarchy was born out of the blood of Caesar. In an attempt to strengthen his relationship with Octavian, Antony married Octavia, Octavian's sister. That did not turn out as Antony had hoped.

Because Caesar had been deified in 42 BC, Octavian required that he be addressed as "Caesar" and then began labeling himself as *divi filius*, "the son of the divine." Good move.

Antony eventually left Octavian's sister and lived with Cleopatra, Queen of Egypt. Bad move. The Romans honored Octavian's public circumspect lifestyle and despised Antony's lavishness in Egypt.

When Antony divorced Octavia, Octavian stole Antony's will illegally and read it aloud in the senate, exposing Antony's loyalties to Egypt. All's fair in love and war. The will promised large inheritances to Cleopatra's children and demanded that when Antony died, his body would be buried in Egypt. The senate declared war on Antony. Octavian's time had come.

The famous battle of Actium. Octavian won. Antony and Cleopatra committed suicide (no serious future outside of Egypt), all the treasures of Egypt came into Octavian's possession and Egypt became a Roman province when Octavian added Egypt into the Roman Empire.

Now that Octavian ruled the entire Roman world, he avoided Julius Caesar's mistake of holding onto absolute power. He symbolically "surrendered" all his power to the senate and restored the republic. Not. He actually kept all the power for himself. He was nothing more than a power-hungry human emperor.

He changed his name from Octavian to "Augustus," which meant "sacred" or "revered." He also kept the name "*princeps*," which meant first citizen and noble man, and he kept the position as the military chief of staff. It was a brilliant political move.

He persuaded the senate to allow him to be head of the Roman Empire, while allowing them to believe that Augustus was barely more than a normal citizen. Cunning and deceptive. And he left them just enough room to achieve their own political goals. He was continually "elected" as consul from 31 to 23 BC. Everyone was happy.

In 23 BC, however, he almost died from illness, and his faith in spiritual forces re-exerted itself. He entered the world of omens and dreams to help him learn how to keep the gods happy so they wouldn't nix his plans. He rejected deformed people as bad omens. Certain days were unlucky to him. Lightning and thunder petrified him. He wondered if Jupiter was angry at him for something. Superstitions controlled all of Augustus's decisions.

He eventually got well, but he remained wary of the supernatural world. Funny that he wanted to be declared deity which was supposed to be part of the supernatural world.

Extremism defined his relationships. He was a strict authoritarian with his troops, severely punishing them for the slightest infraction. He was brutal with the enemy, and he crushed treacherous rebellion quickly and pitilessly.

On the other hand, he was overly generous with his trusted friends. He always exhibited outward humility by stating that he didn't like titles that flattered him, and he melted down silver statues given to him in his honor and gave the money to things like the golden tripods of Apollo.

His lifestyle was more than modest (clothing, food, sleeping quarters), although he seldom rejected praise that proclaimed him as having divine powers.

By 19 BC he held all the military and political power in the entire empire.

A final incident brought him even more fame as a benevolent leader. Lepidus, a general who wanted more power, attacked him. Augustus won the battle but showed Lepidus mercy and took no revenge. The senate wanted to honor Augustus for his mercy toward Lepidus and wanted to take Lepidus's title of *Pontifex Maximus*, the highest religious position in Rome, and give it to Octavian. He had refused the religious title, saying that Roman tradition required that Lepidus be allowed to keep the title until his death. Again, brilliant, since Lepidus was powerless to make use of the title.

When Lepidus died in 12 BC, Augustus assumed Lepidus's religious title of *pontifex maximus*. The pinnacle of his successful grab for power came in 2 BC when the senate gave him the title of *pater patriae*, "the father of the county."

Let's slow down. The father of the country? With all the military, political, and religious power combined in Augustus?

In the Roman worldview, the family god and the national gods were strongly connected. Everything was protected by the gods and the "Father" presided over them all. Roman worship elevated the Roman home, and the Roman city functioned as a religious center above all other functions.

The sacred open space located just inside the wall surrounding the city was home to the local gods that protected the sacred land around the city. The home, the city, and the administration were all centers of worship, and the temples were used to govern the people. Just like every other religion, including Judaism, physical space and buildings were paramount.

Once Augustus received the title of *pontifex maximus*, all the gods supposedly brought their successes together for the Roman state, under their "Father" who had become their "Savior." As a gracious benefactor, he alone received glory and he alone bestowed glory.

I hope by now that the reader can see what's coming. Jesus, in Mark's Gospel, will challenge this false religion. Keep reading.

The Greeks honored their rulers by declaring them to be gods for their individual good deeds, but the Romans could not be outdone.

They took this one step further. With Augustus, in 29 BC, the provinces honored him as a savior who had stopped all wars, brought peace to the realm, and they announced him as "son of god."

Although Augustus was often very brutal with his enemies, many times as the father figure, he would spare the lives of the sons of his enemies and bring them into the educational system to raise them as Romans.

How thoughtful of him. Kill the parents, turn the children against their parents, and make them good Romans. This allowed him to take over vast areas of the Middle East and integrate them directly into the empire.

He was not original. Nebuchadnezzar did the same thing in Dan 1. (It didn't work on Daniel and his friends. They had already committed their souls to the one and only true God, Yahweh.)

Augustus used religion to elevate the status of morality and to regulate it. Civic law determined morality and both sacrifices in the temples and punishment in the courts paid for any sins of immorality. Augustus even attempted to regulate marriage, with strict punishments for adultery, allowing the nobility to marry freedwomen and granting citizenship to their children.

Augustus served as "father" in many ways: giving preference to the senators' sons by inviting them to the senate, building a temple to Mars, and consecrating spoils of war in the temple of Apollo. He was the father who graciously saved his people.

Augustus saturated the politics and the military with a religious nature fully dedicated to worshipping Augustus. Soldiers swore an oath calling down vengeance of Jupiter on themselves for perjury if they ever spoke negatively about Augustus. He had created a realm ruled by peace and unprecedented prosperity. Who would ever think of saying something negative against such a loving father?

He won far-reaching support by hosting games, building new buildings, updating the city's water system, building two new aqueducts, and restoring eighty-two temples in one year, one of those temples being the huge Mausoleum of Augustus. And he built himself a palace on the Palatine Hill, yet outwardly avoiding any signs or symbols of monarchy.

In 27 BC he even gave back the right of coinage, a symbol of sovereignty, to the senate. He allowed the senate to believe that they ran the country while styling himself "*divi filius*," son of the deified Caesar. He avoided, but did not reject, any form of worship directed at himself, even though this was normal procedure for the kings in the world at that time.

The images and symbols of Rome brought all glory to Rome through Augustus. Even the image of his seal was planted on all kinds of written documents: personal letters, passports, and formal communication. His seal started out first as a sphinx, then became an image of Alexander the Great, and eventually an image of himself.

The message was clear: Augustus had saved his people and the empire and was restoring peace to all. The assimilation of this message into the entire realm, especially the private sphere, could not be avoided. Augustus manipulated the official imagery that portrayed the past by the sculptures in the memorials, statues, and their decorative details. He channeled the symbols to all the buildings that gave him high recognition factors. Every monument and building included skulls of sacrificial animals, offering bowls, and priestly tokens.

We have no images of Jesus.

Aeneas and Romulus played a prominent role in gracing the architecture as their imagery portrayed the Roman virtues of *pietas* (loyalty) and *virtus* (virtue—at least outwardly). All the courageous deeds of past heroes were linked with the *Princeps* (noble man) of Augustus. These drew the emotions of the Romans to feel a spiritual association between the present and the mythological past that the Romans so desperately wanted to be true.

Virgil's *Aeneid* became the centerpiece of all such images. It stood in the Forum of Augustus as the most prominent expression of celebration for Augustus's victories over Julius Caesar's murderers. Augustus used Virgil's love for Rome and genius writing ability to further himself as the supreme leader of the Roman Empire. This drove Augustus to have the *Aeneid* published immediately upon Virgil's death. Augustus recognized the impact that the *Aeneid* in the hands of everyone in the empire would have in furthering his political career.

Augustus had harnessed and guided the power-driven nationalistic literature through successful passive-aggressive means. Virgil knew this, but he viewed it as good tactics. Virgil's candidate had won the election, and he rejoiced over the victory of his emperor with few complaints about the politician's methods. Maecenas coddled and spoiled Virgil as the king of literature in the Roman realm.

In the *Aeneid* the mythological symbolism of Aeneas and his family served as a token of loyalty. These images have been found on finger rings, lamps, and terracotta statuettes. Wall paintings in a house from Pompei reflect the imagery of Aeneas and Romulus depicted in the Forum of Augustus. It cannot be overstated how much influence the *Aeneid* had as *the* propaganda instrument in promoting Augustus as everything he claimed to be.

As the invisible values of computer games influence the minds of children who play those games constantly, so subliminal absorption over time controlled the minds of all who were raised in the Roman Empire during Virgil's time. Political symbolism can be found on every imaginable object: utensils, textiles, ceilings, clay facings, burial urns, roof tiles, jewelry, walls, furniture, and tombs. No one anywhere in the entire world that was controlled by Rome could have missed the *Aeneid* or its message: Augustus is our savior.

Augustus's success was unprecedented. No one had seen it coming. Creating a kingship and building a dynasty requires an intricate weaving together of personalities who all eventually find their place in the power structure of the kingdom. Augustus navigated that process in the usual manner by killing his enemies and rewarding his supporters. Virgil presents Aeneas in the *Aeneid* as Augustus's forerunner who preceded Augustus in establishing Aeneas's kingdom in the same fashion.

The impact that Augustus had on the world has no comparison with any of the mundane politicians and rulers whose names disappeared with their funerals. The rise of Augustus initiated an unprecedented Golden Age. Virgil viewed the establishment of Rome as the triumphal entry of Rome rising from the ashes of Troy. Orosius, during Augustine's time, stated that the Roman Empire raised society to higher levels of superiority than ever previously envisioned. Extreme nationalism permeated the Roman world. Augustus's extraordinary success laid the foundation for Roman preeminence.

Augustus died at Nola in 14 AD. His ashes were placed in his Mausoleum. Although deified in life, he did not rise from the dead. And today, few people remember him.

25

Background

Mark, the Author

A NICE REVIEW OF forgotten mythical history taught for nineteen centuries as literature. But what did Mark have to do with all that?

Augustus died. No myth. Everybody dies. No matter how much myth promoted their existence; no matter how many thousands chose to believe those myths.

His death marked the end of an era. He had originated in a prominent family and risen to fulfill Virgil's mythical description of the man who would become the son of god. Although his dynasty lasted two hundred years, his fame receded into the mist of unknown tyrants whom only elite scholars remembered through the ages.

If anyone could recall Augustus and his deeds, it was due to Virgil's *Aeneid*, which morphed from being the Roman Empire's prominent piece of propaganda into a literary creation that transcended its original purpose and which engaged minds of the literate for over nineteen hundred years. People studied the *Aeneid* for its own sake. Augustus had become just another dead emperor whose life after death as a son of god was as fictitious as the poem that had elevated him to prominence.

Mark's birth begins in obscurity in an unknown family in a small conquered group of disjointed Jewish tribes. Somewhere around 14 AD, a Jewish woman named Mary gave birth to a son, Mark, and raised him under the shadow of Tiberius, the adopted son of Augustus. Tiberius eventually degenerated into a tyrannical recluse, killing anyone and everyone he feared was threatening his throne.

Mark surfaces in history as a young man who rose to prominence when he wrote a Gospel proclaiming Jesus as the Son of God. Both Virgil and Mark promoted their leaders through pieces of literature that rivaled one another all the way into the 1900s. The *Aeneid,* in Latin and English, and the Gospels, in Greek and English, have occupied the minds of students in classical education classes throughout the Western world for centuries. Both leaders, Augustus and Jesus, died. The rivalry between these leaders ceased when Jesus rose from the dead.

Jesus was a teenager when Augustus died. Mark was a teenager when people began addressing Jesus as Rabbi. Sometime after the resurrection of Jesus, Mark became the apostle Peter's constant tag-along. Mark may or may not have known Jesus personally, but Mark did not remain an immature teenager who carried Peter's bags everywhere he went. Mark eventually began to write down what he learned from Peter from the other apostles, from his older cousin, Barnabas, and from the apostle Paul.

The debate over the date of Mark's Gospel has vacillated between the extremes of a very early date before the destruction of the temple in Jerusalem (AD 70) to a very late date after that event. No one knows for sure. Robert Thomas edited a book that discussed all the issues involved and arrived at the conclusion that scholars might actually never really discover the answer to the riddle of Mark's date.[1]

Not wanting to give up on this eternal search for an answer, some have resorted to using the Synoptic problem to discover when Mark wrote his gospel. That's funny. To date, no one has solved the Synoptic problem. We still have to discuss it.

The Synoptic problem: did Mark write first and then Matthew and Luke copied from Mark? Did Matthew write first and then Mark just grabbed the stories he thought most interesting and wrote a shorter version? Did Luke write first and then Matthew copied Luke's gentile approach and tweaked it for his Jewish audience?

Scholars refer to this problem as "literary dependence between the three Synoptic Gospels." I just ask, "Who copied whom and why?"

Griesbach held that Matthew wrote first, but of late, Mark has ascended to the throne. It is difficult to believe that Mark rewrote Matthew and Luke by leaving so much important information out, but then adding less significant items. Instead, scholars believe that it is more likely that

---

1. Thomas, *Three Views.*

Matthew and Luke used Mark to write their own Gospels, expanding and broadening the message of Jesus. The true connection between Mark and the other two Synoptic Gospels centers on Mark's theology being more subtle. It needed to be. The Romans enjoyed crucifying those who opposed Augustus.

In any case, neither scholars nor scholar-wannabes have come up with an answer. Maybe nobody copied from anybody. What an idea! The Holy Spirit just spoke to each one independent of the other ones.

Why are there similarities between them then? Because the Holy Spirit told them the same stories? This answer would be too simple for those who have spent their lives getting PhDs on this subject. But William of Ockham (Occam in Latin) reached the logical conclusion that the simplest explanation is best. No wonder that many scholars don't like him.

But consider for a moment the hypothetical common source of the Gospels, Q: that mysterious, elusive document that arose, no one knows when or where, composed by no historically confirmed authors, and that contained within the Gospels whatever stories the scholars declare existed, based on their speculative questions that need conclusions to justify their presuppositions that the Gospel writers did not write the Gospels. The length of that sentence is indicative of a tedious search for the unfindable. (If it was findable, after two thousand years, we would have already found it.) That got us nowhere.

For the sake of this book, it makes no difference. If Mark appeared first then that would lend more emphasis to Mark's impact as the first Gospel to enter the Roman world. Whether Matthew or Mark appeared first is of little consequence, since the purpose of each Gospel was unique yet comprehensive. Many prophecies in Matthew illustrate that Matthew's Gospel was written to the Jewish people of his day to proclaim the arrival of the Messiah, the hope of Israel. Luke wrote his Gospel to Theophilus, a Greek believer, indicating the direction Luke would develop his Gospel. John wrote to everyone with the distinct purpose of bringing people to faith in Jesus as the Christ, the Son of God.

Many, many scholars have defended Mark's audience as including, but broader than, the Jewish environment. Adam Winn makes a strong case for Mark writing to a Roman audience (which included the Jews in Rome), but, going further, Winn also contends that Mark's Gospel was an early Christian response to Rome's propaganda.

So, as stated above, if the future produces some clear evidence of who came first, the date and rivalry of first place among the three authors as it concerns the Gospel of Mark do not affect the content of Mark. The *Didache*, a first century writing known as "The Teaching of the Twelve Apostles" directed at the gentiles, presented us with the same problem: unknown author, no clear date, and no dateable external event, but all the church fathers had an opinion about its importance and use, *based on its content*. We will treat Mark's Gospel in the same manner and let it speak for itself.

Who wrote the Gospel of Mark? Form criticism has postulated that Mark's Gospel was nothing more than a hodgepodge of oral traditions from the first century church. They arrived at that view in the twentieth century. The early church fathers, however, disagreed with the twentieth century experts. Irenaeus, Justin Martyr, Origen, and Papias (all second century) were two thousand years closer to the situation, and they unanimously claimed Mark as the author of his Gospel. No new *factual* information has surfaced to whisk aside the opinions of those who were the closest to the scene. Disagreeing with the second century pastors and theologians teaches us nothing more about Mark nor the content of his Gospel. Thus, Mark wrote Mark.

Scholars have attacked and dissected Mark and his Gospel from every angle possible. Some have promoted the literary-historical perspective. Good stuff. Some have used sociological categories to promote Mark as challenging the dominant society of his day. More good stuff. Some view Mark as a narrative story created in an oral society that needed to be written down later. Possibly, but we'll never really know since we have no direct evidence of this taking place. Plus, this assumes that Mark's earliest audience was mostly illiterate, which has also been hotly debated.

The Greeks got their alphabet from the Phoenicians during the ninth century BC, and the Greeks began writing plays during the eight century BC—which they published! No one publishes something unless people buy it and read it. Nancy Mavrogenes claims that these Greeks produced mass literacy and used a reading curriculum in their schools.

Scholars have also attacked Mark's status among the other Gospel writers. Until recently Mark has been viewed as the younger brother of the other two Synoptic Gospels, Matthew and Luke. Mark's vocabulary and style appeared to be second-rate, as fitting an untrained younger man who randomly scribbled down those nuggets of experience that Peter chose to reveal to his subordinate tag-along. Since the other two

Gospels had written much more about many of the same things, why should scholars spend any time perusing a watered-down version of a secondary source? Mark's Gospel was so short and written in summary form that few viewed Mark as exhibiting any serious and deep theology. It was raw history with no refinement of Jewish (Matthew) or gentile (Luke) insights.

Today those scholars who have recognized the faultiness of their presuppositions have been forced to reappraise Mark's abilities. Mark was probably fluent in four languages: Hebrew, Greek, Aramaic, and Latin. Mary Ann Beavis states that, "Mark is not a transcript of apostolic memoirs but a mosaic of pre-Gospel traditions from various sources, artfully edited together into a connected narrative."[2] What scholars thought was a hodgepodge of short, cryptic stories has turned out to be one long story perfectly pieced together in order to demonstrate that Jesus is in fact the Jewish Messiah and the Son of God (Mark 1:1).

Mark's writing ability? Keep reading.

Why didn't Mark name himself as the author? Simple. He was already well-known by his audience. He had no need to promote himself since he was not the main topic of his Gospel. In addition, it was somewhat unhealthy to promote another Son of God in opposition to Augustus. Putting his name on such a document could lead to crucifixion. And if people who did not know Mark read his Gospel, the Holy Spirit would have drawn them toward Jesus and not toward Mark.

Although the date of Mark's birth is less certain, he would have been younger than Jesus. According to the Coptic Church, Mark died in 68 AD, placing his childhood education within fifty years of the publication of the *Aeneid* (19 BC). Some scholars connect the young man in Mark 14:51–52 with the writer of this Gospel.

Papias, a second-century bishop of Hierapolis claimed that Mark had never heard nor followed Jesus during Jesus's lifetime.[3] However, a thirteenth-century Coptic manuscript (in a footnote) identified the young man as Mark the Evangelist. Neither Matthew nor Luke tell us about this young man, but since they didn't see him run away, why would they mention it?

If he was one and the same, why would Mark tell his readers about his desertion? Assuming that Mark was not forced to relate this incident,

2. Beavis, Parsons, and Talbert, *Mark,* 9.
3. Eusebius, Hist. Eccl. 3.39.15.

he had a reason for including it. The other disciples ran away as well (14:50). Mark uses himself to point out that followers can become fleers when the pressure becomes life-threatening. When they do, the shame of nakedness overtakes them.

An interesting note: the Greek word for "linen cloth" appears four times in Mark's Gospel: twice referring to this young man and twice referring to Jesus's burial shroud (16:46). Both linen cloths covered degradation. Shame buried itself in death. The next time Mark uses the term "young man" is to refer to an angel dressed in white (16:5) at the empty tomb. Jesus had already radiated such brilliance on the Mount of Transfiguration (9:3).

It seems that Mark connected his own failure in the garden to Jesus's shame on the cross and in the grave, and then Mark used the "whiteness" of the linen cloth after the resurrection to connect the radiance of Jesus before the cross with the victory of the resurrection. These connections demonstrate that Mark was capable of using literary devices like innuendos to make a point. Most people don't even recognize such literary devices yet Mark used them. Mark's present-day readers are probably more uneducated that he was.

When Mark wrote his Gospel, he didn't use foreign terms or alien concepts to induce the Romans to evaluate the differences between the two kingdoms, to switch allegiances, and to follow the true Son of God. Mark used Roman vocabulary and concepts that were political, imperial, economic, eschatological, and rhetorical to weave the teachings and works of Jesus into his message to connect with the Romans and motivate them to read and compare Mark's Gospel with the *Aeneid's* portrayal of Augustus.

Augustus was viewed as the emperor who had reached the pinnacle of Roman rule by bringing stability to Rome after five vicious civil wars. Augustus's influence was so great that the emperorship stayed within his family through the next five emperors. His accomplishments were so spectacular that no later emperor accomplished anything of significance in comparison with the two-hundred-year *Pax Romana* (Roman Peace) ushered in by Augustus. Not even Vespasian's Flavian dynasty that only lasted twenty-seven years (69–96 AD) would rise to Augustus's level of fame.

Mark had no need to compare Jesus with any other emperor besides Augustus. The *Aeneid* proclaimed Augustus as the Roman hero who would bring peace to the world and all later emperors basked in the distinctions originated by Augustus.

When did Mark write his Gospel? No one knows for sure. Mark wrote about the recent history of Jesus who had been in Israel from 4/6 AD to 37/39 AD. Jesus arrived in the Roman world just as Augustus was fulfilling his destiny laid out in the *Aeneid*. Mark wrote his Gospel barely sixty years after the death of Augustus (born 63 AD, became Caesar 27 AD, died 14 AD).

Some believe that Mark wrote his Gospel before 70 AD, thus predicting future events. Some believe that he wrote it after the fall of Jerusalem in 70 AD, thus making Mark 13 a description of past events. Some scholars even claim that the discussion is nothing more than a waste of time because there are so many possibilities. Knowing the exact date would not change the text of what Mark wrote anyway.

Who was Mark's audience? Scholars began with the obvious: the Jews. Although Mark was obviously familiar with the Old Testament and the gospel, some scholars wondered if Mark's audience might have encompassed a bit more than just some small Jewish communities in Palestine. They agreed that the Greeks might have stumbled onto Mark's Gospel, since Luke and Paul were traveling companions and Paul took Mark on his first missionary journey.

This led to realizing that Mark certainly spoke Greek. Eventually academia arrived at the conclusion that Mark not only wrote for the Romans but that he probably targeted the Romans as his main audience. Those few scholars who continued to lump the Greeks and Romans together as gentiles were eventually moved to acknowledge that there were some significant differences between those two cultures and that Luke and Mark actually took these differences into account when they wrote their version of their Gospels.

Where did Mark write his Gospel? Eusebius was one of many church fathers who assumed Mark was written in Rome. The alternatives are so numerous and based on mere speculation that the evidence for Rome overwhelms the other options.

What connections did Mark actually have with the key players in the Middle East during Jesus's time? Luke 2:1–2 reads: "In those days a decree went out from Caesar Augustus that all the world should be registered. This was the first registration when Quirinius was governor of Syria." Caesar Augustus (the Augustus of the *Aeneid*) reigned from 27 BC to 14 AD. Matthew 2:1 states that Jesus was born during the days of

Herod the king, who died in 4 BC. Joseph and Mary fled Bethlehem when this Herod ordered all boys under two years old to be killed, placing Jesus between one and two years old at that time. Therefore, Jesus would have been born between 6 BC and 4 BC. He would have been a teenager when Augustus lived and when Virgil wrote the *Aeneid*.

There is no record of Jesus having actually spoken to Mark. Mark may not have been the young man who fled when Jesus was arrested in the garden, but the alternatives are pure speculation. In any case, Mark still had close connections with Peter, who had been extremely close to Jesus. We don't know when Mark and Peter met for the first time, but Peter's relationship with Barnabas, Mark's cousin, in the early part of Acts would indicate that they had more than a short acquaintance between them. And Mark was younger than Barnabas, Peter, and Jesus.

If Mark wrote his Gospel not just to inform the Romans about Jesus but to actually challenge the theology of the *Aeneid*, then we have to demonstrate that Mark had extensive contact with the *Aeneid*. This will require determining just how extensive the *Aeneid* had become during Mark's lifetime.

26

The *Aeneid*'s Place of Supreme Propaganda in Roman History

APART FROM THE BIBLE, no other piece of literature has influenced the societies of the Western world for so long as has the *Aeneid*. The *Aeneid's* genre, literary style, grammar, symbolic hermeneutics, and lasting influence has been thoroughly researched and dissected in literature courses throughout the centuries. It has been translated into numerous languages and widely distributed in terms of geography and nationalities.

Sometime early in the nineteenth century this influence waned considerably. The twentieth century changed the direction of history more than that of any previous generation. Two world wars have eliminated from the English-speaking world the self-perceived responsibility to teach the next generation the necessity of promoting and supporting the empire. Rome's glory at its pinnacle proclaimed the superiority of that nation, but the last two centuries of subsequent writers have demolished the nationalism and the racism read into Virgil and Horace by the merging of Constantine's empire and the Christian church.

The Summary of the *Aeneid*

Homer is the legendary author who wrote the *Iliad* and the *Odyssey* sometime in the eighth century BCE. The *Iliad* described the last fifty-two days of the ten-year battle between the Greeks and the Trojans at Troy, a battle that lasted ten years. The Greeks believe that the war occurred during the thirteenth century BCE. That war was already legend in the fragmentary *Epic Cycle* poems before Homer wrote about it.

The *Iliad* is paired with something of a sequel, the *Odyssey*, also attributed to Homer. The *Odyssey* focuses on the Greek hero Odysseus (knows as Ulysses in Roman myths), King of Ithaca, and his journey home after the fall of Troy. It took him ten years to reach home after the ten-year-war at Troy.

Virgil extended his own epic poem, the *Aeneid*, beyond these two Greek poems. Here's a summary of the twelve books of the *Aeneid*. I have written it with scholars in mind. I have left out a lot of the details. If you choose to read the entire *Aeneid*, you need to remember how prominent the *Aeneid* had become in the Roman world (revealed in the next chapter). The Romans would have learned those details by heart, and many of those details show up in Mark's Gospel as allusions.

This book would be more complete if I could travel back in time, sit down over coffee with a Roman, and read the *Aeneid* and the Gospel of Mark, side by side.

BOOK 1

Virgil summaries his poem in the first seven lines: He will sing of war and the man—Aeneas—who will be driven by fate away from Troy to Italy. Aeneas will found a city there called Lavinium, which will become Rome.

Virgil asks: Why does Juno, the queen of the gods, want to destroy Aeneas? Because she loves Carthage and hates the future Rome which will overthrow Carthage. She has also never gotten over being rejected by Paris, the Trojan, when he gave the golden apple of beauty to Venus instead of Juno. Two minor reasons also plagued her: she was jealous of Jupiter's (her husband) affair with Electra that produced another son and because Jupiter made Ganymede, a Trojan prince, to be the god's cupbearer.

Why was this so upsetting to Juno? Virgil doesn't tell us, but Greek mythology does. Homer described Ganymede as the most beautiful of humans, and Zeus (who became Jupiter) fell in love with Ganymede's beauty and kidnapped him in the form of an eagle to serve as cupbearer (wine). This myth modelled the socially acceptable Greek custom of a romantic relationship between an adult male and an adolescent male (*paiderastia*).

Back to the *Aeneid*: having lost the battle of Troy, Aeneas sails away. Juno commands Aeolus, the god of the winds, to drown them all. Aeolus obeys, and some ships are lost in his storm, but Neptune, the god of the sea, overrules, calms the sea, and informs Aeolus that he had overstepped his boundaries. Seven ships make it safely to Carthage on the North African coast of Libya.

Aeneas's mother, the goddess Venus, is frantically reminding Jupiter of his promise that the Trojans would reach Italy to become the Roman people.

Jupiter calms her down by assuring her of his promise. The Trojans would reach Italy, Aeneas would win a great battle and found Lavinium, and more. Ascanius, his son, also known as Iulus, would found Alba Longa near the future site of Rome, and Romulus will found Rome. Rome will conquer the world, including Greece. Juno will come to love the Romans. (Juno hated that prophecy.) Eventually a Trojan Caesar named Julius, after Aeneas's son Iulus, would adopt Augustus, who would bring peace to the world.

Jupiter supports his reassurance by sending Mercury, the messenger god, to Carthage to put benevolence in the hearts of the Carthaginians and their queen, Dido, to receive the Trojans.

Aeneas and his companion, Achates, explore the coast and they meet Venus (Aeneas's goddess mother), who disguises herself as a female huntress. She tells them all where they are and the rough life that Dido had when she had to run away from the Phoenician city of Tyre. Her evil brother, Pygmalion, murdered her husband, Sychaeus. Venus tells Aeneas to go to Dido's palace and that his missing ships and comrades are safe. No one drowned.

As she goes to leave, Aeneas recognizes her and vents to her that she has disguised herself. She engulfs them in a cloud so that they are invisible to other people.

They head for the city and stumble onto a temple dedicated to Juno. The inner walls show pictures of the Trojan war. Aeneas is sad.

Beautiful and majestic Dido and her attendants show up, but they can't see Aeneas and Achates, and Dido holds court. Aeneas's lost men show up and are greeted warmly and sympathetically received as they relate their tragic trip. The cloud disappears, and everyone greets each other with lots of enthusiasm.

Dido personally welcomes Aeneas (Mercury prepared her heart for this action) and prepares a banquet.

Aeneas sends for his son, Ascanius. Venus, however, fearful that Juno will mess things up again, replaces Ascanius with her own son, Cupid, the god of love, in disguise as Ascanius. She does this to make Dido fall in love with Aeneas, so he will be safe. This does not turn out to be a good idea when Aeneas wants to stay in Carthage forever, but even goddesses, meaning well, make mistakes.

At the banquet, Dido embraces Cupid, thinking that he is Ascanius, and falls in love with Aeneas, his father (Ascanius, not Cupid's father). She then asks Aeneas to describe in detail his wanderings and mishaps.

BOOK 2

Aeneas gives a history lesson of the Trojan War. Most people were fooled by the Greek horse, but Laocoön, a priest of Neptune, figured out that the wooden horse was either full of soldiers or was a war machine. He threw a spear into the side of the horse and asked everyone to remember the last time the Greeks had given a gift to Troy without attempting to deceive them. That had never happened.

A Greek captive, Sinon, showed up and claimed that he had deserted Ulysses's army and the horse was meant to appease Minerva, because the Greeks had stolen her sacred image from her temple in Troy. He said that if the horse was harmed then Minerva would destroy Troy for their irreverence, but if the Trojans brought the horse into the city, Troy would win the war.

He lied. He was part of Greece's counterintelligence unit, sent to deceive and prepare for the Greek invasion.

After two serpents rose out of the sea and crushed Laocoön and his two sons in their coils, the Trojans believed Sinon. They brought the horse inside.

That night, Sinon opened the belly of the horse and the Greek warriors hidden inside opened Troy's gates to the Greek army.

The Trojans lost the war. Hector, King Priam's son, had been killed by Achilles earlier. Hector appeared to Aeneas in a dream and told him to run away, to take Troy's gods with him and to find another city to live in.

Aeneas didn't listen, but armed himself for battle, with every intention of dying in battle. He witnessed the destruction caused by Pyrrhus, Achilles's evil son. Pyrrhus murdered Priam's son in front of Priam and then he killed Priam on Jupiter's altar. Being in a holy place didn't save the religious king of Troy.

Aeneas finally realized that the safety of his family depended on his well-being, so he went home to his father, Anchises, his wife, Creusa, and his son, Ascanius. On the way home he ran into Helen, the Greek beauty. Her elopement with Paris had caused the ten-year Trojan War. Venus kept him from killing her. Venus opened his eyes to the supernatural world of evil. Helen had been nothing more than a pawn in the hands of the gods. The visions she showed him revealed the god's inherent destructive natures.

As they attempted to run away, Anchise (his father) refused to leave. He would rather die there than face exile. His tantrum was interrupted by a flame that appeared around Ascanius's head. Anchises prayed to Jupiter for another sign (one wasn't enough?). Thunder rumbled, and a star flew across the sky toward Mount Ida (three signs!). Anchises agreed to leave with the rest of the family. Aeneas carried him on his back.

They didn't all make it out. Creusa got lost. Aeneas went back to look for her but ran into her ghost. The ghost told him that he was going to marry again after reaching Italy. She faded away.

He returned to the rest of his family to discover that a bunch of other refugees had joined them and expected him to lead them. They headed toward Mount Ida.

BOOK 3

Aeneas continues his story. He describes the journey (where they went), the storm, losses on his sailing trip, and how he arrived at Carthage. They landed first in Thrace (northern Turkey), but Polydorus, Priam's youngest son, spoke from the dead to warn them to leave. As the war was escalating, Priam had entrusted Polydorus to the Thrace king, who had been an ally of Troy. That king had changed allegiances and murdered Polydorus, who somehow was still able to communicate with Aeneas.

Aeneas performed funeral rites for Polydorus, left, and sailed to the island of Delos, which belonged to Apollo. Aeneas asked Apollos for advice. Apollos told Aeneas to seek their "mother of old." Anchises (Aeneas's father, remember?) thought Apollo meant Crete. They sacrifice some animals to the gods and sailed to Crete.

They tried to found a city there, but a plague broke out that killed people and crops for a whole year. Aeneas wanted to go back to Delos to clarify what Apollos had really said, but Troy's gods told him in a vision that Apollo had meant Hesperia, Italy, the ancestral home of another ancestor, Dardanus.

They took off for Italy, but a storm drove them to the Strophadës, a group of islands in the Ionian Sea. Some vicious bird-women, called Harpies, tried to eat them. No one got eaten, but Celaeno, the leader of the Harpies, prophesied that when the Trojans reached Italy, the lack of food would drive them to eat their tables as a punishment for their violence against the Harpies.

The Trojans sailed to Actium along the northern Greek coast, where they decided to hold some athletic contests for a few months.

Then they sailed to Buthrotum, where the prophet Helenus welcomed them. He was a son of Priam, and his wife, Andromachë, was the widow of Hector. Helenus's prophecies were not pleasant. There were lots of hurdles to overcome before they would arrive in Italy and found their city. However, when they would arrive in Italy, Aeneas would stumble over a white sow with a litter of thirty young. This would indicate where he was supposed to found his city.

Helenus told Aeneas how to avoid the monster Sculla and the whirlpool Charybdis. He also told him to ask the sibyl of Cumae for help and to offer a few sacrifices to Juno to appease her hatred.

Andromachë told Aeneas that Pyrrhus had been killed in the same way that he had killed Priam: on his father's altar. As it should be.

The Trojans then sailed north to Ceraunia and crossed over to the heel of the Italian peninsula. Aeneas offered prayers to Pallas and sacrifices to Juno, according to Helenus's instructions. Then they sailed across the Gulf of Taranto and, after escaping Scylla and Charybdis, landed on the coast of Sicily, where they spent a fearful night near Mount Aetna, a volcano.

The next morning, a Greek stumbled into their camp. He begged the Trojans to take him with them or else kill him. He didn't want to be captured by any of the Cyclopes in the area. Then some Cyclopes showed up and they all fled.

They sailed along the coast of Sicily; Anchises, Aeneas's father, died. They buried him, left, and a storm drove them to Carthage. That was the end of Aeneas's story.

BOOK 4

Book 4 is probably the most famous of the twelve books.

They held a banquet, and the next morning Dido told her sister, Anna, that Aeneas was the only man who could motivate her to break her vow to remain single and faithful to the memory of the dead husband, Sychaeus.

Anna said that the dead don't care about the romances of the living and that Dido should follow her dream. Pursue the Trojan to keep him in Carthage for her own happiness and the prosperity and safety of her people, i.e., Aeneas had a small army of soldiers with him.

Dido gets more turned on for Aeneas but doesn't know how to proceed. She begins to neglect her own people and the building projects of her city.

Enter the goddesses: Juno and Venus notice this budding romance between Dido and Aeneas. Juno wants to keep Aeneas from reaching Italy, and Venus wants to keep him safe. Both push the couple to have sex with each other.

Juno cooks up a rainstorm on a day when Aeneas and Dido are out hunting together. They take shelter in a cave and have sex. Dido justifies herself by claiming that having sex means that they are married.

Everybody finds out about their relationship. One of Dido's rejected suitors prays to Jupiter to break it up. Jupiter sends Mercury to Aeneas to remind him that he can't shirk his duty to found a city and a people in Italy. Aeneas must leave immediately. Aeneas and his people intend to sail away secretly and immediately. He doesn't inform Dido, but she finds out and verbally abuses him for wanting to abandon her and for hiding his plans to leave her.

Aeneas tries to justify himself by saying that he did not intend to deceive her and that he will never forget her, but he does not regard Dido and himself as married, and he must fulfill fate's decrees. His pathetic attempt to justify himself only makes Dido angrier. She sends Anna to Aeneas to beg him to delay sailing until she can come to terms with his leaving. Anna does so a number of times to no avail. Aeneas's resolve never waivers.

This leads to maximum despair on Dido's part. She secretly decides to kill herself. She gets Anna to build a pyre and heap on it everything that was associated with Aeneas. She claims that burning these things, with a couple of magic rites added, will either restore him to her or free her of her love for him. She lied.

Naïve Anna obeys. Dido puts a couch on top of everything on the pyre, a picture of Aeneas and his sword, which he left behind.

During the night Dido reviews her options: marry a former suitor or follow the Trojans or kill herself. She decides to commit suicide.

During the same night Aeneas, on board and ready to sail the next morning, gets another visit from Mercury, who tells him to take off immediately. Aeneas obeys.

The next morning Dido sees the Trojan fleet on the horizon and is consumed by rage. Maybe she should pursue the Trojans, but she couldn't catch them. She resorts to a vengeful prayer that Rome and Carthage will hate each other forever, that some avenging spirit will avenge her, and that Aeneas will "fall in battle before his time and lie unburied on the sand."[1]

Dido climbs onto the pyre, lies down on the couch, and stabs herself with Aeneas's sword. Anna shows up, holds Dido into her arms, and Dido dies.

BOOK 5

From his ship Aeneas sees flames lighting the city, but a storm claims his attention and he sails for Sicily, landing at Drepanum. They had been there a year earlier. Full circle. Once again, King Acestës welcomes them.

Because Aeneas's father is buried there, Aeneas celebrates funeral rites for him. Aeneas also orchestrates some athletic games in his father's honor (or to take his mind off Dido).

A giant snake shows up at the funeral rites but appears to be harmless.

A long description of the athletic games follows: a hectic rowing contest, a foot race, a bloody prizefight between two muscular boxers, and a display of archery skills. Not everyone plays fair. Ascanius, who will become the forefather of the Romans, leads a cavalry display by the young men.

Juno shows up. She sends the goddess Iris to upset the Trojan women who are tired of traveling and want to stay there. Iris disguises herself as one of the women and motivates them to set the ships on fire.

---

1. Virgil, *Aeneid*, 4.620.

Aeneas finds out in time and calls on Jupiter for help. He sends rain to put out the fire and thus saves all but four ships.

Aeneas decides to let anyone who wants to stay settle there. It won't be Rome, but whatever.

His dead father, Anchises, shows up and tells him that they will meet soon in the underworld after Aeneas has landed in Italy. King Acestës agrees to have some stay, and Sicilian land is divided among the Trojans who wish to stay.

They spend nine days feasting and sacrificing to honor the site of the new Trojan city. Aeneas and the rest leave after fixing up the damaged ships.

Venus is still concerned for the security of her son and his people, so she asks Neptune to guarantee a safe journey for the Trojans. Neptune promises to do as Venus asks, but he tells her that one Trojan must be sacrificed in return for the safety of the rest. (No one really knows why Virgil wrote that into the plot.)

Somnus, the god of sleep, causes Palinurus to fall asleep during his watch on the lead ship. He falls overboard and drowns. He is the sacrifice that Neptune demanded for safe passage. Aeneas feels bad, takes over the ship, and sees lands in the distance.

BOOK 6

This book is another major turning point in the *Aeneid*: lots of detail remembered by every Roman and many scholars over the centuries. Dante wrote his description of hell based on this book. I am including only the key details in this summary.

Aeneas prays to Apollo, and the sibyl, Deiphobë, predicts lots of trouble for the Trojans in Italy: a bloody war and Juno's hatred. Aeneas tells her that he already knows that. He wants to descend into the underworld to visit his father and asks for her help.

She tells him that he must find and pluck a golden bough from a tree in an adjacent forest. The bough will allow him to enter the underworld. First, however, he has to find and bury the body of the trumpeter, Misenus, who was drowned by the sea god Triton for daring to challenge him in a trumpeting contest.

While Aeneas is building the funeral pyre for Misenus, Aeneas sees twin doves, which he somehow knows were sent by his mother, Venus. The doves lead him to the golden bough and Aeneas takes it to the sibyl's cave. Then he buries Misenus.

Deiphobë leads Aeneas to the underworld's entrance, bypasses a couple of spooky places, and then they descend through a gloomy region haunted by dreadful spirits and monsters. They reach Acheron, one of the underworld's rivers. Aeneas sees Charon, the boatman who ferries spirits of the dead across the river. Then lots of spirits crowd around Aeneas, anxious to cross the river. Some of those spirits have to wait a hundred years to cross or until their bodies receive a proper burial on Earth.

Charon normally doesn't take live humans across but does so when he sees the golden bough.

On the other side they stumble into a bunch of wailing souls of dead infants, then spirits who had been executed for crimes they did not commit, then suicides. At last they come to the Mourning Fields, the final place for those who died of love. Dido's ghost shows up. Aeneas knows that she killed herself because he dumped her, so he tries to justify himself by blaming the gods for forcing him to leave.

She does not forgive him and returns to her dead husband, Sychaeus, who is now with her.

Aeneas and Deiphobë now reach the fields of the spirits of men famous in battle, Trojans and Greeks alike. His own Trojan men warmly greet him, but the Greeks turn away afraid of him.

Aeneas now has to make sure that he doesn't take the path to the left that leads to the region of Tartarus, where the wicked are punished forever. Elysium, Aeneas's destination, lies on the right. He sees lots of really evil dead people suffering for their wicked deeds done on the earth before they died.

When they reach Elysium, Aeneas places the golden bough on its threshold as an offering. They are now in the Blessed Groves, a region of beautiful meadows inhabited by blessed spirits, Anchises included. They find Anchises in a lush green valley, checking out the spirits of his future Roman descendants. They greet each other emotionally.

Aeneas is curious about a river in the distance and the souls that hover "as bees" over it.[2] Anchises tells him that the river is named Lethe, the river of forgetfulness. The spirits there formerly had human bodies on

2. Virgil, *Aeneid*, 6.708.

Earth, but when they drank the water of Lethe, they lost all memory of their former existence. They are now waiting to be born into new bodies. They have already been given their new identities.

Aeneas asks his father to explain reincarnation to him. Anchises describes a bunch of historical people who would have been already familiar to Virgil's Roman readers but who are described from the vantage point of Aeneas and Anchises in Elysium as belonging to the future of a city yet to be founded. Among them were Silvius, Aeneas's son by Lavinia and the founder of a race of kings; Romulus, founder of Rome; and the descendants of Aeneas's son, Ascanius, the Julian family, whose glory will reach its peak with Augustus, "son of the deified." Julius Caesar, the "deified" god, is also there. Young Marcellus, Augustus's nephew and heir who died at the age of nineteen, is there.

After seeing all those future people, Anchises leads Aeneas and Deiphobë to the two gates of sleep, one of horn, the other of ivory. Passing through the ivory gate, Aeneas and the sibyl return to the world of the living.

BOOK 7

This is the beginning of the second half of the epic and the setting is Italy.

The Trojans then sail north, and at dawn on the following day, they reach the mouth of the Tiber River and dock their ships.

King Latinus of Latium is descended from the god Saturn. Latinus and his wife, Queen Amata, have a daughter, Lavinia, their only surviving child. She is of marriageable age and many want to marry her, including Turnus, the leader of the Rutulian tribe. At the exact time that the Trojans arrive at his land, Latinus's dead father tells him to get a foreign husband for Lavinia. Her mate needs to be a non-Latium who will intermarry with his own people, the Latins. Their descendants will conquer the world.

On the shore of the Tiber, meanwhile, the Trojans are so hungry that they eat everything including their plates, which are hardened wheat cakes. This fulfills the prophecy that they will eat their tables in the place they will settle. (Virgil attributes this prediction to Anchises here, but the harpy Celaeno actually made it in Book 3. Virgil died before he could edit and correct this mistake. Oops.)

The next day, Aeneas sends gifts to Latinus to win his favor. He then starts planning his city. Latinus warmly accepts the gifts because he assumes that the Trojans are the strangers his father told him about. He offers Lavinia as a bride to Aeneas and sends his own gifts to Aeneas.

Juno explodes in anger, again. Since she can't stop fate—Aeneas will marry Lavinia and they will establish Rome—she swears to hinder Aeneas any way she can. She uses the fury of Allecto to start a war between the Trojans and the Latins.

(She really needs an anger-management class.)

Queen Amata favors Turnus as her future son-in-law and Allecto motivates her to bitterly oppose Aeneas as her husband's choice. She tells a bunch of lies to the Latinus about Aeneas. She claims that Turnus qualifies as a foreigner since his parents were Greek. Her husband doesn't budge, so she hides Lavinia.

Then Allecto, disguised as an old woman, tells Turnus to defend his right to marry Lavinia by attacking the Trojans. When Turnus does not take this old woman seriously, Allecto drops the disguise and shows her fury to him, and he decides to prepare his army to fight.

Allecto then jumps over to the Trojans and causes Ascanius to wound a Latium family's pet stag, and this motivates the Latium people to retaliate. War starts—casualties. Latinus's subjects want war, but Latinus doesn't, so he goes home to his palace. Juno counters by throwing open the twin gates of Mars's temple, a ritual signifying war.

Book 7 ends with a list of all the people who have come to fight against the Trojans.

BOOK 8

Everyone shows up for the war. The river god of the Tiber appears to Aeneas in a dream and tells him that he will find a white sow and her litter, which symbolically represent Alba Longa, the city that Ascanius will establish in thirty years. There are thirty sucklings in the litter.

This discovery was the sign Helenus foretold to Aeneas: it is absolute proof that the Trojans have come to the right place at last. The river god also told him to sail upstream and get help from Evander, the king of Pallanteum.

Aeneas obeys, but he also sacrifices the entire litter to Juno. The next day Evander and his son, Pallas, warmly welcome him. Evander, a Greek, came to Italy years earlier and established Pallanteum, on the site of the future Rome. Aeneas informs Evander that they both have the same mixed blood of the gods, Atlas and his daughters, Electra and Maia's son, Mercury.

As a young man, Evander had met Priam and Anchises, and thus gives his full support against Turnus. Then they all worship Hercules because he killed Cacus, a fire-breathing giant that victimized Evander's people. Evander also explains that the god Saturn, exiled by Jupiter from Latium, had come to Pallanteum and brought the arts of civilization to all the barbarians there. Evander shows him the sites that will become famous when Rome enters its full glory.

That evening, Venus asks her husband, Vulcan, the blacksmith of the gods, to make weapons and armor for her son, Aeneas. Vulcan agrees. Evander sends Aeneas to another stronghold of the Etruscans to seek their help. They had overthrown their evil king, Mezentius, who took refuge with the Latins. The Etruscans are eager to find him and kill him. A seer told the Etruscans to choose a non-Italian to lead them, so they welcome Aeneas as their leader.

Aeneas hesitates to accept their help until his mother releases lots of thunder. He's convinced. Aeneas takes Pallas and four hundred horsemen and sets off for Agylla. He sends a message to Ascanius telling him what happened.

At Agylla Aeneas connects with the Etruscan force. Venus shows up with the arms and armor from Vulcan. The shield, the most spectacular piece, was decorated with episodes from Roman history which lie in the future. The naval battle at Actium graced the center of the shield. At Actium, Augustus will defeat Antony and Cleopatra and will become Rome's most famous emperor.

BOOK 9

Juno really wants this war. She sends Iris, a lesser goddess, to tell Turnus that he has to attack while Aeneas is gone. Turnus attacks. The Trojans are outnumbered, so they withdraw inside the walls of Pallanteum.

Since Turnus can't get to the Trojans, he decides to burn their ships. Venus objects, and Jupiter intercedes by changing all the ships into sea nymphs who swim away, oblivious to the danger.

Turnus is not surprised by this. He rejoices that the Trojans have no more ships. They can't escape. He orders his forces to rest until morning.

Nisus and Euryalus, Trojans in the camp and inseparable companions (see Book 5), volunteer to break through the Latin forces to go to
Aeneas in Pallanteum to tell him about the siege. Glory-bound and fear-
less, Ascanius promises them a rich reward.

They manage to kill some sleepy warriors, but they are detected
and flee separately into the forest. Nisus gets away, but Euryalus is captured. Nisis sees him in enemy hands and kills two warriors to free him.
It doesn't work. Volcens, captain of the Latins, kills Euryalus; Nisis kills
Volcens; and Volcens's fellow warriors kill Nisis.

The Latins raise the heads of Nisus and Euryalus on stakes outside
the city walls, and the battle begins.

Turnus's forces try to scale the Trojan camp's walls but are beaten
back. Ascanius kills Romulus, Turnus's brother-in-law. Apollo visits Ascanius and praises him for that kill, but tells him he can't kill anymore
because he is intended to promote peace.

The Trojan brothers, Pandarus and Bitias, throw open the Trojan
gate as a challenge to the Latins. Latin warriors attack but lose, and the
Trojans start fighting outside the walls.

Turnus kills Bitias. The Latins manage to close the gates, trapping
many Trojans outside. Turnus, however, gets inside the camp before the
gate is shut and, with Juno's help, kills Pandarus.

Turnus kills more Trojans, but they eventually outnumber him. He
escapes by jumping fully armored into the Tiber River and swimming
back to his fellow warriors.

BOOK 10

Jupiter tells all the gods to stay out of the human war. He overrules both
Venus and Juno. There will be no more divine interference. Fate will determine the outcome of the war.

Lots of casualties on both sides. Thirty ships of Etruscans, Evander's
forces, and Trojans show up and join the battle. As they approach, the sea
nymphs tell them about the siege taking place.

The Trojans are overjoyed to see Aeneas in such beautiful armor.
Turnus attacks. Lots of warriors are killed on both sides.

Pallas courageously rallies the spirits of his men. He attacks Lausus,
Mezentius's son. They are equally young, brave, and good looking. Both
die. Turnus kills Pallas and takes his illustrated sword belt as a trophy.

Aeneas kills Lausus. Hercules had foreseen these deaths and mourned, but Jupiter consoled him by pointing out that everybody has to die—however, dying bravely can bring fame.

Aeneas is enraged at Pallas's death and kills his way to Turnus. Jupiter breaks his own rule of non-interference and allows Juno to save Turnus by creating a shadow that looks like Aeneas. Turnus chases the shadow onto a ship, then Juno pushes the ship out to sea. She didn't want Turnus to face Aeneas in battle at this time.

Turnus is frustrated, and Aeneas, who can't find Turnus, wounds Mezentius, the former Etruscan king. Lausus intervenes. Aeneas warns Lausus not to fight him. Lausus scoffs at this advice, and Aeneas quickly kills him. However, Aeneas pities young Lausus for his bravery and death and selfless love for his father.

Someone gives the body of Lausus to his father, Mezentius. He's devastated. Severely wounded, he mounts his horse and rides off to fight Aeneas. He wants to avenge Lausus's death. His life is meaningless without his son. He fights bravely, but Aeneas wounds his horse, which falls on Mezentius. He begs Aeneas to bury his body with his son.

BOOK 11

Aeneas gets tired of killing, so he hangs Mezentius's armor on a big oak trunk to honor him as the fallen king and to show that he, Aeneas, won that battle. He buries the dead and sends Pallas's body, a thousand men, lots of plunder, captives, and Pallas's horse back to Pallanteum. Aeneas pities Pallas's father, Evander, who doesn't know that his son is dead.

Messengers from Laurentum want peace and ask Aeneas to bring the Latin dead back for burial. He agrees. He says that he is willing to fight Turnus in single combat to resolve the conflict. The Latins agree. The truce lasts for twelve days as both sides honor their dead.

Evander is devastated by the death of Pallas and wishes that he had died in his son's place but does not blame the Trojans. His son died for a good cause—to help the Trojans settle down in Latium. He adds that Aeneas owes him Turnus's death.

Through lots of mourning, the Latins are tired of the war and oppose Turnus's proposed marriage to Lavinia. Since Turnus opposed the Trojans settling in Latium, they want Turnus to fight Aeneas. Queen Amata, Turnus's mother, opposes this idea.

Then the Latins get a message from an ally, king Diomedes in southern Italy, that he will not support the Latins in their fight against the Trojans. He tells them that only evil things have happened to those who have opposed the Trojans. He lists four things that have happened to him: some of his friends were changed into birds, he lost his wife, and he was kicked out of Argos because he had wounded Venus; having fought against Aeneas, he knows how well Aeneas can fight.

Latinus wants to stop the war and welcome the Trojans to Italy or give them ships to go somewhere else. Drancës, who hated Turnus, approves, saying that Aeneas should marry Lavinia and Turnus should engage Aeneas in single combat.

Turnus claims that victory over the Trojans is still possible. If Drancës won't fight the Trojans, Camilla, the famous Volscian woman warrior will join the battle against the Trojans. If no one else sides with Turnus, then he will fight Aeneas personally.

News arrives that the Trojan and Etruscans troops are marching on Laurentum. Turnus calls the Latins to war and a throng of women, including Amata and Lavinia, leave to pray to Athena.

(Virgil knows that his Roman readers will know who Athena is. Modern readers do not. Athena was the goddess of lots of things, but in this case especially, of skill in warfare and wisdom, the patron goddess of heroes. She was born from Zeus after he had an enormous headache, and she sprang out from his forehead fully grown and in battle armor. She had no mother—like a super tomboy.)

Turnus and Camilla join forces to protect Laurentum. Turnus is going to ambush Aeneas's army, and Camilla and her cavalry will engage the Trojan cavalry. Camilla is killed and her forces run for cover. Turnus gives up the ambush idea and returns to Laurentum, stumbling into Aeneas's army. Everyone gets a good night's sleep outside the walls of Laurentum.

BOOK 12

Turnus realizes that Laurentum will fall to Aeneas, so he agrees to fight Aeneas in single combat. The winner gets the girl, Lavinia. Both Latinus and Amata try to stop this, since they know Turnus will lose. Turnus sends a message to Aeneas: Let's do this! That night, Turnus spends his time with his horses and armor while Aeneas hugs his armor that Vulcan made for him.

The next morning everyone gathers in an open field for the fight. Juno sends Turnus's sister to try to save him from death or break the truce. Aeneas vows that if Turnus wins the fight, the Trojans will go back to Pallanteum and they will never again attack the Latins. If he wins, however, he will claim nothing for himself: peace and equality will reign between the Latins and the Trojans. He will marry Lavinia. Latinus, her father, will keep his position of power. Latinus solemnly agrees.

The Rutulians, Turnus being their king, still disagree. Juturna, goddess of fountains, disguises herself as one of their nobles and shames them back into battle. At that moment, a pack of water birds attack an eagle that had seized a swan. The eagle releases the swan. The Rutulians take that as a sign that they will win the battle against the Trojans. A priest who interpreted bird omens throws his spear at the Trojans and the war starts over again.

Aeneas tries to restore the peace but is wounded by an arrow and has to leave the field. Turnus is thrilled and goes berserk killing Trojans.

Venus heals Aeneas with a magic plant. His strength is miraculously restored. He returns to the field, pulls his troops together, and chases Turnus.

Juturna, disguised as a chariot driver, gets control of Turnus's chariot and drives him away from Aeneas. Both Turnus and Aeneas are quite frustrated about not finding each other.

Venus shows Aeneas that Laurentum's citadel stands undefended, and Aeneas and his men attack it immediately. The Latins inside are petrified. Amata, Turnus's mother, thinks that he has been killed and hangs herself.

On the battlefield, Turnus figures out that his chariot driver is a fake. Then a warrior tells him that Aeneas is inside of Laurentum and his mother has killed herself. The warrior mocks him, the famous warrior, for driving over an empty field.

Aeneas and Turnus meet in the open outside of the city and begin the battle. Turnus had grabbed the wrong sword from the chariot, and when he strikes Aeneas's armor, his sword shatters. He calls his men to bring him another sword. Aeneas chases him and throws a spear at him, but Turnus prays to Faunus, the god of the forest, and the spear lodges itself immovably in a sacred olive tree. Juturna brings Turnus his real sword, but Venus unsticks the spear for Aeneas.

From a golden cloud Jupiter and Juno watch this battle. Jupiter tells her that Aeneas will win and that she can't stop it. She promises to stop making Aeneas's life miserable but asks that the Latins retain their language and name. Jupiter agrees and adds that the alliance between the Latins and Trojans will produce an indomitable race (the last prophecy in this epic), which matches Jupiter's prophecy to Venus in Book 1.

Jupiter then sends a fury, disguised as an owl, to attack Turnus, who is petrified. The omen causes Juturna to give up in discouragement. Aeneas throws his spear at Turnus, and Turnus throws an enormous rock at Aeneas. The rock misses, but the speak strikes Turnus in the thigh and knocks him down.

Turnus knows that he is dead and asks Aeneas to return his body to Turnus's father. This sparks pity in Aeneas to spare Turnus's life, but then Aeneas sees Pallas' sword belt that Turnus is wearing as a trophy. In aroused anger, Aeneas stabs Turnus in the chest, and Turnus dies.

THE END

27

The Launching of the *Aeneid*

GREEK EPIC POETRY LAID the foundation for the *Aeneid*. In this type of poetry, mythology controls the story as it explains the past. Symbolism carries the past into the future by repeating visions and prophecies that focus on a central character, supposedly a hero who lives out the political and religious viewpoints of the Greeks. Homer (eighth century BC) wrote the *Iliad* and the *Odyssey*, which laid the foundation for all future epic heroes. Although these heroes were not described as robots, fate became the prime mover of men's actions, and the interaction between men and the gods, who had the same vices as men, became the primary method of describing "historical" events.

Aristotle in his *Poetics* asserts that "poet" (the same word "poet" used in Acts 17:28) is less profound than written history because historians only describe events, while poets reveal what might have happened, a more noble objective. The Greek world's values and national identity rested on Homer's epics. Aristotle treated poetry as an art and a tool for influencing society. Aristotle had a significant influence on Virgil.

Virgil had a higher calling than just contributing to the great literature of his day by furthering Greek myth through Greek epic poetry. Virgil, trained in Homer's style, intended to surpass him. Virgil recognized that he could not simply sweep aside seven hundred years of literary tradition, since it was the most revered type of writing in his day. The cyclic epics that followed Homer evidenced the impact of Homer on the Greek and Roman Empires. Although this tradition waned four hundred years before Virgil, Aristotle attempted to resurrect it one hundred years later.

The mythical figure of Aeneas appears in Roman literature long before Virgil wrote his epic. He shows up several times in the *Iliad*. The *Aeneid* was grounded in the Greek epic traditions. The concept of *pietas*, or loyalty and faithfulness to all relationships, arose in the *Iliad* when Aeneas carried his dying father away from the lost battle of Troy. His act has been imprinted on objects like vases as early as the sixth century BC. Gnaeus Naevius, a poet in 270 BC, began the Roman national epic with a poem about the First Punic War. He wrote the poem in the Saturnian verse, which was a rigid style of poetry, but he connected his poem to the Roman god Saturn who was supposed to bring about a golden age for the Romans. Naevius seems to mention that Romulus was the grandson of Aeneas.

By the time Virgil began writing the *Aeneid*, a myriad of gods, goddesses, and humans had blossomed within Greek epics to the point that everyone understood what a poet meant by some reference to a context that contained some of these characters. For the reader of Virgil's day, comparison between stories became automatic.

As I stated in chapter 1, Mark wrote his gospel with the same intention: intertextuality. This is just a long word for connections. One sees connections between two texts and interprets one in light of the other. Literary techniques used: allusion, quotations, plagiarism, parody.

This intertextuality allowed Virgil to view Homer as his primitive starting point while going beyond him and completing the "history" of the founding of the Roman Empire. There is no doubt that Virgil made extensive use of Homer's style in the *Iliad* and the *Odyssey*, but Virgil was no copycat. Using the form most understood and accepted in his world, Virgil went beyond it to proclaim the Augustan Gospel. Attempting to make sense of the *Aeneid* today without knowing Homer is like missing the secret code in the text. Or understanding *Return of the Jedi* without having seen *A New Hope*. (Let the reader understand.)

Augustus wanted an epic poem written about himself. Although no written documentation verifies this statement absolutely, Rome had an overflow of epic poets who praised the successes of a general or politician. Public relations demanded such a strategy.

The Augustan age produced over two dozen epics that were mentioned in the literature of that day but have since been lost. Augustus was no different than any other emperor. His ego demanded his own epic.

Virgil's closest contemporaries who joined him in the inner circle around Maecenas were Horace and Propertius. Horace was one of the most famous poets of his time. Horace's work, *The Art of Poetry*, revealed his fanaticism for precision. He always wanted the most critical advice from others for his work. He would not write something that did not meet his own criteria. When Augustus requested that a poet write him an epic, Horace politely declined. Propertius wrote four books of love poems. In Book 2 he considers writing an epic, but when Augustus made the offer, he too declined. Perhaps Propertius preferred real history over mythology.

The task of writing an epic for Augustus was a daunting one. Kenneth Quinn believes that they turned Augustus down because of the difficulty of writing what he wanted. Epic poems required more than just a special kind of artistic form. Many believed that poetry promoted high morality in society. In their poems the poets expressed their own ideas and ideals about what was right and wrong with society.

How could a poet promote Augustus's morality through an epic poem? Augustus was not above carrying out his own vicious will against all who opposed him. Everyone hated the civil wars, about which both Horace and Propertius had written. Propertius had grown up close to where Augustus had besieged the forces of L. Antonius in 41 BC and Augustus brutally exterminated the population when he finally took the town. Propertius had lost his own estate due to the civil war. No poet wanted to glamorize a war that everyone so vividly remembered. What, then, was the point of writing an epic for Augustus, an epic that would probably condemn him?

And the "real" history would, in fact, condemn Augustus. Virgil, therefore, had to choose what kind of "history" he needed to write. He could not write history as the total content of time, nor even limiting that content to the past. All written history is, by definition, selective. He could not write history based on everything that had already been discovered and written as a report of the past. He could not base his epic on the popular sense of the word, those different versions and explanations of history that other historians had worked up from their research of the historical facts.

Virgil had to produce something apart from any actual historical facts. He had to integrate some historical facts with enough philosophy to make his story palatable to all levels of society. Instead of staying in the world of hard facts, he had to shift into the land of shadows, so his readers could be guided to draw their "own" conclusions that Virgil intended for them to draw.

As C. S. Lewis commented, when somebody stares at something like the *Aeneid* for too long, they can't help but see shadows take shapes which excite those parts of our minds that bring continuity to incongruity and form mythical themes that weave through fiction. The more vague the object, the more we see a face in the moon until we look through a telescope and just see rocks. Virgil had to avoid the open world of historical facts and enter the vagueness of myth, but he had to appeal to the real world, damaged by destruction and looking for meaning in life.[3]

Virgil tackled the assignment. Courageous! He could begin with a broader context to win the reception of those who had not lost so much in the war. Augustus's achievements could be praised while his vices could be shrouded behind generalities. A broader theme could also include those character qualities presupposed of all good Romans, like *pietas* (faithfulness and loyalty), *dignitas* (personal pride), *firmitas* (tenacity), *humanitas* (cultured), *industria* (hard working), *prudential* (wisdom), *veritas* (truthfulness), and *pas* (peace loving). If the reading audience could be guided to see these things in Augustus, then these traits could potentially overshadow his negative ones.

It's also difficult to write an epic memorial about someone who is still alive.

Virgil could also make use of legend, which was the normal mode for an epic poem, and Virgil did not have to invent his characters for the *Aeneid*, as mentioned previously. Many of Virgil's contemporaries latched onto Virgil's stories with minimal critical thinking. They regarded Virgil's reshaping of them as a poetic presentation of things that actually happened.

Once a legend has become accepted in society, the emperor could have coins molded with his image on them and even become deified. Lewis notes that Virgil wrote an official make-believe world that required educated Romans to accept the ancient legends of divine origins of Roman lineages.[4] Propertius recognized what Virgil had in mind. He saw the brilliance and magnitude of this forthcoming epic. Of the *Aeneid* he wrote, "*Cedite Romani scriptores, cedite Grai! Nescio quid maius nascitur Iliade.*"[5] ("Make way, you Roman writers, make way, Greeks! Something greater than the *Iliad* is born.") He foresaw that the *Aeneid* would

---

3. Lewis, "Historicism"; Lewis, *Fern-Seed*, 52.

4. Lewis, *Fern-Seed*, 39.

5. Propertius, Book 2, 34, 65, http://www.thelatinlibrary.com/prop2.html#34a.

encompass both the victory at Actium, which was Augustus's victory over Antony, and the victory in the person of Aeneas, the Trojan founder of Rome.

Virgil summarizes the entire poem in the first seven lines. He focuses on Rome but insinuates the war and fighting found in the *Iliad* and the story of a hero in the *Odyssey*. Virgil's first six books in the *Aeneid* connect with the *Odyssey*, while Books 7 to 12 address the *Iliad*. Aeneas (*uir* equals "man" in line 1 and in lines 5–7) ties the first six and the last six books together. Virgil recalls Homer's story and constantly uses Homer's methods of expression himself.

Virgil's parallels between the *Aeneid* and its two predecessors jump off the page throughout the *Aeneid* (intertextuality). Virgil even makes use of smaller items, too many to mention. G. N. Knauer published a book that brought together over 550 pages of explications of Virgil's imitations of, and allusions to, Homer. Virgil was a Roman, heavily influenced by the Greeks, but who wrote as a Roman.

His copying of Homer was not plagiarism. Virgil wanted his readers to closely associate Aeneas's travels and victories to challenge and overshadow his predecessors. Virgil brought material together from what is commonly understood and transformed it into the foundation epic for Augustus and the Roman Empire.

When one compares Virgil with other literature of his day, one notices the use that Virgil made of each of them: Greek tragedy, Plato, Apollonius. Quinn declares that Augustus's victory at Actium gave the Romans triumph over the Hellenistic world as well as allowing them to develop their own national literature that rivaled and surpassed the Greek writings of the past.

In fact, the *Aeneid* is an actual reversal of Homer's epics. The gods chose the Greeks as world rulers in the *Iliad* and helped them win the war against Troy. The Trojan Aeneas, almost an insignificant character in the *Iliad*, rises as the hero with help from the gods to found the Roman Empire at the expense of the Greeks. The heroes in Homer embrace the old, while Aeneas leaves the old to establish the new. Odysseus attempts to return home, whereas Aeneas leaves to establish a new kingdom. Odysseus reaches his goal after losing men, whereas Aeneas leads most of his people to safety.

Aeneas's initially impulsive character, like Homer's hero, goes beyond Homer's hero and changes gradually into a leader who exhibits faithfulness for his mission and community over individual emotional love, thus receiving the character qualities of a Roman leader who will be deified. Aeneas's father in the underworld defines the Roman mission being given to Aeneas, that of government and civilization, as opposed to the Greek dream of art and literature and philosophy.

Virgil's premier recipient of Aeneas's characterization, Augustus, appears three times in the *Aeneid*. The first time occurs at the end of Book 1 (1.286–96) with Virgil's embodiment of Roman history. However, Augustus is never directly mentioned, and the evils of the previous civil wars are significantly underplayed.

In Book 6 (6.789–805) Augustus is specifically mentioned and he is praised through seventeen lines. Only one short note surfaces about the civil war, but Augustus receives high praise as the divine general who conquers a greater part of the earth than Hercules ever did, while Julius Caesar is blamed for the civil war.

The third passage (8.671–713), the longest, describes the battle of Actium and then Augustus's return in triumph to Rome (8.714–28). This section includes the revealing of the magic shield[6] upon which Roman history is inscribed. Virgil uses the shield to make his case. If the readers can accept the shield and if those pictures on the shield are truly there on the shield, then those events might have actually taken place.

So, the only "trick" that Virgil slips into his masterpiece is that of presenting the events of recent history as the very probable climax of an extended historical process. Since the Romans viewed history as part of their family record, the readers would have little problem accepting the *Aeneid* as their own personal history.

And since the Romans viewed history as cyclical, in contrast to a present-day linear continuum, accepting Virgil's take on history found wide and grateful acceptance. Virgil rejected the use of an historical epic that connected legendary past and recent events in any kind of chronological sequence. He simply recycled a tale from legend. That was quite acceptable to his Roman audience, who believed that Aeneas's experiences were directly related to their real life.

It becomes obvious that Virgil recognized that, when he wrote of a war and a man in the past, the Romans would recognize the not-so-hidden message of another war and another man. It would be difficult to improve on Quinn's comments on Virgil's success.

---

6. The fire-god made this magic shield for Aeneas at Venus's request in his workshop under Mount Etna.

Virgil had sailed as close as possible to plagiarism, had produced a poem which imitated other poems to an extent that, one would have thought, must preclude creativity. If instead Virgil succeeded in producing an imaginative fiction that arouses and holds our attention, one major reason for his success is that he transcended Homer's objective. In one important respect the *Aeneid* differs from all preceding epic poems: it is no longer a story told for the story's sake. It is a poetic myth, appealing more to our fancy than to our taste for adventure.[7]

The *Iliad* and the *Odyssey* take place in the memorable past, with characters a little stronger than normal people, a story that barely stretches the limits of suspended disbelief. The *Aeneid* reaches into the distant, magical past, written to appeal to an educated, intelligent audience who grasped the world of imagination. Virgil moves away from Homer's narrative tragedy into moral lessons of life that connect the symbolism of fantasy to the concrete world of Augustus, who is a very human deified human and who overcomes his obstacles because his cause is noble.

The fairy tale approach lessens the harshness of the intended propaganda. Aeneas's rivals are not viewed as ruled by evil, and they gain the reader's respect, even if the reader wants Aeneas to win in the end.

The truth of poetry is not the same kind of truth as that of fact. S. H. Butcher believes that things beyond the range of our experience, that never have happened and never will happen, may be more profoundly true in a poetic sense than those things which we expect to happen every day. Virgil masterfully inserted fantasy throughout the realm of facts. Butcher says that those things improbable to reason are disguised enough to allow them to become probable and even necessary.

Without the *Aeneid* Virgil would have slipped into the mist of unknown authors. But the *Aeneid* connected the mythical past with the brutal present and the *Aeneid's* message resonated with the Roman soul. The *Aeneid* took on its own personality and breathed life into death. It achieved something that no other Latin piece of literature could have even envisioned. It became the bedrock foundational piece of propaganda promoting the destiny of the Roman Empire as defined and set in motion by Augustus.

Virgil intended to portray Augustus as the peacemaker of the Roman Empire. It is a well-known fact that Virgil's *Aeneid* contained a political message. Numerous times the *Aeneid* alludes to and promotes the

7. Quinn, *Virgil's Aeneid,* 52.

legitimacy of Augustus's rule based on the life of Aeneas. The Deification of Augustus occurs in The *Aeneid* 6.801. The closure of the *Gates of Janus* in 4.159 demonstrated the peace that Augustus brought. The fate (*Fatum*) of Aeneas steered him toward the priestly office of *Pontifex Maximus*, which became the natural fate of Augustus *Pontifex Maximus* in 10.112–13. The piety of Aeneas became the piety of Augustus in 2.695. Aeneas triumphed as a great warrior, making Augustus his natural successor in 1.283–85 *and* 6.839–40. Both established an empire of peace in 8.678. Aeneas predicted the successful battle of "*Actium*" in 8.679. Augustus brought peace by being the restorer of the golden Saturnian age in 6.793. The shield of Aeneas attributed glory to Augustus in 8.729–31.

The best quotation of all: Augustus will be the natural ruler through a series of legitimate successions in 1.288.

28

The *Aeneid's* Width and Depth of Dissemination throughout the Roman Empire and Beyond

DAVID R. WALLACE'S RESEARCH in his book *The Gospel of God* has uncovered a prominent reason why the apostle Paul wrote the book of Romans: to challenge the theology of the *Aeneid*. Paul never shied away from defending the gospel from any other false teachings, and the most well-known prophetic source in first century Rome, which strengthened Roman ideology and assured Roman salvation, was Virgil's *Aeneid*.[1]

Marianne Bonz discovered the same thing in her research in Luke–Acts. She reveals that Roman literature dominated Augustus's reign. "In no other work is it expressed with such artistic power, clarity, and religious overtones as it is in the *Aeneid*."[2] She also uncovered a letter from Seneca to the imperial slave Polybius[3] in which Seneca points out the high value of Polybius's translation of Virgil's poetry into Greek and Homer's works into Latin. The *Aeneid* was most likely translated into Greek in the mid-first century AD, read and re-read throughout all of Greece, at least during Paul's lifetime.

Paul and Luke travelled extensively together throughout the Roman Empire. They could not have missed hearing about the *Aeneid's* premise of Augustus as savior of the empire as Roman citizens, soldiers, philosophers, and common people retold Virgil's epic story. Both Wallace and

1. Wallace, Gospel of God.
2. Bonz, *Past as Legacy*, 57.
3. Seneca, Consolatio ad Polybium 11.5.

Bonz make a strong case for the wide dissemination of the *Aeneid* soon after its publication.

Christine Godfrey Perkell, Emory Classics professor, has written and published extensively on all aspects of the *Aeneid*. She proclaims that "Yet in its haunting and resonant verse, vivid characters, dramatic confrontations, and melancholy memorializing of tragedy and triumph, the *Aeneid* eclipsed its predecessors in epic, becoming immediately *the* Roman poem and—worst of fates—a standard school text."[4]

She ends her description of the depth of the *Aeneid*'s dissemination down into Roman society by stating, "The long-established fame of the *Aeneid* inclines us to forget how innovative and comprehensive was Vergil's achievement."[5] The *Aeneid* had penetrated deep into Roman society, but how widely had it been disseminated?

Volumes have been written about Augustus's desire to spread his message of salvation beyond the official borders of the empire.[6] When Rome invaded England, Britain was nothing more than a disparate group of peoples with no sense of national identity beyond their local politics.

The research of Alan K. Bowman[7] and Peter Salway[8] have shown that the most important legacy of Rome in England was that every generation of British inhabitants that followed the invasion strove to be Roman. The Saxon, Norman, Renaissance English, and Victorian were all attempting to regain the glory of that age when Britannia was considered to be a grand civilization established by the Romans.

Until 1992 neither Bowman nor Salway made any reference to the *Aeneid*. However, John Creighton believes that, "It is perfectly possible that a foundation myth from LIA Britton did survive through the Roman period to be transcribed at a later date in Ireland, especially if it was associated with the story of the *Aeneid*."[9] Creighton can't prove this possibility, but he states, "It [the *Aeneid*] exemplifies precisely the genre of foundation myth which would have been created within the political context of Britain in the early first century AD."[10]

4. Perkell, *Reading Vergil's Aeneid*, 8, emphasis added.

5. Perkell, *Reading Vergil's Aeneid*, 8.

6. For instance: Winn, *Purpose of Mark's Gospel*; Pollok, "Roman Propaganda"; Allen, "Fasti of Ovid," 250–66.

7. Bowman, *Life and Letters*.

8. Salway, *Roman Britain*.

9. Creighton, *Coins and Power*, 143.

10. Creighton, *Coins and Power*, 143.

Then in 1992, the dream of any historian occurred. Someone discovered the Vindolanda manuscript in northern Britain. Bowman wrote,

> In the *praetorium* at Vindolanda, probably during the occupation of Cerialis and his family, someone took a writing-tablet on which a private letter had been begun, but not finished, and wrote on the back of it in rather good, but degenerating, capital hand a line from the *Aeneid* of Vergil (9.473): a complete line, not a complete sentence and certainly not a readily memorable one, from the second half of the poem which is generally much less in evidence as a quarry for writing exercises; and one with the remarkable form of *e*, hitherto unparalleled in ink texts.[11]

Were texts of Vergil available at Vindolanda? Were they used for writing practice (as is commonly found on papyri) and by whom? Cerialis's children? There is a limit to the value of speculation, and we may yet learn more. But the existence of this text is perhaps the most single remarkable phenomenon of our find. It may, indeed, not be the only literary text at Vindolanda (even if it is the only one of which we can be certain) and one of the fragmentary letters carries a clear reference to "books" (*libros*).

If the imagination may be tickled by a remarkable coincidence, it is worth adding that almost on the same day as the Vindolanda text came to light, a batch of Latin military papyri from Herod's fortress at Masada in Israel was found to include a scrap containing a line from the fourth book of the *Aeneid*.

The Romans had carried the *Aeneid* into northern Britain and as far south as Masada on the eastern edge of the Judean Desert overlooking the Dead Sea. The *Aeneid* legend had reached national importance as *the* Roman poem and had been carried by Roman soldiers to Masada and by Roman nobility all the way to northern Britain.

A new age was dawning. The civil wars were over. History was circling back upon itself. When Augustus rose to power, the Romans grasped onto Virgil's portrayal of an emperor who would bring peace out of the chaos of civil war. In the center of the previous chaos stood Aeneas, and in the new world order stood his descendant Augustus, the spiritual

---

11. Bowman, *Life and Letters*, 91–92. See also Vindolanda Tablets Online, http://vindolanda.csad.ox.ac.uk/4DLink2/4DACTION/WebRequestQuery?searchTerm=118&searchType=number&searchField=TVII.

focus of the *Aeneid*. Thus, the *Aeneid* became the centerpiece of literature for the propagation of Augustan theology.

29

Mark's Knowledge of the *Aeneid*

BEFORE WE BEGIN TO compare the Gospel of Mark's theology with the *Aeneid*'s theology, we need to demonstrate Mark's connection with the *Aeneid*. We will reconstruct Mark's lifelong contact with the *Aeneid* by arranging fourteen pieces of evidence into a cohesive whole. Different pieces carry different weight of importance, but collectively they will reveal the amazing conclusion not seen by scholars to date: Mark had more than just a passing connection with the *Aeneid*.

Mark's Family & Travels

> SUMMARY: Mark's family and his travels placed him in the perfect position to write his Gospel in Rome, where the *Aeneid* was the most prominent.

Mark didn't write his Gospel in a vacuum, but unless we attempt a complete picture of Mark's background and surroundings, then he will retain the image of an obscure teenager who got rejected by Paul for their second missionary trip.

We know nothing of Mark's father, so we have to start with Mark's mother, his cousin Barnabas, and eventually Paul and Peter. Mark's mother, Mary, and his cousin, Joseph, were Jewish. Joseph was also a Levite, and he was born on Cyprus. Apparently, after he had begun to follow Jesus, Joseph gained the reputation as a man who greatly encouraged other people. Thus, he was nicknamed Barnabas (Son of Encouragement). Barnabas was wealthy enough to have sold a piece of property and given it to the church in Jerusalem (Acts 4:36–37).

Some believe that Mark was the young man in Mark 14:51–52. It could have been a different young man, but this incident of a young man running away from the arrest of Jesus is only reported in Mark's Gospel. The unanswered question: why would Mark tell about some anonymous young man running away naked in the garden? A young man who plays no part in the story and never shows up again? It's easier to believe that Mark wanted everyone to know that he had been among the disciples who had deserted Jesus in the garden. Mark wasn't shy about telling the truth.

Since his mother, Mary, lived in Jerusalem at the time of Jesus, Mark had met Jesus and chosen to follow him before Jesus died on the cross. We can only assume that Mark was among the seventy who were sent out in pairs to inform the people that the Messiah was right behind them. We don't know.

Mark's age at that time might be significant for his continuing education, but neither Scripture nor church history records that information. Acts records Peter disappearing from the scene in Acts 12, but Mark accompanied Paul and Barnabas on their first missionary journey in Acts 13. This mission's trip would have certainly enhanced Mark's education as indicated by the word that describes his duty during the trip.

Mark's responsibility on that trip was that of a "helper" (13:5). The Greek word indicates that Mark had much more responsibility than a slave. Mark was not a mere baggage carrier. He was respected enough by Paul to be taken along. Mark held the position of delegated authority while Paul and Barnabas evangelized the people on Cyprus.

These three went to Cyprus first. That makes sense. Barnabas was from Cyprus. He was returning to his home country on the first missions trip, and he took his younger cousin with him. Luke records that the Holy Spirit sent out Saul and Barnabas. Nothing indicates that these two men made a mistake by taking Mark with them. After a number of calm Jewish synagogue presentations, they reached the other end of the island. At that point they encountered an evil Jewish sorcerer. The outcome of that confrontation led to the conversion of proconsul and the Holy Spirit blinding the sorcerer. That must have been an interesting first missionary experience for Mark.

In addition to Mark's delegated authority on this trip, his Roman training in rhetoric and his Jewish education in memorizing the Torah[1] equipped him with the skills of a recorder of everyone's activities, like a designated amanuensis, or secretary who took dictation and copied manuscript.

Luke had not gone with them on that journey. He would have received a report about that journey from them later, which he probably used to write his version of the gospel and Acts.

For some unknown reason, Mark left them and returned to Jerusalem. When Paul and Barnabas returned to Antioch at the end of the trip, they reported everything that had happened, focusing on the salvation of the gentiles (14:27). Did Mark tell his side of the story when he arrived home first? Did Mark write anything down? Did Luke consult Mark as one of his sources for writing about that trip (Luke 1:3)? Mark's experience on Cyprus gave him a first-hand view of how Paul and Barnabas evangelized the gentiles. Somewhere along the line Mark developed enough writing skills to write his own Gospel in Greek.

Time passed before Paul and Barnabas began discussing their second missionary journey. Paul refused to allow Mark to go with them again (Acts 15:3641). We have no information as to the reason why Mark left Cyprus, but Paul accused him of deserting them in Pamphylia and had not continued to work with them in that ministry. This accusation does not refer to Mark's abilities, but to his endurance and commitment. This disagreement led to two different missionary teams—nothing wrong with that.

Paul later came to appreciate Mark, as demonstrated by his request from Timothy in 2 Timothy 4:11: "Get Mark and bring him with you, for he is useful to me for ministry." If Paul wrote 2 Timothy around 65 AD, then over twenty years had gone by since Paul and Mark had been on Cyprus together. Considering their contact with the other apostles and their travels, it seems unlikely that they had had no contact with each other for over twenty years. Paul had revised his opinion of Mark and wanted Mark to come to him either because of previous contact since Cyprus or enough positive communication about Mark from others.

After twenty plus years Paul also came to recognize Mark's literary abilities. In 2 Timothy 4:13 Paul requested that Timothy bring Mark and

---

1. More about Mark's education later.

"the books, and above all the parchments." Why did Paul have such a high interest in the *scrolls* and *parchments*? Which *scrolls* and *parchments*?

This is an interesting question. No one believes that Paul was overly concerned about his bank receipts or fiction novels. *Scrolls* and *parchments*. Valuable. Not cheap paper used for note-taking. The text doesn't say that Timothy had these items, but that Paul had left them with someone named Carpus. The text doesn't say that these scrolls and parchments even belonged to Paul.

That thought makes it even more interesting. Look at the timeline. Paul wrote the book of Romans in 57–58 AD from Corinth. Most scholars now believe that Mark wrote his Gospel before Matthew or Luke wrote theirs. Since none of the Gospels refer to the destruction of the temple in Jerusalem in 70 AD, many scholars assume that Matthew, Mark, and Luke wrote before 70 AD. If Mark wrote first, then his Gospel would have been penned closer to 55 AD instead of 70 AD. Paul wrote 2 Timothy around 65 AD.

Speculation is fun. What if Paul was referring to Mark's own writings?

Speculation number one: Mark wrote his Gospel first, then Paul wrote Romans, then Paul wrote 2 Timothy and wanted to see the scrolls and parchments.

Speculation number two: Paul wrote Romans in AD 57–58. Mark wrote his Gospel after that. Paul wrote 2 Timothy in AD 65, asking to see a copy of Mark's Gospel. If Paul wrote Romans first, then the book of Romans would have been widely circulated by the time that Peter and Mark arrived in Rome.

Speculation number three: They wrote at the same time and Paul wanted to compare notes.

Fact number four: We have no idea.

We don't know when Peter and Mark arrived in Rome. We don't know who arrived first or if they arrived together. Maybe Peter arrived first and asked Mark to join him, or Mark arrived first and found an apartment for both of them, or they both arrived at the same time without informing each other and wondered who was stalking whom. We don't know.

There is no firm evidence that Peter, along with Mark, planted the church in Rome. The Catholic Church claims that Peter and Paul planted the church there. Some of the church fathers seem to agree.[2]

The Protestants protest against Peter and Paul as founders of the church in Rome. They use the book of Romans to prove their point. Paul wrote the book of Romans to an existing church, not to one he was planting. Paul made reference to Peter in the book of Romans because Peter was in Rome at the time. The Protestants make the point that the "visitors from Rome" (Acts 2:10) were among the three thousand saved on that day of Pentecost years before in Jerusalem, and they returned to Rome and planted the church there before either Peter or Paul arrived the first time. This was before the day of Bible schools and seminaries who trained church planters. Back then people started churches without realizing that they were doing the impossible by not having a pastor or an official church planter. They hadn't been educated in the denominational clergy/laity split yet.

The only firm evidence that both the Catholics and Protestants accept is that Peter preached in Rome, and the believers asked Mark to write it all down. In order for Mark to have written everything down, he had to have spent enough time in Rome to disciple the believers and gain the trust of those believers to have them ask him to write down the teachings of Peter. No one disputes that Peter discipled other believers, and Mark was one of those believers. First Peter 5:13 places Mark in Rome with Peter: "The church in Babylon, also chosen, sends you greetings, as does Mark, my son."

When Mark arrived in Rome, he found that many of the church members in Rome were Romans (duh!) and spoke Latin. As in every culture, many people only learn their own mother tongue. Some Romans (at least a few), having grown up and been educated in Latin, saw no reason to learn to read, write, or speak Greek.

Did Peter and Mark learn Latin? If Latin was the primary language of the capital city of the Roman Empire, why would missionaries choose to ignore the major language of the major population? Why would Peter and Mark require the Romans to tolerate the Gospel in spoken Greek? And since Mark was the younger, he certainly learned more Latin than Peter. In fact, it's highly unlikely that Peter, a Jewish fisherman, knew Latin at all.

---

2. Ignatius of Antioch (110 AD), Dionysius of Corinth (later second century AD), Irenaeus (189 AD), Clement of Alexandria, Tertullian (200 AD).

It seems completely unreasonable to assume that Peter and Mark required the Romans to listen and understand the Gospel in Greek, without any Latin, and then to reject Latin as the language they used to teach and disciple the new Roman converts, some of whom only knew Latin.

A modern day experience: My wife and I met some foreign missionaries in Russia who never learned Russian, but used paid translators, some of whom were not followers of Jesus, to "bring people to Christ." One English-speaking missionary chose not to learn Russian and he had been preaching in English for over a year with a Russian interpreter. His interpreter finally asked him if English was a more important language than Russian.

In another instance I was asked to lead a Bible study for a group of elderly Russian believers. I had been studying Russian for some weeks and I attempted to lead the study in Russian. My vocabulary ran out after forty minutes, so instead of continuing in English, I chose to close the study early. Everyone thanked me for the study. As everyone was leaving the interpreter approached me with tears in her eyes. I thought that I had offended her either because my Russian had been so bad, or because I closed the study early.

She replied, "No, your Russian was fine for someone who has only studied it for a few weeks. And I'm not upset that you closed the study early. I've been interpreting Bible studies for English-speaking missionaries for a few years now." She almost choked up. "This is the first time I've ever heard the Bible taught in my own language."

I did choke up.

When I consider the options for Peter and Mark in Rome, I assume that Peter and Mark learned and used the majority language of the Romans (Latin) to communicate the Gospel and then to disciple the new Roman converts. Maybe Peter's Latin was rusty and he used Mark as his key interpreter.

Another tantalizing fact is the existence of the Old Latin Gospels, of which scholars know very little, except that they did exist during Mark's time.[3] The origins of the Old Latin Gospels are lost in obscurity. Having said that, however, their existence raises the question of their origin and their usage.

---

3. http://www.romeacrosseurope.com/?p=6934#sthash.wzANaxol.DqHMPDpi. dpbs.

The believers in Rome had asked (begged?) Mark to write down what they had been taught orally. After his escape from prison in Acts 12, Peter eventually ended up in Rome. Mark joined him there. Peter taught the small church in Rome and discipled Mark during that time.

Because Mark had been educated in all three worlds, he was conversant in Latin and taught the Roman believers in Latin, the Greeks in Greek, and the Hebrews in Hebrew. Peter returned to Antioch in 46 AD due to the tension between Jerusalem (Jewish believers) and Antioch (gentile believers). The believers in Rome wanted the gospel written down.

Paul L. Maier translated *Eusebius: The Church History*, and in chapter 2.15.1–2, Maier wrote:

> In the fourth century Eusebius claimed that the believers in Rome had to almost beg Mark to write his Gospel. And, thus, when the divine word had made its home among them, the power of Simon was quenched and immediately destroyed, together with the man himself. And so greatly did the splendor of piety illumine the minds of Peter's hearers that they were not satisfied with hearing once only and were not content with the unwritten teaching of the divine Gospel, but with all sorts of entreaties they besought Mark, a follower of Peter, and the one whose Gospel is extant, that he would leave them a written monument of the doctrine which had been orally communicated to them. Nor did they cease until they had prevailed with the man and had thus become the occasion of the written Gospel which bears the name Mark. And they say that Peter when he had learned, through a revelation of the Spirit, of that which had been done, was pleased with the zeal of the men, and that the work obtained the sanction of his authority for the purpose of being used in the churches.[4]

Jerome confirms this request with variations: "Mark the disciple and interpreter of Peter wrote a short Gospel at the request of the brethren at Rome embodying what he had heard Peter tell. When Peter had heard this, he approved it and published it to the churches to be read by the authority as Clement in the sixth book of his Hypotyposes (Outlines), and Papias, bishop of Hierapolis, record."[5] Even Papias wrote, "Mark, the

---

4. Eusebius, *Church History*, 2.15.1–2.
5. Jerome, and Gennadius, *Lives*, chapter 8.

interpreter of Peter, wrote carefully down all that he recollected, but not according to the order of Christ's speaking or working."[6]

How does Mark's family and travels connect with the *Aeneid*? Mark's family was not an isolated Jewish group of hermits who ran away and hid from the Romans. Barnabas didn't gain his wealth by hiding in a desert village. Mark's family and his travels clearly point to Mark being in Rome with Peter and writing his Gospel there. Rome was the center of Augustan power, and the location where the *Aeneid* was the most prominent. Mark was brought up to engage the world, not avoid it.

Mark's travels took him everywhere, and he ended up spending time in Rome with Peter and the local church. Did Mark help to plant the church in Rome? We don't know. Did Mark write the first copies of his Gospel in Latin? An intriguing idea, but we don't know. In any case, Mark's family and travels placed him at the heart of the empire. Considering the time and involvement of Mark in the lives of the Roman believers, it is almost absurd to assume that Mark had never heard of the *Aeneid* or had not come in contact with it in Rome.

Hebrew Education

SUMMARY: Mark's Hebrew education in no way hindered his ability to write his Gospel in Greek. In fact, his Hebrew education taught him exactness in his studies, something he would use in his reading and evaluating the theology of the *Aeneid*.

Mark's education played a role in his encounter with the *Aeneid*. The responsibility for the education of Jewish children was placed primarily on the fathers, as commanded in Deuteronomy 6:6–9 and 11:18–20. The fathers were to be the initial channel for teaching Jewish morality based on the commandments (Ps 78:5), as well as the meaning and purpose behind the feasts and customs associated with them (Exod 13:6–8). The mothers took over the responsibility when the fathers went to work.

The education of Jewish boys focused on certain passages of Scripture that each boy was expected to know: the *Shema* (Deut 6:4–9; Deut 11:13–21; Num 15:37–41). *Shema* means "hear." It is derived from the first word of Deuteronomy 6:4: "Hear, O Israel: The Lord our God is one

6. Eusebius 3.39.15.

Lord;" the Hallel (Ps 113–18). Hallel means "Praise [God]!"; the story of the creation and the fall (Gen 1–5); and the basic elements of the Levitical law (Lev 1–8).

The children were also taught to read the Hebrew of the Old Testament, because the Jewish men were expected to read sections of the Hebrew Scriptures in the synagogue service (see Luke 4:16–29).

Aramaic—a language closely related to Hebrew—was also probably taught in the synagogue schools. It was the native tongue of most Jews living in Palestine and the language of the Targums, which were esteemed translations and interpretations of the Old Testament.

The study of Greek was apparently not important in the education of Jewish boys, however the Jews learned Greek through the Hellenization period. It was unavoidable. The second half of the Second Temple period (516 BC to 70 AD) witnessed a rapid increase of Hellenization in Israel. Jewish high priests and aristocrats even took on Greek names. The Hellenic influence pervaded everything. In the very strongholds of Judaism, it modified the organization of the state, the laws, public affairs, art, science, and industry. It affected the ordinary things of life and the common associations of the people.

Mark was educated as a Hebrew, but he wrote his Gospel in Greek. A literature search found no scholar who believes that the Holy Spirit gave ("inspired") the words of Mark's Gospel to a Jewish man (Mark) who had no knowledge or ability in the Greek language. In whatever way that Mark acquired his ability in the Greek language, he was able to handle the language well enough to write down the words inspired by the Holy Spirit. Mark's Hebrew education taught him a thorough knowledge of the Old Testament and exactness in his studies, both necessary for evaluating the theology of the *Aeneid*.

Roman Education

SUMMARY: Mark received as much Roman education as any other Jew, and probably more, since he came from a wealthy family. That Roman education brought him in contact with the *Aeneid* and prepared him to engage the *Aeneid*'s theology.

Rome trusted the myths of the poets, culminating in Virgil's *Aeneid*, to give them their identity and importance. More important than war, ideas brought the Roman people together in their raising and carrying the Roman banner of superiority. The myths of the *Aeneid* contributed significantly to this cause. Rome wanted to rule the world, especially the Greek world. The best method of indoctrination was to put their best literature in the language of the conquered people and to place this literature into the hands of the educators. Thus, the *Aeneid* was translated into Greek. I'll demonstrate this under the section, Books, Publishers and Readers, further on in this chapter.

Eventually some knowledge of Latin became mandatory in the Roman world and the educators used bilingual glossaries and bilingual lists of authors. Most of the glossaries were written with the Greek script, and the vast majority of the bilingual word lists were from the *Aeneid*. The importance of the *Aeneid* functioned as one of the basic texts for education from the beginning of its publication, and it held sway in Roman education long after it was written.

Rome relied heavily on Greek culture in the Roman education of their children. For the most part the Greek culture dominated the Roman world. Rome believed that they owed a debt of gratitude to Greece and Greek culture. Rome praised Athens and Sparta and Olympia as symbols of Greece's glories and classical legacy. The Romans despised the Greeks as weak and decadent but revered their cultural models. In reality, both were decadent, but Rome had won militarily. One result was that the Romans brought Greek tutors into their homes to educate Roman children.

The Romans had no official department of education that required a minimum of schooling for any given age of children. Only the wealthy made use of tutors. A wealthy Roman husband might have married a non-Roman wife, but, as a Roman, he used his wealth to promote the Roman Empire through the education of his own sons. The content of that education included abilities in rhetoric and the propaganda of Roman myths that supported the establishment and continuing existence of Rome as a civilization.

The *Aeneid* held a prominent place in the education of Rome's sons. Quintilian played an active role in supporting the thesis that the *Aeneid* had become part of the fabric of Roman education. Quintilian (born 35 AD, died after 95 AD in Rome) was Rome's leading Latin teacher under the emperors Titus and Domitian. He was entrusted with the education of the emperor's two heirs. His *Institutio Oratoria*, a major work of educational theory and literary criticism, in twelve books, was published shortly before the end of his life. This work shaped Roman education for the next two hundred years.

Quintilian made unique use of the *Aeneid* in his tutoring of students. He incorporated it in his rhetoric classes by using the opening lines of the *Aeneid* to demonstrate specifically how to properly read Virgil's poem in a speech. Quintilian was not teaching the *Aeneid* to students who had no knowledge of that text. The students already knew the *Aeneid* well from other lessons. Quintilian was using a well-known text (the *Aeneid*) to teach his students how to use it in their speeches.

Quintilian was roughly twenty years younger than Mark. Since the *Aeneid* was still prominent during Quintilian's time, it had obviously grown in importance during Mark's lifetime. Since Quintilian was Rome's most prominent teacher, as noted above, this evidence shows a direct connection between Mark and the *Aeneid*.

Edward E. Best, Jr. demonstrates that even the common Roman soldier was required to read. He shows from Livy's Latin that the *tessera* was used throughout the Roman Empire. A *tessera* was a small tablet used for a number of functions, one of which was to send non-vocal messages to the troops.

Marcus Valerius Martialis, a Roman poet, boasted about his own popularity when he discovered that centurions were reading his poems. He claimed that they read so much, they were wearing out his books.

Best also mentions that Roman soldiers had written lots of graffiti on the barracks walls at Ostia during the second century suggesting that reading and writing on the walls was one of the main ways these troops entertained themselves.

We know little of Mark's formal Roman education, but unless his parents had whisked him away and stuck him in a desert monastery in southern Judea, he encountered the *Aeneid*.[7] And even in that monastery, some rebellious monk was probably reading the love story between Aeneas and Dido in chapter 4. It's gets very lonely in monasteries.

---

7. Buddhist monasteries appeared around the fourth century BC, as a haven for the monks during the South Asian wet season, roughly three months mid-July to mid-October. They didn't want to trample down new plant growth or get stranded in bad weather.

Mark's Personal Education

SUMMARY: Mark wrote his Gospel in Greek, but he spent time in Rome with Peter. In order to evangelize and disciple Romans, Mark spoke and read and wrote Latin. It was easy for him to engage the *Aeneid* in both of those languages.

As noted above, the Jews took the education of their children very seriously. No evidence exists revealing any information about Mark's education. Although Rome dominated the Middle East, the older disciples of Jesus, like Peter, probably did not receive an intense Roman education. They had already become established in their professions. It cannot be argued conclusively that Mark's *official* education encompassed both the Hebrew and Roman worlds.

However, Mark's parents played a vital role in his education. Let's look at the evidence of his family.

There is no official record of Mark's father. The Orthodox Church holds the tradition that Mark's parents were Jewish. However, outside the Coptic Church, no scholars have substantiated this view of Mark's parentage nor even agree with it.

Another theory is that Mark's father was Roman. The first piece of evidence for this theory is Mark's name. Several apostles had two names. Mark (Markus) was his Roman name (Acts 15:39; 2 Tim 4:11), whereas John was his Jewish name (Acts 13:5, 13). Mark uses a number of Latin words in his Gospel that indicate a good knowledge of Latin. If this is true, then Mark would have received a *thorough* education in both worlds: Jewish and Roman.

Since no solid evidence of parentage clarifies Mark's education, we will have to look elsewhere.

Money.

Mark came from a wealthy family, and wealthy Jewish families did not get rich by avoiding the Romans. The Jews studied the Romans and their economy and did everything possible to get rich off the Romans. The upper classes within Judaism, such as the Pharisees and Sadducees, hoarded their wealth. And the wealthy, both Romans and Jews, educated their children well. Mark fell under that category of children required to tolerate a deeper and broader education than less fortunate children.

The evidence for his family's wealth comes directly from the New Testament. When the apostle Peter realized that an angel of the Lord had released him from prison in Acts 12:12, "he went to the house of Mary, the mother of John who was also called Mark, where many were gathered together and were praying." There did not seem to be a strong middle class in Palestine at that time in history. Apparently, only wealthy people owned houses. Although the text does not clearly state that Mary owned her house, the connection of wealth can be made with Barnabas, her brother.

As mentioned earlier, Barnabas was a Levite (Acts 4:36–37) from Cyprus, living in Jerusalem at the time of Pentecost. Every city has its share of poor and rich neighborhoods. Barnabas probably lived among the wealthy on Mount Zion, a wealthy neighborhood inhabited by King Herod as well as the high priest.

As the believers were helping one another financially in the church in Jerusalem, Barnabas "owned a tract of land, sold it and brought the money and laid it at the apostles's feet" (Acts 4:36).

The Jewish believers consisted of a tight community that supported one another (Acts 2:44–45). Barnabas's sister also shared in the wealth exhibited by Barnabas's financial standing in the community. The Romans allowed their subjugated peoples to retain wealth to the point of owning houses and owning slaves. Owning a slave was also evidence of wealth. Mary apparently had at least one female slave, Rhoda, who was the first person to realize that Peter had been freed from prison (Acts 12:13–14).

No evidence exists explaining how Barnabas and his sister came into their wealth. One could postulate that Barnabas was a businessman from Cyprus and moved to Jerusalem to secure a business deal but chose to buy a house and stay.

The wealthy educate their children. Because Mark came from a wealthy family, he likely received the best education possible. That education would have included Roman as well as Jewish content.

The Romans were overly zealous about educating everyone using Greek textbooks. The Romans laid a premium on education, and especially education in the Greek language, in order to teach everyone the basics of writing and speaking. Greek was so important to the Romans that they began with four main Greek works (*Progymnasmata*), and then translated them into Latin as needed.[8] These Latin translations were far less important than the Greek originals.

8. The *Progymnasmata* were handbooks of Greek preliminary rhetorical exercises. The term first appeared during the late fourth century BC.

The program of study laid out in these four works contained a progression of Greek exercises that increased in difficulty as they trained students (and adults) in writing and public speaking. More importantly, these exercises included cultural values and everyday literary forms for those choosing to become teachers.

The Romans used the Greek language in their education system to spread their propaganda to all their subject peoples. Even more significantly, George Kennedy notes that the Roman's educational system used secular literature of the Greeks and Romans, the writings of early Christians beginning with the Gospels, and other documents through the early church fathers to mold the habits of thinking and writing among the young.

The Romans wanted to influence the world with their vision of Augustan as savior of the world. The New Testament writers (Luke, Paul, and the author of Hebrews) wrote their inspired works as a direct challenge to the "habits of thinking" of Rome.[9]

Further, these four Greek works were so tightly structured in the progression of difficulty, from simple stories to debates of logic, that the Romans used these stories to give their students lists of things to say on many subjects. They didn't teach them to think on their own, but the Romans were *indoctrinating the students in traditional values.* The Romans did have a clear agenda of propagating their Augustan theology to the rest of the known world. The *Progymnasmata* was used the most during the Roman period, when freedom of speech was curtailed (Augustan propaganda).

However, during that time philosophical skepticism still flourished in the schools, and the context of the student exercises were distinctly political and nostalgically promoted the previous period of Greek history when Athens was democratic. Even some Romans struggled against the strict Augustan theology in the realm during the time that Mark wrote his Gospel (50–70 AD). Someone during the high point of Roman power who disagreed with Augustan salvation would not have been completely out of the mainstream. The Gospel of Mark was a refreshing alternative for some of those gentiles who were not completely captivated by Augustan propaganda.

Mark's education intersected three worlds: Jewish, Greek, and Roman.

---

9. Luke and Acts: Bonz. "Best of Times"; Romans: Wallace, *Gospel of God*; Hebrews: Mark Reasoner, "Divine Sons," 152.

1) The Jews viewed the world differently. Religion dominated the Jewish education. The Law, its observance, and the practical implications involved in following the Law influenced every activity in life, and if intellectual ability happened to improve, so much the better, though it was not a necessary result. Detailed memorization played a large part in Mark's education. Character development before God was more important than Greek or Roman nationalism. Moreover, physical and military education was treated with hostility.

2) Greece aimed for "good citizens" through their educational endeavors. Individual excellence was paramount as applied to public usefulness. Virtue, the supreme goal of all education, was always connected with civic duties. Gymnastics was for physical and military training, and music for the arts. Although Plato focused on society and Aristotle on the individual, the final goal was a combined effort to produce a well-organized state. Socrates was enthralled with the power of thinking that was intended to produce fundamental universal moral principles. If contemplative thinking was unique to humans, then the pursuit of knowledge was man's highest function. Where Greek philosophy dominated, nothing practical surfaced, only philosophical speculations seeking ultimate truth.

A true liberal education was required by the Greeks for all who could afford it. The Greek *Paideia* system of education mandated training in Greek and Hellenistic (Greco-Roman) cultures that included almost everything: gymnastics, grammar, rhetoric, music, mathematics, geography, natural history, and philosophy. This Greek *paideia* became known as *humanitas* in Latin and founded the model for European Christian institutions of higher learning.[10]

3) Rome's goals were similar: preparation for Roman citizenship, which included military, civic duties, and economic acumen. Oratory eventually became the superior aspect of their education, and the finest citizen was the orator, but the underlying Greek philosophy still dominated. Pertaining to Roman education before the birth of Jesus, the "Twelve Tables" made up the main content of Roman education in the very early days of Rome.

The "Twelve Tables" was an Old Latin written law code, c. 450 BC, that applied to every person in the Roman Empire, from the patricians (Roman nobility) to the plebians (common people). There were no

---

10. The education of the ideal children of the population.

social distinctions within this law code. These laws were committed to memory, then understood and mastered as practical guidance for the life after death. They affected every aspect of Roman life. History, including biography and the study of Roman law, comprised the subject matter of early Roman education.

How did these three educational systems form Mark's character and writing?[11] Once a child reached the age of six or seven and entered a school "system," the major difference between the Jewish and Greek/Roman elementary schools was one of content. The Jewish system focused entirely on the Torah and Jewish daily conduct. Science was practically looked down upon by the rabbis. The Greeks and Romans worshipped the sciences (like many do in the West today), and they pushed aside the study of ethics to inferior theoretical speculation about the nature of man and the universe.

Another major difference between the Jewish educational system of children and the Roman system was the social positions of the teachers. The Jews placed the highest priority on knowledge of the Law, the teacher's piety and sincerity, and the respect of the community for the teacher. The Romans were far more practical. They didn't care about the teacher *per se*. They just wanted their money's worth. Therefore, the Romans used highly educated slaves as mentors for their children. And most of these highly educated slaves were Greeks. This is important. If Mark's father required a tutor for Mark, that tutor probably would have been a Greek. This would have enabled him to read and interact with the *Aeneid* in Greek, while writing his Gospel in Greek.

The story of the *Aeneid* was very widely known and Mark had not been an isolated Jew who had rejected Roman influence and education. Mark received enough of a Greek and Roman education to enable him to engage the concepts and theology of the *Aeneid* in both languages.

Some believe that Mark's education was irrelevant when he wrote his gospel. They claim that Mark simply wrote down what Peter taught. And why would Peter care about the *Aeneid*? He probably had never even heard of it.

This view simplifies the writing of Mark's Gospel too much. Peter gave the teaching, but then he left Rome and returned to Jerusalem for a time. While he was gone, the believers in Rome begged Mark to write down what Peter had taught them. Mark obliged and finished his Gospel

---

11. Barrow, *Greek and Roman*; Drazin, *History of Jewish*, 137–43.

before Peter returned. When Peter read what Mark had written, Peter approved. His approval does not assume that Mark wrote down word for word what Peter had taught. Mark had the freedom to write down what he had understood from Peter's teaching, and Mark easily *contextualized his Gospel* to address the current wrong theologies of his day. The Holy Spirit would have guided Mark's writing in the same way that the Holy Spirit guided Peter. "No prophecy was ever produced by the will of man, but men spoke from God as they were carried along by the Holy Spirit" (2 Pet 1:21).

The confluence of the three educational systems gave Mark a breadth and depth of education that influenced his understanding of the *Aeneid*. When Mark eventually ended up working with Peter in Rome, Mark was not a Jewish hermit hiding out in Rome among a small group of Hebrews. Mark used his Roman education to simply contextualize his Gospel in order to draw the Greeks and Romans away from Augustus and toward Jesus. If, as proposed, Mark had extensive contact with the *Aeneid*, then he also had a deep enough understanding of it in Greek to present counterarguments of the *Aeneid* in his Gospel.

The Date of Mark's Gospel in Relationship to the *Aeneid*

> SUMMARY: Mark wrote his Gospel after the *Aeneid* had reached the outer rims of the realm and penetrated down into the Roman school system. Knowledge and contact with the *Aeneid* could not be avoided.

The date of Mark's Gospel and its proximity to the *Aeneid* also supports Mark's encounter with the *Aeneid*. Virgil got sick in 19 BC and demanded that the *Aeneid* be burned and not published. Then Virgil died. Augustus ordered Varius, Virgil's friend, to publish it anyway. Varius complied, and the *Aeneid* entered mainstream Latin literature in the same year, 19 BC. The authority of the emperor carried more weight than pleasing a dead friend.

Mark wrote his Gospel between 55–68 AD That was roughly eighty years after the *Aeneid* was published. Within that eighty years the *Aeneid* had achieved extensive prominence throughout the Roman Empire and penetrated all the way down into the Roman school system. Mark could have stumbled over copies of the *Aeneid* discarded by careless school children on their way home from their tutors.

Jewish Knowledge of the *Aeneid*

SUMMARY: The Jews knew Greek and Roman literature as well as their own. This included the *Aeneid*. Mark could not have missed the *Aeneid*.

Mark was a Jew. If other Jews had encountered the *Aeneid*, then Mark can't be left out. The content of Hellenistic primary education focused on classical literature, with moral education being passed along through the myths and stories. The main Graeco-Roman genre was biographical, which promoted the great deeds of this or that hero presented as a model *for everyone to follow, not just the Roman children, at all levels of society.*

Roman schools existed all over the Middle East. In Asia Minor and Syria, and even in Palestine, but more importantly, in Greek areas to facilitate the process of Hellenization. Previously the Jewish Maccabees had revolted against the Seleucid Empire when the Greeks demanded that the Jews worshipped the Greek gods. Being ultra conservative, the Maccabeans revolted for a number of reasons, one of which was to protect their own school systems which promoted a more exclusive moral and religious training.

In every generation, believers have attempted to protect their children from the deceptive education of false religions. Some have attempted to escape the cities to find refuge in the countryside. Mark's generation was no different. But even if some Jews (Mark, included) had fled from Roman centers of influence to avoid contamination by Greek literature, they could not have escaped every vestige of the culture of the Roman world.

Awareness of the literature and culture was passed down the social ladder from the upper educated classes through numerous channels: public debates, the theater, courts, the philosophers and in the marketplace, and even after-dinner entertainment for the wealthy, in which servants and slaves (the lower classes) learned about Roman literature by simply being in the room. A culture-gap between the highly literate aristocracy and the masses simply did not exist.

The early manuscripts of the Gospels were probably not written by people of the lower classes; the gulf between the education of the upper and lower classes has been exaggerated. No educational chasm existed between the Gospels and Graeco-Roman literature. Early Christians permeated every class in the Roman culture. The names in the New Testament, along with indirect evidence about travel, slave ownership, money, and tensions within Pauline communities, show that believers existed in every level of society and every level of society existed in the local churches. Only the extremely poor and the extremely rich were missing in large numbers.

The Jewish community was as literate in Greek literature as in Jewish literature. The Gospels can no longer be considered as simply popular fiction listened to by illiterate Christians. All the evidence reveals highly educated Jews and Christians in the Roman literary world. The literary ability, the education, and the social and cultural setting of the Gospel writers placed them in the perfect position to even write Graeco-Roman literature. Mark was raised among those highly educated Jews and Christians. He received a dual education in the Jewish and Roman worlds of literature. He knew Roman literature, which included the *Aeneid*, as well as any Roman.

Mark's Broader Audience: Rome

SUMMARY: Scholars started targeting small Jewish communities, added the Greeks, and eventually included the Romans as Mark's main recipient for his Gospel. It's only one more step to see the *Aeneid*, Rome's premier piece of propaganda, as his main target.

Ages ago scholars declared that Mark had written for his Hebrew community. Later scholars recognized that the Hebrews had lots of contact with the Greeks, so it was declared that Mark had written his Gospel for the Greeks as well, or at least as an afterthought. Eventually, a few dozen scholarly books and hundreds of academic articles appeared in numerous literary journals proclaiming that Mark actually had a lot to say to the Romans, as well as the Greeks and the Hebrews. Let's look at some of those journal articles and scholarly books.

Mark's style of writing required the audience to read (and listen to) the text a number of times. Why is this important? Because this view assumes that Mark's audience had a high level of education. This included Christian traditions, important theological terms, people in Mark's Gospel, and most of the locations mentioned. If Mark's audience had a high level of education, then it is likely that the same audience was quite familiar with the Roman educational world, which included the *Aeneid* as its premier piece of literature.

Many scholars believe that Mark wrote his Gospel for a much wider audience than just a few hundred people. The original readers of Mark, whoever they were, had far more knowledge about the events surrounding the gospel than later readers had. Because Mark's Gospel progressively reveals new information and upcoming events, the original readers would have understood far more than what Mark wrote in his Gospel, since Mark did not have to communicate to them what they already knew. This is important. This background knowledge allowed them to evaluate Mark's Gospel in more precise detail than later readers, building on the reader's knowledge and understanding of their Hebrew and Greco-Roman world.

As discussed previously, the Romans carried the *Aeneid* all the way to Vindolanda, a fort in northern Britain. As far as we know, neither the Hebrews nor the Greeks were interested enough in the *Aeneid* to carry it that far out of the empire.

Maybe Mark wrote his Gospel for a number of small communities throughout the Roman world. These communities were everywhere from Rome to Galilee to Syria and beyond. Most scholars posit a general audience rather than specific communities (with little concrete evidence as to which community), but no scholar has clearly ruled out any of the other options proposed. Given all this data, we can assume that Mark wrote for a number of audiences. Mark wasn't hindered by present-day scholars vying for prominence with their limited geological viewpoints.

The largest audience was the Romans. As noted earlier, the Romans wanted everyone to read the *Aeneid* and accept it as true history. It's interesting that *none of the scholars who have weighed in on this topic of Mark's audience make any connections between Mark's Gospel and the* Aeneid.

Craig Evan's article, "Mark's Incipit and the Priene Calendar Inscription: from Jewish Gospel to Greco-Roman Gospel," makes a clear and detailed connection of Mark's opening verse to Augustus Priene Calendar Inscription (OGIS 458; c. 9 BC). Mark intentionally used the phrase "son of God" as a comparison with the Priene. Mark could have been comparing Jesus with all the evil Roman Emperors, beginning with Augustus. Mark, born around the time of Augustus's death and dying before the destruction of the temple in 70 AD, lived through seven or eight evil such emperors (Tiberius, 14 AD; Caligula, Claudius, Nero, Galba, Otho, Aulus Vitellius, and maybe Vespasian, 69 AD). Augustus's golden age had deteriorated and the emperors became more and more decadent and violent, even though each one had been given the title "son of God." Whether Mark was thinking of all the emperors during his lifetime or just Augustus, it makes no difference. The *Aeneid* remained the key piece of propaganda for the Roman Empire, no matter who sat on the throne as emperor, and Mark intended to present Jesus Christ as the true, divine Son of God.

Although Augustus had been in the grave fifty years when Mark wrote his Gospel, every Roman emperor was attempting to convince the world of Rome's superiority: the Roman-Parthian War of 58–63; Nero; the first Jewish-Roman War beginning in 66; then Roman forces conquered Britain and entered Scotland. Rome was still extending its realm beyond its borders and forcing its will upon its conquered subjects. We don't need to choose one over the other. Mark might have been challenging all of the evil Roman emperors, but every emperor relied on the *Aeneid*'s propaganda for support. The *Aeneid* ruled far beyond any one specific emperor.

Adam Winn claims that Mark wrote his Gospel as an early Christian response to Rome's imperial propaganda. He surveys New Testament scholarship's search for Mark's purpose in writing his Gospel and provides some excellent comparisons between Jesus and the Roman propaganda. Without realizing it, he comes the closest to connecting Mark's Gospel to the *Aeneid*, which was Rome's main piece of propaganda.

If Mark intended the Romans to be his ultimate target, then the Romans understood more of what he wrote than we realize. The Romans understood the saying about the cup in Mark 14:24, where the blood of Jesus was poured out for many. If the Romans were familiar with the Hebrew customs, then they understood these sayings as referring to the death of Jesus as a ritual sacrifice for the sins of many people.

Dio Cassius's comments also reveal that the Romans understood Mark 10:45: "The Son of Man did not come to be served, but to serve, and to give His life a ransom for many." The Romans defined the word *lutron* (ransom) as a transaction between humans and gods when the humans needed to appease the gods and receive forgiveness of their sins.

Cassius's work, *Romaika*, a history of Rome, had become one of the most valuable manuscripts about the last years of the Roman Republic and the early empire. This work is important for two reasons.

He wrote it in Greek indicating how much the Romans wanted the rest of the world to know about the Roman civilization. Cassius also made a reference to Otho, a Roman emperor, born in 32 AD who died in 69 AD. Otho is claimed to have said, "I shall free myself [that is, take my own life], that all may learn from the deed that you chose for your emperor one who would not give you up to save himself, but rather himself to save you."[12] Otho only claimed to give his life for the people, a noble and honorable thing to do, but there is no connection to being a "ransom" for the people.

The Hebrews understood the term "Son of God" differently than the Romans. However, the fact that Augustus first coined the phrase "Son of God" to refer to himself demonstrates that the theology was already known to everyone in Mark's day. For Mark and the other Gospel writers to appropriate that term for Jesus would have caught the immediate attention of anyone who read it, regardless of how they interpreted it. The term "Son of God" would open the door for discussing Jesus, no matter who was reading the text.

During Mark's day, a heavy depression pervaded Rome that deepened the city's social and political climate and led to the severe persecution of the Christians, both Jewish and Roman. When we read Mark's Gospel with Rome in mind, a large number of allusions about Rome appear, and so many indirect references are not coincidental. Seen together, they indicate that Mark wrote his Gospel to speak to the pressures on the Roman believers during his lifetime.

Incigneri's book is the most in-depth study and expression of Mark's underlying motive to reach out to the Romans with the gospel. His book has shown conclusively that Mark wrote his Gospel for a wider audience than the Jewish nation, that Rome was paramount in Mark's mind as he penned each narrative, miracle, and conclusion in his Gospel.

Another strong indication that Mark wrote for the Latin world appears in Mark's use of Latin words in his Gospel. The obvious words in Mark are "poll tax," 12:14; "centurion," 15:39, 44, 45; *denarius* (a Roman

---

12. Cassius Dio, *Dio's Roman History,* vol. VIII, 214–17.

coin), 12:15; "legion," 5:9, 1; "peck measure," 4:21; "governor's official residence," 15:16; *quadrans* (a Roman coin), 12:42; "pitcher," 7:4; "executioner," 6:27; and "to flog," 15:15. Mark lived in Rome, the place where the ordinary Greek and Roman had to deal with both languages, Greek and Latin, in daily life.

As noted earlier, Mark Reasoner connects the book of Hebrews directly with the *Aeneid*. Mark and the author of Hebrews had been thinking along the same lines, but from a different angle. The writer of Hebrews was challenging the divinity of Augustus in the *Aeneid*, whereas Mark was challenging the salvation that Augustus offered as put forth in the *Aeneid*. Hebrews compared the persons, while Mark compared the theologies of Augustus and Jesus.

David R. Wallace's wrote *The Gospel of God: Romans as Paul's Aeneid* because no one had ever connected the apostle Paul's political and religious response to the message of the *Aeneid*'s message of salvation for Rome as opposed to the salvation of Israel. He shows that both the *Aeneid* and the letter to the Romans were written to send a message to people who had been divinely elected to receive a promised, victorious future brought about by the prophetic fulfillment of a divine son.

Stating the obvious, if Paul wrote for the Romans, with his close connections and Roman citizenship, then Mark would have also had similar motives as Paul in writing for the Romans. The difference between Paul's Romans and Mark's Gospel is significant. Paul wrote like a prosecuting attorney: point, counterpoint, building his case into an airtight theological proclamation that the gospel is superior to the *Aeneid*. Paul, however, was not countering Virgil's myth, but the *Aeneid*'s theology.

Mark approached the *Aeneid* from the actual events of Jesus during the last three years of his adult life. Mark builds and interweaves his theology through the narratives and miracles, in comparison to Paul's theological discourse, and in contrast to Virgil's myth which was interspersed with a few historical details, Mark begins a new epoch: "The time is fulfilled, and the kingdom of God is at hand." Mark writes his open epic story but based on historical fact with no myth added.

Marianne Palmer Bonz wrote in her dissertation comparing Luke and Acts with the *Aeneid*. After analyzing the *Aeneid* in detail, along with its direct literary descendants, she launches an exhaustive exegetical analysis of Acts 2, and concludes by confirming the view that a divinely ordained mission began with Jesus in Nazareth and with Paul in Rome (Acts 28). The death of God's son was the rebirth of God's people.

Without knowing the extent of the connection, all three writers, Luke, Paul, and the writer of Hebrews, had access to, and interacted with, the *Aeneid*. It is absolutely inconceivable that Mark never came into contact with *Aeneid*.

If Mark wrote his Gospel later (69 AD), then Luke/Acts, Romans, and Hebrews had already entered the arena of challenging Roman theology in the *Aeneid*. If Mark was written early (50 AD), then Mark would have been the first discordant voice speaking out against the *Aeneid*.

Virgil's Sources and His Knowledge of the Old Testament

> SUMMARY: This point does not directly support Mark's connection with the *Aeneid*, but this point does impact how Mark responded to it. He would have seen the connections that Virgil made with the Old Testament.

In attempting to assess Mark's connection with the *Aeneid*, scholars have generally overlooked Virgil's sources for the *Aeneid*.

His most obvious source was Homer. Generally, Virgil held to Homeric conventions in writing the *Aeneid*. Literary composition demanded strict adherence to the accepted forms in order to be understood by his Roman audience.

Virgil also used what he called fulfilled prophecies. The setting of the *Aeneid* was the Trojan War. Writing hundreds of years later allowed Virgil to prophesy future events that had already come true. Easy and convenient. Looking back from Virgil's standpoint, those prophecies had already occurred, but writing ancient history as current events allowed Virgil to invent prophecies for his hero to fulfill after the fact. If a Roman could suspend disbelief and accept the *Aeneid* as actual history, then those prophecies Virgil had already invented as completed deeds, had been correct and would become "factual history" in the minds of the Romans. Climbing out of five vicious civil wars, the Romans needed hope, even if it was pure myth.

An example of the difference between Old Testament prophecies and the *Aeneid*: Isaiah prophesied the death and resurrection of the Messiah in Isaiah 53, eight hundred years *before* the actual event. Virgil wrote about a fictitious Aeneas who foretold the coming of Augustus, who had already appeared when Virgil wrote about Aeneas.

When Dido (chapter 4 of the *Aeneid*) foretells the Roman victory of the wars between Rome and Carthage, Virgil was asking his audience to believe that his other prophecies would also come true. These included universal peace yet unrealized under a united Rome. Since everyone wanted peace, especially when nationalism reigned, it was a logical step to gain the Roman populace's support of the *Aeneid's* message.

Virgil used this apocalyptic style for political and religious reasons. The reader should note that the prophet Daniel used the same apocalyptic style of writing to comfort the Jewish people and to strengthen their faith in their God, who had revealed the future to Daniel.

Mark's Gospel, on the other hand, shows Christ fulfilling prophecies given hundreds of years before, including some of Daniel's, to confirm God's underlying and overarching control of all past, present, and future events. Mark's prophecies did not use myths nor pseudo-proofs to promote Jesus, but actual historical events that could be evaluated based on the logical understanding of history. Whereas Virgil combined myth with facts and presented his poem as true, Mark did not distort any facts in order to fit in with the genre of the day.

Virgil also used the lives of leaders who experienced extremely successful careers. Silvius, the son of Aeneas and Lavinia, produced the Alban kings, who ruled over Italy four hundred years before Romulus (who was a much later descendent of Aeneas). Romulus founded the city of Rome as the first king and established the house of Augustus. Aeneas became *the* parent of the Roman people, who are called "children of Aeneas." Virgil implanted in Aeneas all the virtues (an important Latin word and Roman human attribute) his descendants would inherit. Aeneas's character was sacred and holy. Virgil had raised patriotism to the status of religion. He proposed that the gods blessed and guided the Romans with a divine plan.

There is no doubt that Virgil's creation and development of the Aeneas legend is unique to classical literature, but Virgil was not isolated within the Roman world, nor was he immune to the past. It is not to be contested that Virgil was brilliant, but very few brilliant people start a movement for no reason. Virgil's predecessors abound.

Consider Alexander the Great. When he conquered the Hellenistic world, he was not able to eradicate all the conquered cultures and amalgamate them into one world culture. Political independence and religious freedom remained a cauldron of dissention everywhere. The antiquity of national traditions began to appear in fictionalized forms and these fictional characters often returned nationalism back to its former glory. The heroes within these stories all performed supernatural deeds and gave the people hope of survival and pride in their past.

Moses Hadas developed this cultural survival aspect of Rome's conquered peoples more thoroughly. He researched *all* the literary efforts intended to support cultural survival of conquered peoples in the Hellenistic world, and he uncovered the fact that *the Jews and the Jewish community, especially in Alexandria, produced the most extensive reports about the cultural survival under the Romans.* This is important.

Virgil's most prominent source will surprise us: Moses, the primary hero figure promoted by the Jewish community. Moses was more significant than any other biblical figure, since he saved his people from the Egyptians. *Hadas states: "Of the series of legendary heroes celebrated by the descendants of the non-Hellenenic peoples of the Near East, it is Moses who is most likely to have become known to Vergil, and certainly Moses who provides the clearest pattern for Aeneas."*[13] Hadas then shows clear parallels between Moses's deeds and Aeneas's deeds. Both were unique heroes. Hadas admits that if the deeds of Aeneas are judged apart from Moses, then scholars will concede that Virgil's imagination was more independent from all other cultures than any other known writer of fiction, but Hadas, an expert in the classics, states more cautiously than the evidence indicates that "taken together, however, they would seem to argue very strongly that Virgil was deeply influenced by Jewish tradition."[14] Hadas gives further support by quoting Virgil's first draft of the *Aeneid*, where Virgil writes:

> All lingering traces of our guilt shall be erased, and the earth released from its continual dread. He shall have the gift of divine life (. . .). The earth untitled shall pour forth her gifts (. . .). Uncalled the goats shall bring home their udders swollen with milk, and the herds shall not fear huge lions; unasked thy cradle shall pour forth flowers for their delight. The serpent too shall perish (. . .).[15]

13. Hadas, "Vergil, Hebrew Prophecy." This work was originally written in 1959.

14. Hadas, "Vergil, Hebrew Prophecy."

15. Virgil, *Eclogues of Virgil*, 4.4. The so-called *Fourth* (of ten) or "Messianic" written between 37–40 BC. Virgil took the Greek *Bucolica* ("on care of cattle") by Theocritus (poet of *idylls*, or "little scenes," "vignettes") and modified it into a Roman version that gave a political and mythic (and dramatic) explanation of the troubles in the Roman Empire between 44 and 38 BC. *Eclogues* means "draft" or "selection," to be performed as herdsmen's singing imagined conversations in the country about

Hadas notes, "This poem has been more widely discussed than any other piece of similar length in classical literature. From Constantine and Augustine until the age of modern criticism, Christian writers have interpreted the *Eclogue* as a prophecy of the birth of Jesus,"[16] and they connect it with Isaiah 7:14. Hadas concludes that "there is no reason to exclude the possibility that Virgil may have known of it or at least of the Messianic speculations that derived from it."[17]

Hadas then lists all the contacts Virgil had had with that Jewish culture that would have given him more than merely a summary of ideas for the *Aeneid*. Virgil's wanderings often took him to the Campania coast which had a Palestinian flavor and a large Jewish population. Petronius, a Roman citizen and a contemporary of Seneca (died 66 AD), wrote a comic novel, *Satyricon*, in which he mocks the lifestyles of Roman citizens who formerly had been slaves. In his novel he mentions locations of Syrian and Hebrew communities that had inhabited those regions for a long time. He expected his Roman readers, Virgil included, to recognize those locations and those who lived there. Horace, the leading Roman lyric poet during Augustus's time, was supposedly of Jewish origin and Virgil's friend, and he also assumed that his readers had some knowledge of Judaism.

Hadas connects those ideas with the seriousness, strength, and epoch-making ideas found within the *Aeneid*. Religion merging with politics fits the theocracy of the Pentateuch well. "Belief in the supernatural sanction of a specific national group and in the supernatural authority of its founder, and concomitant convictions of national election as the special instrument of providence and of responsibility to a divinely ordained mission"[18] fit perfectly with the message Moses brought to Israel, and these ideas are very foreign to classical Greek literature.

More scholars have stumbled onto the connection between Aeneas and Moses. Patrick V. Reid connects Virgil with Moses in his book, *Moses Staff and Aeneas's Shield: The Way of the Torah Versus Classical Heroism.* He compares a number of Moses's actions among the Egyptians with Virgil's thoughts through Aeneas. He does not state that Virgil copied Moses, but simply demonstrates Virgil's actions as mimicking Moses.

suffering or revolutionary change or love. Virgil became a legend because they were wildly successful on the Roman stage, combining far-reaching politics and eroticism.

16. Hadas, "Vergil, Hebrew Prophecy."

17. Hadas, "Vergil, Hebrew Prophecy."

18. Hadas, "Vergil, Hebrew Prophecy."

Hadas believes that Virgil, "depressed by a century of incessant war and by the knowledge that Rome was ruining peoples more cultured than herself, would grasp at the new promise like a drowning man at a straw."[19] All past wars could be accepted, and even justified, if the result was an orderly world peace that preserved and spread Roman culture throughout that peaceful world. Augustus brought the politics to the table, but Virgil, borrowing and modifying the Jewish idea of a messiah, inserted religion into the mix, thus giving Rome a divine mission to conquer the world.[20] The agent of that plan was Aeneas, who symbolized Augustus. Hadas's conclusion is that Virgil "introduced the immortal values of Moses and the prophets into the political life of the Western world."[21]

Mark's Hebrew education rendered him well-versed in the Old Testament, and especially the story of Moses. Mark quotes the Old Testament twenty-eight times in his Gospel. If Mark had no connection with the *Aeneid*, then Virgil's source in Moses is irrelevant. If Mark, well-versed in the story of Moses, had read the *Aeneid*, the connections and allusions would have stunned him.

Virgil can also be connected with Moses from a historian's viewpoint. All historians arrange their material and positions in a way that attempts to interpret the meaning of historical events. The Gospels were also written with that purpose in mind. Historical time presents the past as rigid, as opposed to myth and legend which represent no specific time frame. Virgil establishes a historical destiny for the Romans, and this parallels and contrasts with the Hebrew destiny of the promised land found in the Bible.

Both the Hebrew Bible and the Roman poets previous to the time of the New Testament based their existence on land they assumed had been promised to them and the divine election of deity. The term "epochality" refers to history that has reached a major turning point when destiny will be fulfilled. Virgil makes use of this idea by proclaiming a new unparalleled era under Augustus. The Roman poets based their entire philosophy and theology of the future on the belief that the ascent of Augustus Caesar had begun a golden age that had no predecessor.

Virgil's major poem, the *Aeneid*, mimics the epic tradition of Homer and offers the establishment of Rome as the story of triumph in which

19. Hadas, "Vergil, Hebrew Prophecy."

20. The different authors arrived at the idea separately, or similarities are read into the texts, or the Jews borrowed the idea from an earlier people.

21. Hadas, "Vergil, Hebrew Prophecy."

Rome rises from the ashes of Troy and becomes an empire by destiny that upholds laws and rules by military might.

There are differences between Virgil's concept of the Roman Empire and the Jewish view of their future kingdom. First, the *Aeneid* was written by one author, whereas the Hebrew Bible came into being from many sources over one thousand years. Second, Rome rose as the victor over adversity, whereas the Hebrews were assured of victory in the future, if they would obey in the present. Yahweh was the Creator God, as opposed to Augustus who made himself into a god. Jewish history taught the Jewish people that Yahweh keeps his promises, and those promises included the promised land and the providential divine election as the people of God. The subjugation of the Jewish people to the Romans during that time had nothing to do with Augustus or his self-proclaimed deity. Yahweh had also promised that if the Jewish people disobeyed God's Law (Deut 27–28), then God would punish them by allowing them to be subjugated by gentile nations. The time of the Judges and Israel's seventy years in Babylon chronicled this direct experience of God's promise. Subjugation to the Romans was simply another experience of their disobedience to Yahweh, this time, for rejecting their Messiah.

The *Aeneid* appeared on the historical stage after the Old Testament had been written. Virgil's *Aeneid* took the position within Roman history that the Hebrew text held in Jewish history: driven by destiny, pushed to overcome suffering, promised some land and prosperity, based in morality, forced to overcome the opposition by military power, thus having initiated an epochal turn in history. Where the Hebrew text presented a future Messiah, the *Aeneid* went a step further and added a son of the gods, Augustus Caesar.

Enter the New Testament age and the clash of ideologies, i.e., theologies. As Jesus entered Roman history, the Romans had built and refined their propaganda for the purpose of convincing the subjugated world that the myths of Virgil were factual history. Everyone under Roman domination had been presented with the *Aeneid*'s version that Augustus had been divinely appointed to save and rule the world. With the death and resurrection of Jesus, this Roman theology began to be challenged.

The Old Testament came first, then Virgil, then Mark—interesting!

Books, Publishers and Readers

SUMMARY: Since Ecclesiastes was *written* between 450–200 BC, long before Augustus, there is every reason to believe that the Romans were readers.

Could people read during Virgil's day? For a long time, scholars assumed that they couldn't, since book production was so primitive. That would mean that poets only became famous through oral presentations on stage. However, Virgil did not write a twelve-book poem for an illiterate audience. Book production was more advanced than previously believed and well underway by the time Virgil wrote the *Aeneid*.

David Diringer demolishes the naive view that most Romans were unable to read beyond the third grade. Beginning with the fifth century BC, Diringer lists some famous Greek authors—Aeschylus, Sophocles, Euripides, Aristophanes, Herodotus, Thucydides, and Xenophon—and then says that Greek literature had reached its zenith during that century. Book production and book trade were highly organized. No original Greek manuscript has survived today, but Diringer discovered that the Greeks had been using several sources for producing, selling, and reading books from the fifth century BC onwards.

Diringer offers a couple examples and then mentions that the Greek comic playwright, Aristophanes, implied that books were easily procured in his time. Diringer tells the story about one of Xenophon's expeditions against the Thracians. The Greeks who went with him discovered at Salmydessus, on the shore of the Black Sea, boxes, written books, and many other things, such as seamen carry in their wooden store chests (*Anabasis*, vii, 5.14). During the Graeco-Roman period, Aristotle quoted Dionysius of Halicarnassus in *Isocrates* 18 (*c.* 25 BC) saying that the speeches of famous orators were sold in Athens by the hundreds.

Aristophanes even said that every man in his audience had purchased a personal copy of the play to read and follow along during the performance. Greek book production had spread over the entire Hellenistic world during the last three centuries BC; there was a large output of literature, and most of the population had read the great works of previous ages. The great works of previous ages were obviously prolific enough to have been preserved after their age had morphed into a new one. Once the Romans had conquered the Greeks, the mixed population increased enormously, as did book production and the practice of reading.

Augustus took serious advantage of this situation and had the *Aeneid* translated into Greek immediately after Virgil's death. Diringer's work takes it for granted that all literature: dramas, tragedies, lyric poems, epics, and historical works were available in abundance and accessible to those who wanted them. This implies a reading public and the circulation of books in manuscript form.

Greek models of literature became the basis for Latin literature, and Roman education consisted of teaching Greek and Greek literature. The Greeks had taken their education seriously, and when the Romans made them slaves, especially in Rome, the Romans used them as teachers.

Atticus's slaves were not only highly educated men, but many of them were excellent copyists.[22] He actually published works of many authors, including Cicero, and sold them in Rome, Athens, and other Greek cities. Lucian, a second-century writer, said that the works published by Atticus and by Callinus were in demand everywhere in the world. Diringer shows that Varro's works were sold in the farthest corners of the world.

There is no doubt that Rome was the commercial center of the civilized world in the West. The ancient book trade in Latin books permeated the famous bookshops in the Argiletum, in the provincial cities of Brindisi, Lyons, Rheins, and many others. New and secondhand books were everywhere. There were so many books being produced during this time, that readers were constantly complaining about copyists' mistakes. Cicero grumbled about the fact that he no longer knew where to turn for Latin books because the copies available for sale were so inaccurate. The preservation of important works began in earnest.

Leo Duel's book, *Testaments of Time,* presents an exquisite history of the search for lost manuscripts and books. The miracle of finding such treasures overshadows the tragedy of having lost an innumerable number of manuscripts and books since the dawn of *written* history. The most amazing miracle surrounding the *Aeneid* is that it was never lost. It survived the downfall of Rome, the Dark Ages, the Reformation, all the

---

22. Titus Pomponius Atticus (born 110 BC, Rome—died 32 BC), a wealthy but non-political Roman famous for his correspondence with the important Roman statesman and writer Cicero, and for his positive personal relationships with the major political figures of the time. Atticus had highly educated slaves who he used to copy and distribute several of Cicero's philosophical and oratorical works.

way into the twentieth century. Why? Because it had immediately upon publication become so prominent inside and outside the Roman world, that it dwarfed all other writings and helped push them into obscurity and oblivion.

Before Virgil's time, books existed everywhere, and everyone was reading everything. The *Aeneid* entered this world of literacy and became an instant hit. It was published in Latin and Greek and "went viral," as they say today. One even wonders if the Silk Road took the *Aeneid* beyond the Roman Empire. Is it not obvious that Mark had access to the *Aeneid* because he had spent enough time in Rome with Peter?

The *Aeneid* in Greek

SUMMARY: The *Aeneid* appeared in Greek early and "went viral" quickly, years before Mark wrote his Gospel in Greek. Since the Greeks were reading the *Aeneid* in Greek, then Mark would have been confronted with the *Aeneid* in both Latin and Greek.

There are no direct quotations of the *Aeneid* in the New Testament. However, although Latin was the Roman language, Greek was revered by the Romans. Dionysius of Halicarnassus, a teacher in Rome during Virgil's time, wrote his *Roman Antiquities* in Greek.

C. Iulius Polybius,[23] a freedman Greek historian, was the person who "translated" the *Aeneid* into Greek. He had a significant influence in literary circles during the reign of Emperor Claudius (41 AD–54 AD). Seneca (c. 4 BC–AD 65) praised that translation as well. This led some scholars to date that translation as early as 42 or 43 AD, which would indicate a wide distribution of the *Aeneid* in Greek *before* Mark wrote

23. Mistakes happen. I confused the real C. Iulius Polybius with a different Polybius (c. 200–c. 118 BC), who was born the son of Lycortas, a distinguished Achaean statesman. He was reared as the son of a rich landowner. As a Greek statesman and historian, he wrote prolifically, but the book that made him famous was *The Histories*, a landmark piece of forty books about the rise of Rome from 264 BC to 146 BC. He showed that Rome wanted to rule the entire inhabitable known world. He also revealed how far Rome went to destroy Carthage for political and economic purposes. He is so famous that I had to include him in this book, but he is *not* the person who translated the *Aeneid* into Greek. Since he died in 118 BC, and the *Aeneid* was published in 19 BC, it couldn't be translated into another language before it was written. I think I confused this Polybius with the one in the next paragraph in my dissertation. Since few people will actually read my dissertation, I'm not worried about anybody noticing.

his Gospel. The Greeks no longer had to learn Latin to read the *Aeneid*. That's important.

Harold Attridge claims that the author of Hebrews most certainly had read the *Aeneid* in either Latin or Greek for the simple reason that Hebrews is dated by most scholars between 54 and 90 AD. As noted earlier, Bonz connected Luke and Acts with the *Aeneid* because Virgil's works have been translated into Greek by the middle of the first century. She recognized that Luke-Acts and the *Aeneid* both arose from the same set of historical circumstances. Mark's Gospel shared the same set of circumstances.

Augustus wanted to rule the entire world, and especially the Greek world. Augustus would have naturally promoted a Greek translation of Virgil's *Aeneid*, and as quickly as possible.

As noted above, Reasoner ("Divine Sons: Aeneas and Jesus in Hebrews") uses Homer's *Odyssey*, written in Greek, to connect the book of Hebrews and Virgil's *Aeneid*. Reasoner claims that the author of Hebrews would have been schooled in Greek literature, and the literary influence from Latin epic poetry influenced the writing of the book of Hebrews.

Reasoner doesn't quit there. He goes further to show that Hebrews is more closely aligned with the *Aeneid* than with the *Odyssey*. Virgil's *Aeneid* was steeped in Homer and his Greek world. Peter Levi notes that Virgil "was essentially a Hellenistic poet to the marrow of his bones, a stylist who had learnt to apply his dazzling ability to a long narrative."[24]

Levi draws the conclusion that one should think of Virgil "as a Greek poet who just happened to write in Latin."[25] Reasoner shows that Augustan theology in the *Aeneid* makes three direct connections between Augustus and Jesus in Hebrews. "The divinely born Aeneas is presented as pious son, priestly son, and founding son in Augustan theology."[26] The connections are obvious between the two pieces of literature.

Since many scholars have connected the *Aeneid* to the Greek world, and Reasoner connects the book of Hebrews to the *Aeneid*, it's evident that Mark, traveling throughout the Roman Empire and living in Rome, had encountered the *Aeneid*. After all, Mark lived in the years nearer to the writing and publication of Virgil's *Aeneid* than the writer of Hebrews.

24. Levi, *Virgil*, 236.

25. Levi, *Virgil*, 236.

26. Reasoner, "Divine Son," 154.

Could Mark read Greek? He wrote his gospel in Greek. If the Greeks were reading the *Aeneid* in Greek, then Mark would have been confronted with the *Aeneid* in both Latin and Greek.

Genre: Biography

SUMMARY: Mark used the genre style of his day in his Gospel, thus conforming to the literature of his day. The Romans would easily understand Mark's message.

Until the 1970s, few scholars believed that Mark wrote his Gospel as a Greek and Roman biography. The actual genre of Mark's Gospel has been debated and disputed since the middle of the nineteenth century. In 1880, Heinrich Holtzman summarized the state of affairs in the study of Mark's genre by stating that Mark's Gospel was a reliable report and a coherent whole.

The next theory postulated that Mark was similar to biographical literature during its day, but this viewpoint was soundly rejected by the next wave of speculations that mandated agreement within the theological community.

Then the form critical theory arose. It proclaimed that each small unit of text had no coherent connection with any other small unit of text. Therefore, Mark had no connections with any of the literature of his day, thus making Mark an entirely original creation of Christianity. Rudolf Bultmann (1921) supported that speculation so firmly that his first analysis presented an "absolute stance" against the previous views.

This absolute stance lasted until redactional criticism rose to prominence in the 1950s. Redactional criticism replaced the no-connection theory of form-criticism with fictional people who shaped and molded the stories in Mark to express their own personal theological and ideological goals. Proponents of this theory couldn't believe that Mark wrote the Gospel of Mark.

Bultmann's absolute stance lasted less than thirty years, until the human cycle of unnegotiable theories came full circle and returned to the view that the Gospel of Mark is actually a consciously coherent piece of writing.

Eventually scholars realized that the Gospel of Mark was a combination of two cultures, Jewish and Graeco-Roman. The Graeco-Roman background placed Mark in the biography category, and the Jewish background placed it among apocalyptic literature.

In the 1970s Gilbert G. Bilezikian finally saw the connection between Mark and the Greek Tragedies. Greek tragedies, as biographies, had become the entrenched literature of Mark's day. Mark used the Greek form but did not compromise his own message. Mark used the Greek and Roman biographical form for three reasons.

First, it was the most well-known to his gentile audience. Second, Mark needed to inform his Jewish comrades that God was also interested in bringing the gentiles into the Kingdom of Jesus. Third, Mark used Greek tragedy because it fit perfectly with Virgil's usage of Greek tragedy by Homer. Every Roman would recognize the form of Greek tragedy in Mark's contextualization of the gospel and be comfortable with the form.

Ancient society was well aware of the various genres and taught them to all the school children as the minimum rhetorical tools used by any literate person within the Roman Empire. The biographical genre form was part of the Greek literature which was familiar to everyone.

Although the Jewish and Roman literatures were each somewhat rigid in genre, Mark's biography of Jesus connects with the biographical genre within Roman literature. The Greek biography dealt with a specific individual but focused on the social background of community and emphasized the character and accomplishments as a public example for the children to emulate.

Because Mark wrote an ancient biography, the same genre of the literature of his day, the similarities and differences with the *Aeneid* would jump off the page, like two videos running side by side showing two saviors: Augustus and Jesus.

Allusions work that way. Someone makes a statement that triggers another statement from an entirely different context in our thinking. Our minds do this all the time. If someone says, "You're my only hope," most people today will immediately recall the entire line, "Help me, Obi-Wan Kenobi, you're my only hope."

When people of Mark's day read his gospel where Jesus was called the Son of God, their minds would have immediately thought of the *Aeneid* and Augustus. And the more they compared the Gospel with the *Aeneid*, the more the magnificence and authority of Augustus would pale into insignificance as the holiness and eternal power of Jesus arose and provoked them to look beyond the shallowness of a temporary earthly kingdom.

Genre: Rhetoric

SUMMARY: Mark used rhetoric in his Gospel, thus conforming to the literature of his day. The Romans would have easily understood Mark's message.

Rhetoric is the art of persuasive speaking or writing, designed specifically to motivate an audience to agree with the message of the speaker or writer. Rhetoric was originally used in the courtroom. When a rhetor planned his speech or manuscript, he worked his way through the five stages of rhetoric.

Invention—He found the information and facts for his speech or manuscript.

Arrangement—He chose a form for his presentation.

Style—He chose the best words to express the message.

Memory—He attempted to memorize the presentation.

Delivery—He planned his presentation to stir the emotions of his audience.

Once he had the presentation planned, he put his message together using the three parts of every rhetorical speech or manuscript.

Ethos—Established the speaker's credibility and motives.

Pathos—Appealed to the emotions of the audience through their values and interests. It played to their expectations.

Logos—Used logic and reason to convince the audience to agree with the speaker.

The ultimate goal of rhetoric was to persuade the audience that the speaker/writer was telling the truth.

Rhetoric permeated the world in which Mark lived and wrote. The teaching of rhetoric began at the elementary level to teach moral values. These values had the function of clarifying the difference between good and evil, between being a virtuous person and being a wicked one. The rhetorical education continued through childhood into adulthood.

A good teacher starts where his students are in order to lead them in a different direction. Thus, the Roman educators studied the culture of their conquered students and then contextualized the theology of Rome, the deity of Augustus, and his salvation of the realm.

The prominence and importance of the *Aeneid* in Roman society and beyond overshadowed all other sources using rhetoric that influenced Mark's Gospel. The *Aeneid*'s popularity easily motivated Mark to deliberately use the specialized tools of Graeco-Roman rhetoric as a direct challenge to the *Aeneid*.

Both Mark and Virgil incorporated all three stages of rhetoric in the Gospel and in the *Aeneid*.

In Virgil's case, he vigorously applied rhetoric in the *Aeneid*. Virgil's writings belong to an era that devoted itself to the art of using words to create a desired effect, a rhetorical era. Roman rhetoric changed during Virgil's lifetime. It moved away from the courts into the public theaters, which were widely attended, thus taking on more of an entertainment function. The rhetor's ability and the audience's enjoyment began to outweigh truth and virtue. Hard and cold facts became less important, to be replaced by romantic stories and plots.

How did Virgil relate to this shift? He no longer had to present solid facts to make his case. He could dispense with the first stage of rhetoric, invention, because he had no need to prove anything. The *Aeneid* became his playground. His characters spoke to communicate an attitude or an emotion, not facts, not to win an argument, but to "move" the audience into the story, regardless of the truthfulness of the story's content. Virgil made good use of rhetoric under these new conditions.

If you have not read the *Aeneid*, the following examples will mean nothing to you. Read the *Aeneid* first.

Virgil's use of rhetoric: the speech of Sinon in Book 2, the debate between Venus and Juno where the gods become eloquent orators, Dido's first speech to Aeneas where she uses lots of arguments and entreats that he not leave her. When Homer's *Iliad* is compared with Virgil's *Aeneid*, it becomes evident that Virgil used rhetorical questions in the speeches four times more than Homer in the Iliad.

Virgil's emphasis centered on the emotional passages that required no logic, just tears or anger. Of the sixteen methods of *pathos* to arouse pity, fifteen examples have been found in Virgil. He understood the

Greeks and the Romans and used that knowledge to sway their emotions significantly. He put himself in their place and forced them to abdicate their reason in favor of myth.

Virgil used *pathos* in all the key locations in the *Aeneid*: the terror of fleeing from Troy; the heartbreak of leaving Dido; the anger of remembering the death of Pallas and killing Turnus; the realization that the gods were going to allow him to fulfill his destiny and establish the Roman Empire.

How much rhetoric did Mark use in writing his Gospel? The New Testament writers (Paul, Peter, Luke, the writer of Hebrews) used all kinds of rhetoric, and they shaped their materials in a rhetorical-saturated culture to persuade their readers of the truthfulness of their message. Orators were taught to write out their speeches, memorize them, and present them. If an orator could not be present to give his speech then his written speech would stand in as his speech. All aspects of rhetoric were included in these written speeches. Only body language and voice intonation were missing. This resulted in the epistles becoming the major form of transcribed oral rhetoric, read aloud by someone who had not written it, absent the original writer of the speech.

Mark used rhetoric because the biographical style of writing was intended to teach content and morality. Writers of ancient biographies didn't simply give boring investigations of important people. They persuaded their audiences by storytelling and giving speeches. Rhetoric was a perfect fit for the Gospels. Mark wanted to persuade the world, and especially the Roman Empire, that Jesus was superior to Augustus in every way.

Rhetoric in Mark surfaces in numerous forms. Plutarch, Tacitus and Mark all used *cheria*, which are short pithy stories that did not include every detail of the central figure but made a statement that summed up the story in one sentence, enough to present a clear picture of the person's character. Mark records Jesus using a *chreia* when he referred to the rich young man: "It is easier for a camel to go through the eye of a needle than for a rich person to enter the Kingdom of God" (Mark 10:25).

The very use of *chreia* indicated the intention to persuade the audience of the person's character and mission. The shortness of this style fit Mark's Gospel perfectly. The Olivet Discourse in Mark 13, the longest speech of Jesus in that Gospel, took on the form of a rhetorical speech with all the properly functioning tools of rhetoric.

Mark intended his Gospel be read by individuals, not just in groups. In Mark 13:14, Mark wrote, "let the reader understand," in which both the noun and the verb are in the singular. This indicates that Mark wanted his Gospel to be read as a narrative, not just as a series of speeches. Mark wrote a biography in rhetorical form. His Gospel is like a textbook that pulled together the memoirs and recollections of Peter and reshaped them into persuasive form.

Mark used the *ethos* aspect to demonstrates the intelligence, virtuous character, and good will of Jesus. Mark's credibility rested on his personal knowledge of his subject. This is well illustrated by Mark's use of Aristotle's rhetoric.

Aristotle used an enthymematic process of presenting his arguments, that is, he would leave out a key premise or conclusion, forcing the listener or reader to discover the missing piece and draw their own conclusion. In the *Aeneid* Virgil used enthymematic rhetoric by employing myth to convince the reader to draw his own conclusions. The mythical form allowed the reader to see what he wanted to see. Mark made extensive use of this approach in relating the Lord's parables and incomplete stories. Mark's Gospel is famous for being mysterious. "The secret of the Kingdom of God" (Mark 4:11) is mysterious.

Jesus is mysterious. At times, Jesus intentionally keeps people from understanding who he really is. He shuts up demons and does not allow them to reveal his true identity. He performs a miracle and tells people to keep quiet about it. Why? Aristotle might answer that question by exclaiming that Jesus was using enthymematic rhetoric. Jesus was forcing the people to draw their own conclusions as to his true character, the main premise and conclusion of his life, miracles, and teaching.

The second stage of rhetoric, *pathos*, uses emotional appeals to change an audience's viewpoint. The speaker can use metaphor, stories, and other literary devices. The end objective is to invoke strong emotion from the audience.

Of the many stories Mark used to persuade his audience through emotions, the injustice of the Cross stands out as a supreme example of a *pathos* appeal to the emotions.

The third stage, *logos*, concentrates on the argument itself by using inductive and deductive reasoning to build the argument. Aeneas claimed logic when he listed the reasons for leaving Dido, but "logos" was never a strong element in Aeneas's life and actions. Mark challenges the *Aeneid* by using *logos* in numerous contexts twenty-four times. Mark

2:2 is one example: "he was speaking the word (*logos*) to them." Mark used an imperfect verb ("was speaking"). That kind of verb shows Jesus's consistent ongoing activity throughout the Gospel, as well as the content (*logos*) itself.

Aristotle had even divided rhetoric into subgenre. Mark used all of Aristotle's three subgenre of rhetoric: the forensic scene at the trial of Jesus in Mark 14, the deliberative aspect when Jesus is speaking about decision-making in the context of light in Mark 4:21–25, and the epideictic praise and blame in the Lord's accusations of the Pharisees in Mark 7:1–23.

Virgil presented Aeneas as a virtuous man who was willing to reject the culture of being led by his emotions, and who chose to follow the gods out of duty. Jesus was the epitome of a virtuous human being, and he challenged the culture at every level by demanding that his followers (Mark 8:34) "deny themselves," the opposite of self-centeredness, "take up the cross," a complete rejection of Roman superiority, "and follow Jesus," a repudiation of following Augustus.

Rhetoric had permeated every culture ruled over by the Roman Empire. The *Aeneid* was used as one of the texts to teach rhetoric. Mark would not have been able to avoid it, even if he had wanted to. Just as Virgil used rhetoric throughout the *Aeneid*, so Mark used rhetoric throughout his Gospel.

Dominant Civilizations Acculturating Conquered Societies

SUMMARY: The Romans were more than glad to have every Jew read the *Aeneid*. Mark complied with their demands.

Conquering nations have always attempted to force their conquered subjects to submit to their new cultures. That's called forced acculturation of the dominant culture. One of the best examples of this comes from Babylon around 600 BC. When Nebuchadnezzar took the Jews into captivity, he chose the best prisoners to indoctrinate into the culture and literature of the Babylonian kingdom. Nebuchadnezzar ordered his chief official to choose the best young men taken as prisoners from Israel and from Israel's royal families who were "without any physical defect, good-looking, suitable for instruction in all wisdom, knowledgeable, perceptive and capable of serving in the king's palace—and *to teach them the Chaldean language and literature.*"[27] Not every culture did this, but the Babylonian practice of forcing their language, literature, and culture onto their conquered subjects is an example of an ancient civilization whose dominant civilization acculturated their conquered subjects.

The Romans were no different. They intentionally indoctrinated their slaves and the slaves's children. The *Aeneid* had become one of the main textbooks in the Roman education of everyone.

An unintentional event also helped the *Aeneid* to infiltrate Roman society. During the mid-120s BC, the leading Romans abused their power over their captives, and this resulted in a brutal civil war in central Italy. The Gaius's revolutionary reforms arose and Rome enacted legislation in 90 BC that gave full citizenship to almost the entire peninsula.

The effects were dramatic. The number of Roman citizens skyrocketed to three times the original number, rising to over a million people. This opened the door for previously non-Romans to become citizens who wanted equal rights within the Roman culture. The Romanization of subject peoples has been researched and established in a number of areas in Europe.[28]

With new rights and privileges, almost six hundred thousand new citizens wanted what they had been previously denied. The best way to lay hold of such benefits was to climb higher in society. The best way to climb in society in a new culture is to become more educated in the new culture.[29] No document states that new Roman citizens were required to read the *Aeneid*, but since the *Aeneid* promoted Augustus and Roman religion more than any other document, and the *Aeneid* has been discovered as far away from Rome as northern Britain and Masada, Mark, living in Rome, would have had to have been deaf and blind to not have come in contact with the *Aeneid*.

---

27. Daniel 1:4, Holman Christian Standard Bible.

28. Curchin, *Romanization*; D. J. Mattingly, "Being Roman," 5–26; Haverfield, *Romanization*; M. Millet, "Romanization," 35–44.

29. This author has interviewed numerous refugees in America who want to get a college education more than anything else. A Muslim refugee from Afghanistan told me, "I want to get a college degree and become an American citizen as soon as possible. I love this country." Gaining citizenship in America requires knowledge of the U.S. Constitution and passing some history exams.

The Church Fathers's Contributions

SUMMARY: The *Aeneid* had to grow in its prominence, which it held for centuries, as shown by quotes from the church fathers. Mark wrote his Gospel during the time of that growth. Mark could not have missed coming in contact with the *Aeneid*.

Did the church fathers comment in any way that Mark might have come in contact with the *Aeneid*, or even intentionally targeted Rome, and Augustus, with his Gospel? A number of church fathers place the writing of Mark's Gospel in Rome. There is no solid evidence from the church fathers that Mark wrote his Gospel in Rome, but no one in the early church disagreed with this location. The external evidence points to Rome.

Rome was the center of the empire. The *Aeneid* was the most prominent piece of literature in the bookshops and the schools. If Mark chose to challenge the *Aeneid*, then he did so in Rome, the center of the empire, the source of Augustus's propaganda. None of the church fathers, however, make any reference to Mark's motive for writing.

How Virgil affected the church fathers does not directly speak to Mark's connection with the *Aeneid*, since the church fathers appeared after Mark finished writing his Gospel. Since none of them make any references to Mark being involved with or connected to Virgil's *Aeneid*, little needs to be added from their point of view for this book.

Having admitted that, one point of indirect support can be seen through the eyes of the church fathers. When Peter and Mark arrived in Rome, the Romans had been educated through the study of Horace and Virgil. The value of such classical studies (as termed today) was not only invaluable—it was all they had.

Peter and Mark had also lived and breathed Roman culture. Their everyday world consisted of working with gentiles who had been steeped in mythology and ancient religious traditions. No one questioned the source of Peter's and Mark's education and life experiences. Peter and Mark simply had to evangelize in that world of myth and false history.

As the church expanded, the church fathers recognized the benefits of what the pagans were bringing with them. The church fathers used those myths to contextualize the gospel and to attack paganism. One of the best examples of this can be found in the sermons of Ambrose. He used the *Aeneid* in a sermon on Psalm 118 (119). Ambrose borrowed exact phrases from Virgil, not just to add literary adornment to his sermon but to illuminate and deepen the theological points he was making. Those phrases, which came directly from the *Aeneid*, were used to make his point about the need for higher moral purity among believers and the arbitrariness of the Greco-Roman gods. Showing just one such phrase, Ambrose referred to Laocoön's cruel end to subtly underscore God's compassion and justice, thus showing Christianity's superiority over paganism.

The church fathers were trained just as much to listen to the text as to read it. This training allowed them to see more allusions throughout the larger biblical narrative. We don't see those allusions today. We don't read as much as the church fathers did.

The church fathers were raised on these stories in the Greek culture. The way they had learned to read Homer and Virgil directly influenced how they read Scripture. This pagan literature was well known by the church fathers. Virgil's writings, classified as pagan, permeated the known world during Mark's time. Even when the church fathers began to reject these writings as pagan, their comments reveal the depth and intensity to which these writings had infused themselves into the people's hearts and minds.

Jerome found fault with people who took more pleasure in reading Virgil than the Scriptures, even though he admits that the youth had to study him. Augustine moaned that some Greek-speaking children had to study Virgil in Latin. Augustine is noted for saying that he despised pagan literature. It seems that the Latin fathers had embedded Virgil in their minds so much that they could not have removed him from their souls without doing themselves psychic injury.[30]

Even though Augustine understood the negative aspects of this literature, he still claimed that these pagan classics lead to a more perfect understanding of the Scriptures, and that pagan literature is actually an introduction to the Scriptures. The church fathers could not do without this literature because Virgil and others had become ingrained in society long before the church fathers were born.

So what? The *Aeneid* had permeated the Roman world and beyond immediately after its publication, but it didn't stop there. It continued to influence the church fathers for centuries. Although no church father

---

30. Guite, "Common Elements."

connected Mark's Gospel with the *Aeneid*, the staggering proliferation of Virgil's propaganda piece clearly existed during Mark's lifetime. The influence it had on the church fathers came from its widespread appearance even among non-Roman societies. One could compare the extended influence of the *Aeneid* with *Romeo and Juliet*, whose author everyone still recognizes today. There is little reason to believe that Mark had no contact with the Aeneid. Since the church fathers were steeped in the pagan literature of their day, even if they came to hate it, how can anyone believe that Mark somehow avoided all contact with the most prominent piece of Roman propaganda throughout and beyond the empire?

30

The *Aeneid*'s Theology in Roman History

Pre-*Aeneid*

GREEK AND ROMAN MYTHOLOGY portrayed a forest filled with fleeting fairies and harmless nymphs, a peaceful world of contentment. One could witness Proteus rise from the sea and old Triton blow his wreathed horn from the security of an outdoor aquarium built for the pleasure of an audience seeking a safe adventure.

Reality is cruel. The jungle and desert people today and ages ago in humanity's prehistoric past had no such luxuries. Terror of the gods ruled their universe, and senseless but powerful magic, supported by human sacrifice, pain, and grief, was their only escape.

Greek mythology began with Homer's *Iliad*. Pre-Greek mythology is shrouded in the Babylonian mystery religion, which Hesiod copied extensively in his work *Theogony*. Charles Penglase in his book, *Greek Myths and Mesopotamia: Parallels and Influence in the Homeric Hymns and Hesiod,* shows direct connections where Hesiod "borrowed" the Babylonian gods and turned them into Greek gods.

However, the Greeks made a major change in the god world. Instead of fearsome dragon-like man-eaters, mankind took center stage, and the Greeks made the gods into superhumans. Before that, the Egyptian monstrous sphinx stood outside human reason, the cat-woman's inhuman cruelty tortured men in their dreams, and the half-humans with bird's heads, lions with bulls's heads, all with eagles's wings existed in a non-human unapproachable unreality. The Greeks brought reason to the universe. The invisible could be understood by the visible. Didn't the apostle Paul say that (Heb 11:3)?

The Egyptians were petrified of their gods. The Greeks could laugh at their gods. Their gods were actually attractive, manly, feminine. Somehow the Greeks has managed to break free of the paralyzing terror of an all-powerful unknown. No need for magic. The gods could be understood. Media and Circe, the only witches among the Greek gods, were young and gorgeous and enjoyable. Ghosts evaporated from existence. Astrology gave way to astronomy. The priest faded into unimportance. The poet took his place of eminence. Mythical monsters earned their right of existence as the obstacles to be overcome by superhuman heroes.

The Romans stole all the Greek gods, translated their names into Latin, and borrowed a few gods from the Far East that the Greeks had overlooked.

Roman Religion

Since you, the reader, will probably stumble over all the names of the Roman gods, I've left the names out. I hope I have not offended any of them.

The Roman gods drove the Romans away from blatant worship of nature into the Greek world of gods and goddesses. Nature was permeated by innumerable impersonal beings, faceless and formless, but with the power to influence human activity. The Greeks contributed to this religious system by sharing the human form and personalities of their gods. Eventually, the Roman pantheon outnumbered that of all previous cultures. Nature worship still controlled the minds of the Romans as they constantly sought to interpret natural phenomena (weather, seasons, etc.) as the hidden will of the gods, thus constantly paying attention to the perceived omens and portents exhibiting their obtuse (unclear) messages with every conscious event.

Required worship, with the appropriate offerings, rituals, and prayer formulas, saturated the Roman's everyday life with religion. Forgiveness for involuntary offenses against the gods could be atoned for, but intentional acts brought dire consequences. Sins against humans however, and their inherent immorality, meant nothing to the gods. Human courts had to deal with such minor issues. As with basic nature worship, equilibrium had to be kept in balance.

Daily religion was more concerned with daily life than with the future. Because Roman religion never completely jettisoned nature worship, new gods and goddesses were accepted from other incoming cultures and absorbed into the Roman pantheon. The Second Punic War (218–201 BC) brought more novel gods with their religious ceremonies. These events told the souls of the Romans that their gods were deficient, therefore, they needed additional new ones.

The merging of the Greek gods, overall, had a positive influence on Rome. The Roman gods had become more personal, but this was offset by the flamines. The flamines were human intercessors who performed the magic rituals required by the gods. However, since the flamines had been entrusted with the sacred deities and their formalities, the normal citizen became disinterested in any of the gods that were not directly connected to a person's specific profession. On the other hand, Rome was more interested in a religion that cemented the corporate nature of the empire, which required a heavier emphasis on ritual than on personal belief.

One of the more negative Hellenistic cults to arise was Bacchus (Dionysus to the Greeks, the Greek god of wine), which threatened the entire social order of the Roman Empire. Imagine wine having that effect on society!

This cult was excessively personal, brutal, and immoral. In 186 BC the Roman Senate reacted by suppressing this cult and replacing it with a less-menacing one that would affirm the moral superiority of the Romans over the Greeks. After all, the Romans had won the war over the Greeks. Strict observance to an inflexible set of rituals was imposed by the state, and many of the Bacchus followers were imprisoned or executed. A religion that threatened the empire's unity had been destroyed.

The religious cult that was accepted by the official government sanctioned to replace Bacchus came from Asia Minor: Cybele, who was an early goddess. The Romans identified her with the goddess Rhea, the mother of the Olympians, and Demeter, the goddess of the harvest. They believed Cybele was instrumental in helping the Romans win the Second Punic War. She eventually became known as *Magna Mater*, or "Great Mother." She was worshipped as a deity of rebirth and resurrection in connection with her son, Attis.

Cybele was associated with the mystery religions and she eventually appears during Augustus's time and is included in Augustan theology. He restored her temple which was located next to his palace on the Palatine

Hill. Her cult was especially popular in Rome, and she bears some resemblance to the mother of harlots who rides the beast in the book of Revelation.

Cybele illustrates the downward direction of the failed older religion under the pressure of the Roman wars. Collapse and decay would continue for the next 170 years. Greek literature began to reassert itself publicly mocking the Roman gods. Greek art began representing Roman gods, and if an old deity had no Greek counterpart, that deity began to fade in recognition. Greek philosophy's atheism, skepticism, and rationalism grew in importance among the educated Roman classes. The priests became less educated and degenerated in quality, and the upper classes, the aristocracy, having been devastated by the wars, had dwindled to the point of no longer being able to hand down the old religious rituals. When the Roman high priest was murdered in 82 BC on Vesta's sacred altar, the myth of protection by the Roman gods evaporated.

If Rome was to survive and return to a prophesied "Golden Age," then the "peace of the gods" had to be revived. The gods would agree to protect and safeguard Rome's public welfare, and the Romans would provide the gods their desired worship and cult. If Julius Caesar had intended such an undertaking, his death precluded it happening. Not until Augustus had won the battle at Actium did the Roman Empire begin to see their religious revival. Augustus had new temples built and many restored. He raised the office of priesthood and financial support back to its previous level of position and dignity. He re-instituted extravagant and dazzling religious ceremonies to attract public attention.

The *Aeneid* rose to the occasion to represent the obvious signs of spiritual revival. The *Aeneid*, the predominant religious poem, "proves" that the origin of the Roman was connected with the gods. It incorporated the old religion with a new literary form to build a Roman world that would appeal to and convince both the ignorant and the educated.

Augustus's religion had to become the religion of the empire. Assimilation of other gods was acceptable, as long as none of the foreign gods challenged Augustus and his authority. Nothing was allowed to stand independent of Augustus. Virgil needed to incorporate the divine decree of Rome's destiny and morality, as a result of religion, into the *Aeneid*'s message.

Theology of Determinism

What role did the gods play in the affairs of the Romans? Did the gods determine everything that happened, or did a Roman have free will to make his own decisions?

Since no omniscient and omnipotent God existed within the Roman religion, absolute sovereignty was ruled out. Whenever Jupiter proclaimed the fate of something or someone, it supposedly could not be changed, but prayer to some other god could modify fate, as long as it did not contradict the big picture, and man could still contribute to the outcome by using his own judgment. Fate and free will were compelled to work together. Romans needed the security that comes from believing that life has meaning beyond the monotonous routine of daily life. The universe cannot be completely arbitrary. Someone had to be directing Rome's rise to prominence, helping it fulfill its destiny to rule the world. The gods had ordained Augustus as their champion to complete what they had started with Aeneas in the *Aeneid*.

However, few people want to believe that they have no part in the affairs of life. As important as fate was, it could not be completely fatalistic, since that would contradict and devastate Roman self-determination, fortitude, and the pride of having been a part of their destiny. The human will had to be allowed some room to make a positive impact, even if prayer was viewed as something the gods had already taken into account before setting fate into action.

If the reader wants more depth in this subject, compare Epicureanism, which denied determinism, and Stoicism, which placed man at the complete mercy of the gods. Epicureanism wanted to do away with all the useless gods, and the Stoics wanted no responsibility for their own actions. The tension placed the gods in a position of a vague and distant relationship to everyday life. If the gods affected humans, there was nothing humans could do about it, and if the gods had no effect on humans, then the Romans needed to look elsewhere to discover what part their empire was playing in history. The gods had fallen into oblivion, as evidenced by the fact that almost one hundred temples needed to be repaired long before Augustus rose to power. Rome needed a philosophy that promoted their empire while giving them credibility in their efforts. The gods must return, but not arbitrarily, to give Rome her deserved destiny.

Theology of Prophecy

Virgil used prophecy to promote Augustus. The Sibylline Books were the only organized prophetic system at that time. They came from a sibyl who got them from a deity. Nothing vague about that.

Many had been lost, and many were intentionally destroyed. They were not always supportive of the Roman government, so the Roman Senate kept them away from public use by placing them in the care of various members of the ruling class whose only job was to protect those books. What a cushy job.

They were consulted only in dire circumstances to discover the religious rituals necessary to avert a larger disaster. They were never used to predict future events. When the temple in Rome was burned in 83 BC, the collection was destroyed. The Roman Senate obtained another collection from various quarters and handed it over to the Roman officials to determine which ones did not contradict the Roman religion. In 12 BC Augustus had them sorted out, had over ten thousand burned in order to properly censor them, and had the rest transferred to the temple of Apollo Patrous on the Palatine.

What part did these books play in the *Aeneid*'s theology? They kept the concept of prophecy alive without being viewed as false prophecy. Every one of those prophecies began by presenting a past truth that gave confidence in a future improbability, and most important of all, each prophecy was extremely vague. This protected the blind faith of those who chose to believe the prophecies.

The Romans believed that the gods sent vague signs that had to be interpreted. From this came the belief that a semi-deity or deity would make statements about future human events that had nothing to do with the gods themselves. At this point prophecy was conditional. Man still had a free will to act or reject whatever the gods wanted. Augustus's burning of the Sibylline Books ignited the idea that the old standards of prophecy had enough potency to strike fear in the heart of the Roman elite. By the time Virgil penned the *Aeneid*, prophecy had risen to prominence between the gods and men.

Virgil avoided counterfeit prophecies and made excellent use of "legitimate" prophecy throughout the *Aeneid*. A counterfeit prophecy claimed fulfillment of something that had happened in the past. When Venus disguised herself and informed Aeneas that the ships were safe, that was simply stating what had already happened, not what was going to happen.

Virgil also rejected any general statements of hope about the future, or things that were already known, as masquerading prophecy, like when Hector tells Aeneas that he will establish a famous city.

Virgil's actual use of prophecy occurs early in his first book, when Juno, having heard of Rome's destiny, attempted to use her goddess abilities to hinder Aeneas in order to alter the future. From this point forward, Virgil used three kinds of prophecy to build his myth: omens, oral prophecies, and those focused on the history of Rome that would evolve into power and prominence throughout the known world.

Omens dealt with the present. The Romans felt at home in the world of omens. When Anchises noticed the burning fire on the head of Ascanius, who was sleeping but unburned, Anchises demanded that Jupiter confirm that omen. Jupiter granted his "request" with thunder and a shooting star. Romans were more familiar and comfortable with this type of prophecy, mainly because they were explainable by experts, who however, more often than not, misinterpreted them.

The second type of prophecy, the most numerous, centered on events within the story. Aeneas struggled throughout the *Aeneid* with a balance between duty and selfish passion. Duty required that he serve the gods and country and family above himself. The selfish passion that raged in him pushed him to reverse those priorities. He eventually grew into the Roman hero that fate intended for him, but his journey was fraught with choices of priorities that concerned his family, his emotional love, his country, and his divine calling.

Aeneas's wife Creusa was a model of the Roman woman, who stood for duty. When she died, her ghost soothed him to choose duty over selfishness. His duty was calling, and he had a kingdom to establish. Creusa herself set the example for Aeneas to follow. She was the only woman in Aeneas's life who lived and recommended a life of duty.

Her death was a tool in the hands of gods to move fate in the right direction. Her final appearance to Aeneas and her son placed him on the right path by releasing him from any pain and guilt. He now had to use his love for Creusa as the foundation for his love for their son, Ascanius, who symbolizes the establishment of Rome.

This second group of prophecies all come from Apollo, who was well qualified to give guidance to Aeneas. Apollo was extremely popular at that time as the Olympian god of prophecy and oracles, as well as song and poetry, archery, healing, and protector of the young. Apollo was depicted as an ancient, but youthful, beardless sun god of great beauty. Although Venus is the protector of Aeneas, and she often guides her charges with her star, neither she nor her star are mentioned in saving Aeneas from the Greeks in Book 2. The protection of Aeneas and his ensuing expedition comes from Apollo. Apollo does not compete with Venus, but Virgil sees Apollo's role as emphasizing Augustus, and therefore, Aeneas should be protected by the one god closest to the image of Augustus.

The third type of Roman prophecy focused exclusively on the future of the Roman people. Three famous prophecies delineate the history of Rome to its apex under Augustus and end with concise and stirring promptings of renown victories, which illuminate the vision and mission of Rome to the known world. Rather than specific accounts of linear history, these prophecies choose random, but important, names and episodes.

Jupiter's first appearance in the *Aeneid*, through Venus, prophesies the coming prominence and magnitude of Rome. Anchises, Aeneas's father, utters the second prophecy when he visits him from the afterlife. The third prophecy appears on the shield that Vulcan made for Aeneas, an historical event that applies to several scenes in Rome's legend, which reaches its height when Augustus won the battle of Actium, a battle orchestrated by Apollo when the Roman gods devastated the gods of Egypt. At the end of the story, the most isolated and secluded races bow to Augustus and his army.

The final result of these prophecies centers on Rome's destiny under the leadership of Augustus Caesar. Virgil "dignified" prophecy, raised it above the mere possibility of opportunities and risks, and made it a banner of hope and dreams. He took it beyond the individual private utility to be quickly forgotten with the next meal and elevated it to imperial significance. The Hebrew style of prophecy had become firmly established in the Roman religion and now Virgil could use prophecy, through the *Aeneid*, to influence more than just the Roman world.

Theology of Astrology

Astrology underscored the *Aeneid*'s theology. The faithful uneducated masses were among the faithful adherents. The populace had become so enamored with astrology's potential that, in 139 AD, all astrologers were banished from Italy, due to the threat to the state religion, as evidenced also by the expulsion of the Jews who were accused of promoting worship of Jupiter Sabazius.

The Stoics eventually brought some philosophical respectability to astrology, teaching that the stars were divine. The apex of astrology came with Manilius's *Astronomicon* in which he proclaimed to the growing public that the stars determined man's fate. Soon, an eclipse of the sun and a comet were interpreted to be Caesar's soul traveling through the heavens and Caesar's divinity rose sharply in the minds of everyone. Astrology had become a strong support for the worship of the gods, and Augustus viewed his own popularity through the public's interest in the stars. Numerous poets read the stars to find their destiny. Astrology thus paved the way for the public to accept a limited form of determination, which was vital for Virgil's proposed destiny of Aeneas and Augustus and the Roman Empire, a destiny sanctioned by the divine through the stars.

Theology of *Fortuna*

Virgil incorporated anti-deterministic Fortuna into the *Aeneid* as well. Fortuna was a goddess worshipped mainly by the lower classes and slaves. She took on the attribute of a goddess of luck, especially when humans resorted to seeking their fate through divination by lots under her watchful direction.

The Second Punic War raised the level of fear in everyone, and fortune-telling became a solace and short-term escape from the horrors of war reaching the people. When the wars were over, Fortuna's temples remained in place, and she was given the title of "Luck of People Original," and "Luck of the Roman People."

Although Fortuna was a foreign goddess, she managed to become thoroughly embedded in the Roman state religion, and she was especially attractive to married women and those in childbirth. Married women as a group claimed Fortuna as their own. She became the goddess of the individual in all of life's uncertainties, then the goddess of a special season, and finally, she was adopted as the goddess of Catulus, a Roman general who had been "fortunate" in battle. Julius Caesar followed Catulus by adopting Fortuna for himself. She came to be associated with general luck, wealth, and most important, oversight and protection of a special group of people and individuals. Fortuna had intertwined herself in the destiny of groups and individuals.

Virgil recognized Fortuna's importance in determining the fate of Augustus and the Roman Empire. A fertility goddess had made herself indispensable among the people and gained more prominence than most of the other gods.

Theology of Caesar Worship

The Greeks contributed considerably to helping the Romans accept the idea that man could become a god. Virgil made good use of deified humanity in the *Aeneid*. Evidence of the deification of man is overwhelming in Roman religious thought, and Julius Caesar wanted that status. He did not receive that title until immediately after his death, a process that Augustus fully supported and encouraged.

Virgil had gained fame for himself as promoting Caesar worship long before he wrote the *Aeneid*. He openly presented himself as deifying the young Augustus. Virgil advocated more than private worship toward Caesar. Caesar will become a god. This is not simply an altar sacrifice to honor Caesar, but a temple to be built and garnished with tokens of the most important successes and achievements by Caesar abroad and at home. Caesar is more than a mortal victor; he is moving into the heavens. Julius Caesar's official and popular deification was Virgil's launching pad for Augustus to follow suit. Augustus would be compared to none other than Jupiter himself.

Virgil had already deified Augustus as his personal god, but now he had to insert Augustus's divinity into the life of Aeneas through a national epic poem. How could Virgil do this? Many gods already existed, but Augustus could not simply replace one of them. He had to be a new god, not an old inactive one.

Therefore, Virgil had to resort to prophecy, as demonstrated previously. Virgil's short revelation of Jupiter's communication to Venus, the divine mother, is intentionally placed in the first prophecy of the *Aeneid*. Virgil needed to begin the deification process of Augustus early in the poem. And Venus makes no objections. Caesar worship will enter human history at the proper time.

Although the Romans believed in the idea that a human could become a god, many Romans were repulsed by it. Virgil won them over by *not* explaining how it was possible. He produced no simplistic theory to be presented for blind acceptance, nor did he present an explanation of how what he wanted everyone to believe could actually happen: a man becoming a god. Virgil presents a human who had already achieved deification: Anchises, the father of Aeneas.

Even though Anchises is dead, Aeneas views Anchises as his divine parent. After Aeneas establishes Rome, he goes beyond honoring his father by simply praying to him, offering sacrifices to him and dedicating temples to his father—an act carried out, not for humans, but for the gods. All of Aeneas's friends follow suit with their own offerings. Just like Jupiter and Venus, Anchises receives and accepts mortal prayers. Thus, Virgil circumvented any logical explanation of how humans can become divine and presented Anchises as an example (not explanation) of the deified Julius Caesar.

Aeneas and his struggles to establish Rome and bring his gods to Rome would be a palatable parallel to Augustus, who had just spent twelve years keeping Rome on the foundations set by Aeneas and restoring the prestige and dignity of Aeneas's gods to Rome. Aeneas is obviously human, but his divine mother has destined him for divinity, as his father was. Just before the last drama closes, Jupiter announces Rome's future fame and prominence and adds that Augustus is both divine race and mortal. Augustus has not yet arrived at a state of complete divinity, but he will, just like the experiences of Aeneas, and all Roman citizens will bow to divine kingship.

Theology of Afterlife

Every religious system attempts to answer the question about life after death. The old Roman religion had vestiges of an afterlife shrouded in its theology as Cicero and funeral ceremonies vaguely referenced.

The good Lares were the souls of good men returning to the upper world to have their needs met. They required propitiation gifts. The evil larvae were wicked souls who returned to injure the living. They only accepted human sacrifices.

The good Manes were deified souls of dead ancestors and had similar needs as humans. The living brought them food and prayed for them, after which the relatives celebrated the facts that they, the relatives, were still alive.

None of the spirits were very powerful and could be appeased with the proper religious rite. Few spirits ventured very far from their graves. Overall the dead required that they not be forgotten, indicating that the living chose to believe that a person's personality remain intact after death.

No clear distinction existed in the Roman mind about the differences between the spirits, nor their relationship to the living. Very little evidence implies that the Romans and their religion had any interest in probing further into the next life by engaging the spirits. It should be noted that those who might have wanted to spend their retirement years in philosophically pondering the afterlife usually died a sudden death and were accorded little leisure to produce any written literature documenting their theology on the matter.

The civil wars had not motivated thought about the afterlife, but instead a cynical rejection of a next life. Poets wrote from the standpoint that death led to a dark night of nothingness, therefore one must enjoy life and love while living in time.

The Epicureans viewed death as the ultimate end of a human being's soul, thus extinguishing the personality of the individual, while the Stoics rejected any belief in eternal bliss after death. With no clear theology of the afterlife, the fear of hell also evaporated. To the Romans, the dream of everlasting fame far outweighed everlasting personal existence of the soul and personality. The only people to hold a firm view of the afterlife were the Hebrews, whose beliefs were well-known to the Romans during Virgil's and Augustus's time.

In the *Aeneid* Virgil developed a deeper picture of the underworld. His descriptions stormed into literary prominence almost immediately and have influenced many writers since. According to Virgil's afterlife, both moral uprightness and ritual are necessities. Vagueness permeates most of that world because too many details would derail Virgil from his overall task of using the underworld to promote Aeneas's mission to found Rome against all odds, even against some of the gods who would defy fate.

So, where are the dead? The dead were expected to remain in the underworld or in the vicinity of their burial place. No one seems to have raised the question, nor answered the question, as to why a dead person should be obligated to stay close to his bones, and Virgil's afterlife theology is vague as to what the dead know of the activities on Earth.

Virgil supported the theology that every person has an appointed death day. Unhappy people wanted some enemies to die before their death day, like Dido wishing it upon Aeneas, although ironically Dido herself died too soon. The death day would come, whether anticipated or not; it was unavoidable, and it signified a clear and permanent change in a person's existence.

If a child died too soon, or an injustice caused a death at the wrong time, a new trial was held by Minos, the judge of the dead of the underworld. Anyone else was lumped together with a depressed group of suicides, all of whom regretted having ended their previous lives too soon. Those included people who did not experience violent deaths, like unhappy lovers, or dead warriors.

If anyone died on time, they were judged on their good and bad deeds. The gods determined and meted out the punishments, depending on who committed crimes against the gods and those against Roman morals.

Virgil had reached a middle ground. The old Roman religion held no expiation possible for sinning against the gods; the new religion came with its own hell for moral offenders, and a moral purification in a purgatory was included in the punishment. On the opposite path came the righteous and the blessed: the mythical heroes, like Aeneas; the founder of the Trojan race; and those who lived exemplary lives on Earth, who could receive a reincarnation as their reward.

Anchises overlooks the unborn and assigns those just previously judged to their different forms, which they will take on in the next life. They forget their past, and it is assumed that they forget the future as prophesied. Virgil has combined the old with the new without offending the old by using just enough vagueness to still establish a definite system.

The Stoics rested securely in their beliefs, while the oriental religions kept their afterlife with its punishments and rewards, all dressed up in Roman clothing. Astrology kept its reputation, and the unborn remained under their determined destiny. The Epicureans were left out, but their eschatology of no life after death never allowed them to be satisfied anyway.

Virgil's genius mapped the underworld, and the Roman Catholic Church adopted it *en bloc*. The church thought that the Fourth Eclogue predicted Christ's coming, and that the sixth chapter of the *Aeneid* was a forerunner of Christian teaching on hell. Similarities still exist between

Virgil's rendition of hell and the teachings within the Roman Catholic Church.

Theology of The Relative Ruling Relationships Among the Roman Gods

Uncertainty ruled the gods from Jupiter on down. Some authors attributed absolute sovereignty to Jupiter and that fate was identical to the will of Jupiter.

Other scholars claim the opposite to be true. Virgil had received some training as a Stoic, which taught that Jupiter was omnipotent, omniscient, and the embodiment of fate, but no such ideas are found in the *Aeneid*. Does the answer lie between these two extremes? If not, then either Virgil wrote the *Aeneid* with abandon and carelessly without thinking through any underlying continuity as to how the gods and fate work together or against each other, or Virgil intentionally left the reader in the vague world of apparent inconsistencies and nebulous passages with debatable interpretations. Recognizing the genius with which Virgil was endowed, and the length of time (over ten years) that he spent writing the *Aeneid*, it is more probable to assume the latter.

Virgil faced the apparently insurmountable task of uniting all the conflicting theologies throughout the realm: The Stoics and the Epicureans held the extreme position and all the non-philosophical worldviews. Every group would be difficult to please completely. They would have to discover supporting texts that made them feel included, texts that would allow them to overlook the other texts that could be viewed as disagreeing with their worldview.

If Virgil could write an epic poem that accomplished this feat, then everyone would endorse the underlying theology of the *Aeneid* with its inconsistencies specific to each theology. As long as there were no glaring contradictions that demanded only one interpretation, general conformity would suffice.

As an example, the astrologers needed to be convinced that astrology was a vital part of the Roman religion. Once they found some references to their views in the *Aeneid*, they would be more willing to overlook contrary statements. The murky fusion of the conflicting views allows each person to feel that the Roman state religion is, in fact, his religion, with Augustus standing at the pinnacle, supporting each view and carrying the torch into the world.

Virgil's vagueness is not a confusion of incoherence, but a well-written combination of conflicting viewpoints presented in a palatable way to appeal to and win the support of all. His principle underlying this synthesis surfaces in two passages.

The first, its importance underscored by its position, occurs when Venus intercedes for Aeneas with Jupiter. Jupiter has made some spectacular promises about the superiority of the forthcoming Roman Empire, and his feelings cannot be changed. Although Juno foresees her desire for the destiny that Jupiter has prophesied against, and that a collision of "destinies" will erupt, she wonders how Jupiter will bring his "happy ending" to completion.

Jupiter affirms that her race will not be changed, because Jupiter has not changed his mind. She will be reassured when he reveals the secrets of fate. He wants Rome's prominence to have no boundaries because he has given Rome unrivaled power on the earth. As the highest ruler among the gods, Jupiter uses his own name to speak in the first person.

The second passage occurs near the end of the poem. Venus, in favor of Aeneas, and Juno against Aeneas, have passionately argued their cases. Jupiter concludes the council of the gods by stating that he will not take sides, that fate will decide the outcome.

Fate and Jupiter have their own separate wills[1] and neither seem to be superior to the other. At the end, Jupiter will evaluate fate in two evenly balanced scales to see which was doomed by death, not because he did not know their outcome, but to demonstrate by a clear indication that the issue was much bigger than just a battle between two men.

Once Jupiter has given his decree of fate, it cannot be withdrawn, but it can be modified. Jupiter gave the Trojans the end game, but he could grant Juno's request that the Trojans keep the Latin name. Delay of a decree was also possible, even by Juno. She is a god after all. She knows, however, that when fate is specific, it cannot be changed. Natural laws cannot be broken, and wooden ships cannot be kept in shape indefinitely, but Jupiter is not violating fate by turning the ships into nymphs. Even though some gods rebel against Jupiter's veto, the prophesied war will still occur.

---

1. *Aeneid* 4.614.

The *Aeneid* teaches a contradictory balance between fate's ambiguity and Jupiter's sovereignty. The clash between the goddesses, Venus and Juno, changes nothing of the outcome of the two destinies. Their role simply attempts to move within fate to the best benefit for their chosen party. Like coaches who know before the end of the game who is going to win, they manipulate what they can to give their team the best experience and score of the game.

Humans can know they are in a war, but they cannot see the outcome of the battles. Turnus cries, "I'm not afraid of all the fateful omens from the gods,"[2] which is not a rebellious statement against the gods, since he does not know the outcome. Therefore, he forges forward by stating, "I have my own counter destiny, to root out the guilty race."[3] When it becomes clear that he has lost, he owns it: "Whatever fate is here, is mine."[4]

Dido also recognized fate as a major influence in her life: "Fortune, pursuing me too, through many similar troubles, willed that I would find peace at last in this land."[5] Fate taught her to grieve her negative experience, and when life came to an end, she acknowledged the place of fate in her life: "I have lived, and I have completed the course that Fortune granted."[6]

Aeneas's destiny rises to its fulfillment in the *Aeneid*. Troy's destiny had been wicked and Aeneas's father, Anchises, knows that Aeneas is still burdened with that experience and talks to him twice about it. Although Aeneas initially saw himself as a victim of his fate that drove him to reject what he had really loved, he overcame Carthage and began to live in accordance with his promised destiny. Fate has moved him from the ashes of Troy to the splendid destiny of Rome. Religion and patriotism combine to form one glorious power: Rome with Augustus at the helm.

Theology of the Place of Prayer in Virgil's Theology

Every religion attempts to communicate with their gods. The people either want something, or out of fear they attempt to appease the anger of the gods. The *Aeneid* makes use of both reasons. Aeneas asked for

2. Virgil, *Aeneid*, 9.133–34.
3. Virgil, *Aeneid*, 9.137.
4. Virgil, *Aeneid*, 12.694.
5. Virgil, *Aeneid*, 1.628–29.
6. Virgil, *Aeneid*, 4.653.

things and he feared the gods. Aeneas had lots of needs, and he prayed throughout his story, but he feared the gods at the same time. They often used their power like humans: greed and envy ruled. Aeneas never attempted to reconcile the contradiction between the usefulness of prayer and determinism, which seemed to make prayer nothing more than an exercise in futility.

In spite of these philosophical problems, the hero Helenus warned Aeneas to pray to Juno and recite his vows to her in an attempt to win over that powerful goddess, so Aeneas could reach Italy victorious. Further, the god Tiberius warned him in the same way to pray to Juno, but Tiberius added that Aeneas's prayers were needed to possibly overcome her anger and threats.

Helenus reveals to Aeneas the key to how Virgil views prayer. After the prophecy of eating tables, Helenus tells Aeneas to not worry about the prophecy because "the fates will find a way, Apollo will be there at your call." In spite of Juno's threats, destiny will be fulfilled as planned. This cannot be stopped, and Apollo will listen to further prayers that do not directly contradict fate. The general results are set in stone, but the details depend on the prayers of men and the will of the gods. Not even Jupiter can change a decree, but prayers may modify the method of fulfillment.

Aeneas calls out to the gods for help three times in the poem, but he does not reveal his attitude or belief that his prayers and requests will be answered, either positively or negatively. In one instance Aeneas is searching for the golden bough and he verbally states that he wishes that it might become visible to him. His prayer is answered immediately, maybe by pure coincidence, when two doves enter the scene. Aeneas prays that they direct him to the bough, and that he might count on his divine mother always being there to support him.

Even though the birds do take him to the bough, apparently proving that his prayer was answered, the sibyl has already informed the reader that the right person will find the bough if fate calls that person. His prayer seemed to have no effect on the ultimate outcome, but only on the ease with which he found the bough.

Jupiter's decrees were absolute, but if Aeneas prayed for something that could be changed, then he received a positive response from the gods. Death is fixed and cannot be changed, therefore the gods and men mourn, but they do not protest against *fata*.

The theology of prayer in Virgil's universe was simple. Fate controlled the outcome because decrees had been made and could not be changed. The details of those decrees, however, were open for manipulation by the gods, and humans could request, beg, petition, and even mildly motivate the gods to make human lives easier as they moved toward their fate. Based on their own preferences, those gods could choose to grant or reject those requests.

Understanding that the gods worked this way, humans were well-advised to make worship and offerings to the gods a priority in their lives, either before the prayer request, or making promises to do so after the request was granted.

The status of the human requesting help from the gods made no difference in whether the gods helped or not. No intermediaries existed, except when Venus prayed through Aeneas. How could Jupiter refuse a request from a mother for her son?

No priests were necessary to make propitiatory sacrifices, i.e., no sacerdotalism permeated Virgil's theology. The priests themselves also functioned as warriors and kings. The only magic used, but not actually carried out, in the *Aeneid* was done by Dido who tried to get Aeneas to return to her. Apparently, Virgil viewed magic in mostly a negative light, since Dido eventually apologized for attempting to make use of the magic arts.

Although Virgil was brilliant, he didn't develop his ideas in a vacuum. He made good use of two hundred years of previous theology. He wrote to his own culture. Everyone understood and most agreed with Virgil's theology in all areas. His brilliant synthesis of the many incongruous views of the numerous philosophies resided as worldviews within the hearts of very different groups of people. He mingled and merged foreign deities into the Roman Pantheon. He served up a religion that each person wanted to consume, and thus succeeded in convincing everyone to gleefully accept the whole as the official Roman state religion.

Virgil rejected a theological treatise or a philosophical argument. He chose instead an historical narrative poem. This form allowed the reader to overlook the conflicting details between the different viewpoints. The enjoyment of reading a poem, and the thrill of coming to believe that it was true, captured the hearts and minds of every Roman and many non-Romans who wanted Rome to rule the world. Randomness and sloppiness were not part of Virgil's approach. He did not want his reader to overlook the details of the poem, but through a coherent story he wanted his poem to be accepted as truth that needed no facts for support.

The big picture: Virgil developed Caesar worship beyond any previous old Roman religion. He deified Julius Caesar, raising him from a political figure to a god, a divine king. Augustus would follow. Virgil established the divine right of kings because they were divine kings. Virgil developed a much more elaborate afterlife than had existed before his time. The underworld was the place the dead received their reward for virtue and punishment for evil. Virtue was a necessity, but it had to be accompanied by the proper and exact rituals. Jupiter was supreme as a god, and Augustus would stand supreme among men. Men may enjoy the protection of the lesser gods, but only if they obeyed Jupiter, had the human virtue of duty, and offered the proper sacrifices and prayers.

Virgil, however, as stated above, was not a creator of a new religion, nor a new theology. He arranged and rearranged what already existed. He imitated Homer's poems but surpassed them. He began with the "sacred scriptures" of the Greeks, Homer's *Iliad* and *Odyssey*, and superseded them by codifying his new and improved religion, writing it down in a form that was extremely appealing to everyone who was tired of the wars and wanted a savior. Virgil provided them with that savior: Augustus.

31

Conclusions and Further Research

THIS THESIS HAS SOUGHT to discover if 1) the *Aeneid* had permeated the entire Roman world and beyond, that 2) Mark had knowledge of, and access to, the *Aeneid*, and that 3) Mark wrote his Gospel to address the *Aeneid*. This research builds on the previous work of other scholars who have demonstrated that the *Aeneid* was widely disseminated immediately after its publication, that it permeated deeply into the Roman world and beyond, that other NT authors were at least confronted with concepts and theologies of the *Aeneid*, and that those NT authors addressed the *Aeneid* in their writings (Bonz—Luke, Wallace—Romans, Reasoner—Hebrews). Through fourteen pieces of independent but interlocking pieces of evidence, the case has been made that these other scholars are correct in discovering the *Aeneid*'s extensive circulation and entrenchment into Roman society, that Mark had knowledge of and access to the *Aeneid*, and that he addressed the *Aeneid*'s concepts and theology in his Gospel. Virgil wrote the *Aeneid* to woo the whole world into the mythology that Aeneas had laid the foundation for the Roman Empire, and Augustus had brought it to full fruition. Mark wrote his Gospel to counter this epic myth with the historical truth of Jesus's life, death, and resurrection. The *Aeneid* captivated the hearts and minds of people for centuries. Only recently has its existence and influence begun to wane. Mark's message confronts the *Aeneid* with the words of Jesus: "Heaven and earth will pass away, but my words will never pass away" (13:31).

Bibliography

Abdale, Jason R. *Four Days in September: The Battle of Teutoberg.* Barnsley: Pen and Sword, 2016.

Aberdein, Andrew, and Adina Arvatu. *Rhetoric: The Art of Persuasion.* New York: Bloomsbury, 2016.

Adams, J. N. *Bilingualism and the Latin Language.* Cambridge University Press, 1665.

Adcock, Frank Ezra. *Roman Political Ideas and Practice.* Michigan: University of Michigan Press, 1964.

———. *Roman Political Ideas and Practice.* Jerome Lecture, no. 6. Whitefish, MT: Literary Licensing, LLC, 2012.

Aeschylus. *Eumenides.* Edited by Alan H. Sommerstein. Cambridge Greek and Latin Classics. Cambridge: Cambridge University Press, 1989.

Alcock, Susan E., Jas Elsner, Simon Goldhill, and Michael Squire. "Greek Culture in the Roman World." *Series* (blog) *Cambridge Core,* accessed October 26, 2017, https://www.cambridge.org/core/series/greek-culture-in-the-roman-world/9CBACE392 5A75AA8332C258A5065D02A.

Allen, Katharine. "The Fasti of Ovid and the Augustan Propaganda." *The American Journal of Philology* 43 (1922) 250–66.

Alston, E. B. *The Adventures of Anchises.* Chapel Hill, NC: Writer Book Publishing, 2012. Kindle.

Alter, Robert, and Frank Kermode, eds. *The Literary Guide to the Bible.* Cambridge:Belknap, 1990.

Ambrozic, Aloysius M. "New Teaching with Power (Mk 1:27)." In *Word and Spirit: Essays in Honor of David M. Stanley, S.J. on His 60th Birthday,* 113–49. Willowdale, Toronto: Regis College, 1975.

Anderson, William James, and Richard Phené Spiers. *The Architecture of Greece & Rome: A Sketch of Its Historic Development.* San Bernadino,CA: Ulan, 2012.

Anonymous. *The Twelve Tables.* Los Angeles: HardPress, 2016.

Aphthonius, and Ray Nadeau. *The Progymnasmata of Aphthonius in Translation.* Vol. 19, no. 4. London: Brill: Speech Monographs, 1952.

Aristotle. *On Rhetoric: A Theory of Civic Discourse.* 2nd ed. Translated by George A. Kennedy. New York: Oxford University Press, 2006.

———. *Poetics.* Translated by Malcolm Heath. London; New York: Penguin, 1997.

———. *The Art of Rhetoric.* Reissue ed. Edited and translated by Hugh Lawson-Tancred. London; New York: Penguin, 1992.

Aristotle, and Anthony Kenny. *Poetics*. Reprint, Oxford: Oxford University Press, 2013.

Aristotle, and Stephen Halliwell. *Aristotle's Poetics*. 1st ed. Chicago: University of Chicago Press, 1998.

Aristotle, Longinus, and Demetrius. *Poetics*. Revised ed. Loeb Classical Library. Edited and translated by Stephen Halliwel et al. Cambridge: Harvard University Press, 1995.

Attridge, Harold W. *Hebrews: A Commentary on the Epistle to the Hebrews*. 1st ed. Philadelphia: Fortress, 1989.

Augustan Poets. *Golden Verses: Poetry of the Augustan Age*. 1st ed. Translated by Paul T. Alessi. Newburyport, MA: Focus, 2003.

Augustine. *Confessions*. Oxford World Classics. Translated by Henry Chadwick. Oxford: Oxford University Press, 2009.

———. *On Christian Doctrine*. 1st ed. Translated by D. W. Robertson, Jr. London: Pearson, 1958.

Augustinians Australia. "1311 Greek Language." *Augustine in General* (blog), *Augnet*, 2013, http://www.augnet.org/en/life-of-augustine/augustine-in-general/1311-greek-language/.

Aune, David Edward. "Genre Theory and the Genre-Function of Mark and Matthew." In *Jesus, Gospel Tradition and Paul in the Context of Jewish and Greco-Roman Antiquity: Collected Essays II*, edited by Eve-Marie Becker and Anders Runesson, 25–56. WUNT. Tübingen: Mohr Siebeck, 2011.

———. *Jesus, Gospel Tradition and Paul in the Context of Jewish and Greco-Roman Antiquity: Collected Essays II*. Vol. 2. WUNT. Tübingen, Germany: Mohr Siebeck, 2013.

Aune, David Edward, and Robin Darling Young, eds. *Reading Religions in the Ancient World: Essays Presented to Robert Mcqueen Grant*. Leiden; Boston: Brill, 2007.

Bagnall, Roger S., ed. *The Oxford Handbook of Papyrology*. 1st ed. Oxford Handbooks. Oxford: Oxford University Press, 2011.

Baker, Rosalie F., and Charles F. Baker. *Ancient Romans: Expanding the Classical Tradition*. New York: Oxford University Press, 1998.

Balleine, G. R. *Simon, Whom He Surnamed Peter: A Study of His Life*. London: Skeffington & Sons Ltd., 1958.

Balz, Horst. *Exegetical Dictionary of the New Testament*. Edited by Gerhard Schneider. Grand Rapids: Eerdmans, 1994.

Bammel, Ernst, ed. *The Trial of Jesus: Cambridge Studies in Honour of C. F. D. Moule*. London: SCM, 1970.

Barclay, William. *Educational Ideals in the Ancient World*. Reprint, Grand Rapids: Baker, 1974.

Barker, Ernest, ed. *From Alexander to Constantine: Passages and Documents Illustrating the History of Social and Political Ideas, 336 B.C.-A.D. 337*. New York: Lanham, 1985.

Barnett, Mary. *Gods and Myths of the Romans*. New York: Smithmark, 1996.

Barrett, Anthony A. *Caligula: The Corruption of Power*. 1st ed. New Haven: Yale University Press, 1990.

Barrow, Robin. *Greek and Roman Education*. New York: Bloomsbury, 2011.

Baswell, Christopher. *Virgil in Medieval England: Figuring The Aeneid from the Twelfth Century to Chaucer*. Cambridge: Cambridge University Press, 2006.

Bauckham, Richard, ed. *The Gospels for All Christians: Rethinking the Gospel Audiences*. Grand Rapids: Eerdmans, 1997.

Beard, Mary. *The History of Rome*. New York: Liveright, 2015.

Beavis, Mary Ann. *Mark's Audience: The Literary and Social Setting of Mark 4.11-12*. London: Bloomsbury, 2015.

Beavis, Mary Ann, Mikeal Parsons, and Charles Talbert. *Mark*. Grand Rapids: Baker, 2011.

Best, Edward E. "The Literate Roman Soldier." *The Classical Journal* 62 (December 1966) 122–27.

Betz, Hans Dieter. "Jesus and the Cynics: Survey and Analysis of a Hypothesis." *The Journal of Religion* 74 (October 1994) 453–75. https://doi.org/10.1086/489459.

Bilezikian, Gilbert. "The Liberated Gospel: A Comparison of the Gospel of Mark and Greek Tragedy." In *Baker Biblical Monograph*. Grand Rapids: Baker, 1977.

———. *The Liberated Gospel: A Comparison of the Gospel of Mark and Greek Tragedy*. Reprint ed. Eugene, OR: Wipf & Stock, 2010.

Billmayer, Karl. "Rhetorische Studien zu den Reden in Virgils Aeneis." PhD diss, Universität Würzburg, 1932.

Binkley, Roberta, and Carol S. Lipson. "The Rhetoric of Origins and the Other: Reading the Ancient Figure of Enheduanna." In *Rhetoric Before and Beyond the Greeks*. New York: State University of New York Press, 2004.

Bird, Michael F. "The Markan Community, Myth or Maze? Bauckham's The Gospel for All Christians Revisited." *JTS* 57 (October 2006) 474–86.

Bird, Michael F., Dr. Craig A. Evans, Simon Gathercole, Charles E. Hill, and Chris Tilling. *How God Became Jesus: The Real Origins of Belief in Jesus' Divine Nature—A Response to Bart Ehrman*. Grand Rapids: Zondervan, 2014.

Birley, Robin. *Vindolanda: Everyday Life on Rome's Northern Frontier*. UK ed. Stroud: Amberley, 2009. http://vindolanda.csad.ox.ac.uk/.

Black, C. Clifton. "Was Mark a Roman Gospel?" *Expository Times* 105 (1993) 36–40.

Black, David Alan. *Rethinking the Synoptic Problem*. Edited by David R. Beck. Grand Rapids: Baker, 2001.

———. "The Last Twelve Verses of Mark: A Bibliography," August 17, 2015, http://www.daveblackonline.com/last_twelve_verses_of_mark.htm.

Blomberg, Craig L. *The Historical Reliability of the Gospels*. 2nd ed. Downers Grove, IL: InterVarsity, 2007.

Blunt, John James. *Undesigned Coincidences in the Writings Both of the Old and New Testament, an Argument of Their Veracity: With an Appendix, Containing Undesigned . . . and Acts, and Josephus*. London: Forgotten, 2017.

———. *Undesigned Coincidences in the Writings of the Old and New Testament*. Ann Arbor: University of Michigan Press, 1869.

Bolt, Peter G. *Jesus' Defeat of Death: Persuading Mark's Early Readers*. 1st ed. Cambridge: Cambridge University Press, 2008.

Bonz, Marianna Palmer. "The Best of Times; the Worst of Times: Luke-Acts and Epic Tradition." PhD diss., Harvard Press, 1997. https://www.cambridge.org/core/journals/harvard-theological-review/article/div-classtitlesummaries-of-doctoral-dissertationsa-hreffno1-ref-typefnadiv/88E3C086D386585B781B22B4B338A85C.

———. *The Past as Legacy*. Philadelphia: Fortress, 2000.

Boring, M. Eugene. *Mark: A Commentary*. Reprint, Louisville: Westminster John Knox, 2006.

Botha, Pieter J.J. "The Historical Setting of Mark's Gospel: Problems and Possibilities." *Journal for the Study of the New Testament* 51 (1993) 27–55.

Bowman, Alan K. *Life and Letters on the Roman Frontier*. New York: Routledge, 1998.

Bowman, Alan K., Edward Champlin, and Andrew Lintott, eds. *The Cambridge Ancient History, Vol. 10: The Augustan Empire, 43 BC-AD 69*. 2nd revised & enlarged ed. Cambridge: Cambridge University Press, 1996.

Braun, Herbert. *An Die Hebräer*. Tübingen: Mohr Siebeck, 1984.

Brink, C. O. *Horace on Poetry: The 'Ars Poetica'*. Cambridge: Cambridge University Press, 1985.

Brooks, Otis. *Virgil: A Study in Civilized Poetry*. Norman: University of Oklahoma Press, 1995.

Brown, Michelle P. *The British Library Guide to Writing and Scripts: History and Techniques*. Toronto; Buffalo: University of Toronto Press,1998.

Brown, Raymond E. *The Death of the Messiah: From Gethsemane to the Grave: Commentary on the Passion Narrative in the Four Gospels*. 1st ed. New York: Anchor Bible, 1999.

Brummer. *Vitae Vergilianae*. Edited by Lacobus. Leipzig: Teubner, 1912.

Bryan, Christopher. *A Preface to Mark: Notes on the Gospel in Its Literary and Cultural Settings*. New York: Oxford University Press, 1997.

Burkill, T. Alec. *Mysterious Revelation: An Examination of the Philosophy of St. Mark's Gospel*. Ithaca, NY: Cornell University Press, 1963.

Burridge, Richard A., and Graham Stanton. *What Are the Gospels?: A Comparison with Graeco-Roman Biography*. 2nd ed. Grand Rapids: Eerdmans, 2004.

Burton, Philip. *The Old Latin Gospels: A Study of Their Texts and Language*. 1st ed. New York: Clarendon, 2001.

Butcher, S. H. *Aristotle's Theory of Poetry and Fine Art With a Critical Text and Translation of the Poetics, with a Prefatory Essay Aristotelian Literary Criticism by John Gassner*. 4th ed. Translated by John Glassner. Mineola, NE: Dover, 1951.

Butterfield, Bruce J. "Titus Livius: The History of Rome," 1996, http://mcadams.posc.mu.edu/txt/ah/Livy/.

Buttrick, George Arthur. *The Interpreter's Bible, Vol. 7: New Testament Articles, Matthew, Mark*. Nashville: Abingdon, 1951.

Buxton, Richard. *The Complete World of Greek Mythology*. London: Thames & Hudson, 2004.

Cadbury, Henry J., and Paul N. Anderson. *The Making of Luke-Acts*. Peabody, MA: Hendrickson, 1999.

Cairns, Francis. *Generic Composition in Greek and Roman Poetry*. Revised ed. Ann Arbor, MI: Michigan Classical, 2008.

———. *Virgil's Augustan Epic*. Revised ed. Cambridge: Cambridge University Press, 2006.

Callimachus. *Callimachus: Hymns, Epigrams, Select Fragments*. Translated by Stanley Lombardo and Diane J. Rayor. Baltimore: Johns Hopkins University Press, 1987.

Callimachus, Lycophron, and Aratus. *Callimachus: Hymns and Epigrams, Lycophron and Aratus*. 2nd ed. Translated by A. W. Mair and G. R. Mair. Cambridge: Harvard University Press, 1921.

Calmet, Augustin, Edward Wells, and Charles Taylor. *Calmet's Great Dictionary of the Holy Bible: Historical, Critical, Geographical, and Etymological*. Charleston, SC: Nabu, 2013.

Calvin, John. *Calvin On Mark: John Calvin's Bible Commentary*. Seattle: Amazon Digital Services LLC, 2015. Kindle.

Cameron, Averil, Mark J. Edwards, Markus Vinzent, and Jane Ralls Baun, eds. *Tertullian to Tyconius, Egypt before Nicaea, Athanasius and His Opponents*. Vol. 46. Studia Patristica. Leuven: Peeters, 2010.

Campbell, Joseph, and Bill Moyers. *The Power of Myth*. New York: Anchor, 2011.

Cartwright, Mark. "The Twelve Tablets." https://www.ancient.eu/Twelve_Tables/.

Casali, Sergio. Review of *Virgil's Homeric Lens*, by Edan Dekel. *Bryn Mawr Classical Review*, July 18, 2012, http://bmcr.brynmawr.edu/2012/2012-07-18.html.

Cassius Dio. *Complete Works of Cassius Dio*. 1st ed. Delphi Classics, 2014.

———. *Dio Cassius 63.13*. 9 vols. Edited and translated by Earnest Cary. Cambridge: Harvard University Press, 1925.

———. *Dio's Roman History*. 6 vols. Translated by Herbert Baldwin Foster. New Zealand: Halcyon, 2010.

———. *Dio's Roman History: With an English Translation*. Vol. VIII: Books 61-70. Translated by Earnest Cary and Herbert Baldwin Foster. Cambridge: Harvard University Press, 1925.

Casson, Lionel. "Speed Under Sail of Ancient Ships." *Transactions and Proceedings of the American Philological Association* 82 (1951) 136–48.

Castle, E. B. *Ancient Education And Today*. 1st ed. Gretna, LA: Pelican, 1961.

———. *Ancient Education And Today*. London: Penguin Classics, 1964.

Catullus, Gaius Valerius. *The Poems of Catullus: A Bilingual Edition*. Translated by Peter Green. Berkeley: University of California Press, 2007.

Cecilia, Madame. "Notices of Books." *The Downside Review, Sage Publications* 25 (April 1906) 78–83. https://doi.org/10.1177/001258060602500108.

Charlesworth, James H., ed. *The Messiah: Developments in Earliest Judaism and Christianity: The First Princeton Symposium on Judaism and Christian Origins*. Minneapolis: Fortress, 1992.

———. *The Old Testament Pseudepigrapha*. Translated by O. S. Wintermute. Garden City, NY: Doubleday, 1985.

Chevallier, Temple. *Translation of the Epistles of Clement of Rome, Polycarp and Ignatius: And of the Apologies of Justin Martyr and Tertullian*. London: Forgotten, 2017.

Christman, Angela Russell. "Biblical Exegesis and Virgil's Aeneid in Ambrose Milan's Expositio Psalmi CXVIII." *Studia Patristica* 46 (2010) 149–54.

Cicero, Marcus Tullius. *Delphi Complete Works of Cicero*. 1st ed. London: Delphi Classics, 2014.

———. *Epistulae: Volume III: Ad Quintum Fratrem, Ad M. Brutum, Fragmenta Epistularum, Commentariolum Petitionis, Pseudo-Ciceronis Epistula Ad Octavianum*. Edited by W. S. Watt. 1st ed. Oxford: Clarendon, 1958.

———. *On Divination: Book 1*. Edited by David Wardle. 1st ed. Clarendon Ancient History. Oxford: Oxford University Press, 2007.

———. *On the Nature of the Gods*. Translated by Francis Brooks. London: Methuen & Co., 1896. http://oll.libertyfund.org/titles/cicero-on-the-nature-of-the-gods.

———. *Rhetorica Ad Herennium*. Loeb Classical Library 403. Translated by Harry Caplan. Reprint, Cambridge: Harvard University Press, 1954.

Clark, Donald Lemen. *Rhetoric in Greco-Roman Education.* 2nd ed. New York: Columbia University Press, 1957.

Clarke, M. L. *Higher Education in the Ancient World.* 1st ed. London: Routledge, 2012.

———. "Rhetorical Influences in the Aeneid." *Greece & Rome* 18 (January 1949) 14–27. https://doi.org/10.1017/S0017383500010366.

Clausen, Wendell. *Virgil's Aeneid and the Tradition of Hellenistic Poetry.* 1st ed. Berkeley: University of California Press, 1987.

Clemens, Raymond, and Timothy Graham. *Introduction to Manuscript Studies.* 1st ed. Ithaca, NY: Cornell University Press, 2007.

Coleman-Norton, Paul Robinson. *The Twelve Tables.* Princeton: Princeton Univ. Dept. of Classics, 1948.

Collins, Adela Yarbro. *Mark: A Commentary.* Edited by Harold W. Attridge. 2nd ed. Hermeneia: A Critical and Historical Commentary on the Bible. Minneapolis: Fortress, 2007.

———. "Mark and His Readers: The Son of God among Greeks and Romans." *Harvard Theological Review* 93 (April 2000) 85–100.

———. "The Signification of Mark 10:45 among Gentile Christians." *The Harvard Theological Review* 90 (1997) 371–82.

Columbia College. "Moses Hadas." *The Core Curriculum* (blog), *Columbia College,* 2019, https://www.college.columbia.edu/core/oasis/profiles/hadas.php.

Comparetti, Domenico. *Vergil in the Middle Ages.* 2nd ed. Translated by E. F. M. Benecke. Princeton: Princeton University Press, Allen, 1996.

Conington, John, Henry Nettleship, and Virgil. *The Works of Virgil with a Commentary, Vol I: Eclogues and Georgics.* 4th ed. London: George Bell & Sons, 1898.

Conley, Thomas. *Rhetoric in the European Tradition.* Chicago: University of Chicago Press, 1990.

Cranfield, C. E. B. *A Critical and Exegetical Commentary on the Epistle to the Romans.* ICC. Edinburgh: T. & T. Clark, 1975.

———. *A Critical and Exegetical Commentary on the Epistle to the Romans: Introduction and Commentary on Romans I-VIII, Vol. 1.* 6th ed. London; New York: T. & T. Clark, 2000.

Crawford, H. Michæl. *Coinage and Money under the Roman Republic.* 1st ed. Berkeley: University of California Press, 1985.

Crawford, Peter. *The War of the Three Gods: Romans, Persians, and the Rise of Islam.* 1st ed. New York: Skyhorse, 2014.

Creighton, John. *Coins and Power in Late Iron Age Britain.* Cambridge: Cambridge University Press, 2000.

Croally, Neil, and Roy Hyde, eds. *Classical Literature: An Introduction.* New York: Routledge, 2011.

Crook, J. A. *Law and Life of Rome, 90 B.C.–A.D. 212.* 1st ed. Ithaca, NY: Cornell University Press, 1984.

Cumont, Franz Valery Marie. *After Life in Roman Paganism.* New Haven: Yale University Press, 1922. http://archive.org/details/afterlifeinromanoocumouoft.

———. *After Life in Roman Paganism.* London: Forgotten Books, 2016.

Curchin, Leonard A. *The Romanization of Central Spain: Complexity, Diversity and Change in a Provincial Hinterland.* 1st ed. London: Routledge, 2011.

Cyrino, Monica S. *Aphrodite.* 1st ed. Milton Park, Abingdon, Oxon; New York: Routledge, 2010.

Dante, Steven Botterill, and Anthony Oldcorn. *Inferno*. Edited by Stanley Lombardo. Indianapolis: Hackett, 2009.

Demosthenes. *The Public Orations of Demosthenes, All Volumes*. Translated by Arthur Wallace Pickard. Seattle: CreateSpace, 2015.

Dewey. "Mark as Interwoven Tapestry: Forecasts and Echoes for a Listening Audience." *Catholic Biblical Quarterly* 53 (1991) 224.

Dickson, T. W. "Lost and Unwritten Epics of the Augustan Poets." *TAPhA* 63 (1932) lii–liii.

Dillon, John, ed. *The Greek Sophists*. Translated by John Dillon and Tania Gergel. London; New York: Penguin Classics, 2003.

Dionysius of Halicarnassus. *The Roman Antiquities of Dionysius of Halicarnassus*. Vol. 1, Books 1–2. Translated by Earnest Cary. Rochester, NY: Scholar's Choice, 2015.

Diringer, David. *The Book Before Printing Ancient, Medieval and Oriental*. New York: Dover, 1982.

Donahue, John R. "A Neglected Factor in the Theology of Mark." *Journal of Biblical Literature* 101 (December 1982) 563–94.

Douglas, J. D. *Who's Who in Christian History*. Edited by Philip W. Comfort. 1st ed. Wheaton, IL: Tyndale House, 1992.

Downing, F. Gerald. "A Bas Les Aristos. The Relevance of Higher Literature for the Understanding of the Earliest Christian Writings." *NovT* 30 (1988) 212–30.

———. *Order and (Dis)order in the First Christian Century: A General Survey of Attitudes*. Novum Testamentum, Supplements. Lieden; Boston: Brill, 2013.

Drazin, Nathan. "Full Text of 'History Of Jewish Education From 515 B C E To 220 C E,'" accessed October 7, 2016, http://www.archive.org/stream/historyofjewishe027853mbp/historyofjewishe027853mbp_djvu.txt.

———. *History of Jewish Education From 515 B.C.E. To 220 C.E.* London: Nabu, 2011.

———. *History of Jewish Education From 515 B.C.E. to 220 C.E.* Baltimore: Johns Hopkins University Press, 1940.

———. *History of Jewish Education from 515 B.C.E. to 220 C.E.* Plano, TX: Mottelay, 2007.

Drogin, Marc. *Medieval Calligraphy: Its History and Technique*. Revised ed. New York: Dover, 1989.

Editors of the American Heritage Dictionaries. "Indo-European and the Indo-Europeans." In *American Heritage Dictionary of the English Language (4th Ed.)*. Boston: Houghton Mifflin Harcourt, 2000.

Edwards, Catharine. *Writing Rome: Textual Approaches to the City*. 1st ed. Cambridge; New York: Cambridge University Press, 1996.

Edwards, James R. "The Authority of Jesus in the Gospel or Mark." *JETS* 37 (1994) 217–33.

———. *The Gospel according to Mark*. Grand Rapids; Leicester: Eerdmans, 2002.

Elliott, Susan M. Review of *Cybele, Attis and Related Cults: Essays in Memory of M. J. Vermaseren.*, by Eugene N. Lane. *Bryn Mawr Classical Review*, June 18, 1997, http://bmcr.brynmawr.edu/1997/97.06.18.html.

Elsom, Helen. "The New Testament and Greco-Roman Writing." In *The Literary Guide to the Bible*, edited by Robert Alter and Frank Kermode, 561–78. Cambridge: Harvard University Press, Belknap, 1990.

Epicurus, Cicero, Lucretius, Robert Drew Hicks, and William Temple. *Stoic Six Pack 3–The Epicureans: On The Nature of Things, Letters and Principal Doctrines of*

Epicurus, De Finibus Bonorum et Malorum, The Garden of Epicurus and Stoics vs. Epicureans. Seattle: Amazon Digital Services LLC, 2015. Kindle.

Eusebius. *The Church History*. Translated by Paul L. Maier. Grand Rapids: Kregel, 2007.

———. *The History of the Church: From Christ to Constantine*. Edited by Andrew Louth. Translated by G. A. Williamson. London: Penguin, 1990.

Eusebuis Pamphilus. *Eusebius' Ecclesiastical History: Complete and Unabridged*. Updated ed. Translated by C. F. Cruse. Peabody, MA: Hendrickson, 1998.

Evans, Craig A. *Eschatology, Messianism, and the Dead Sea Scrolls*. Edited by Peter W. Flint and Craig A. Evans. Grand Rapids: Eerdmans, 1997.

———. "Jesus and the Dead Sea Scrolls from Qumran Cave 4." In *Eschatology, Messianism and the Dead Sea Scrolls*, edited by Craig A. Evans and Peter W. Flint, 91–100. Grand Rapids; Cambridge: Eerdmans, 1997.

———. "Marks Incipit and the Priene Calendar Inscription: From Jewish Gospel to Greco-Roman Gospel." *Journal of Greco-Roman Christianity and Judaism* 1 (2000) 67–81.

Everitt, Anthony. *Augustus: The Life of Rome's First Emperor*. 1st ed. New York: Random House, 2006.

Fandel, Peter. *The Judgment of Paris*. London: Forgotten Books, 2015.

Farrell, Joseph, and Michael C. J. Putnam. *A Companion to Vergil's Aeneid and Its Tradition*. Hoboken, NJ: John Wiley & Sons, 2010.

Fears, J. Rufus. "Rome: The Ideology of Imperial Power." *Thought: Fordham University Quarterly* 55 (February 1980) 98–109.

Feldman, Louis H. "Biblical Influence on Virgil." In *Shoshannat Yaakov: Jewish and Iranian Studies in Honor of Yaakov Elman*, edited by Shai Secunda and Steven Fine, 43–64. The Brill Reference Library of Judaism 35. Leiden: Brill, 2012. http://booksandjournals.brillonline.com/content/books/b9789004235458_005.

Fishwick, Duncan. *The Imperial Cult in the Latin West: Studies in the Ruler Cult of the Western Provinces of the Roman Empire*. Leiden: Brill, 1987.

———. *The Imperial Cult in the Latin West: Studies in the Ruler Cult of the Western Provinces of the Roman Empire*. Leiden: Brill, 1992.

Fitzhugh, Thomas. *The Literary Saturnian, the Stichic Norm of Italico-Keltic, Romanic, and Modern Rhythm, Vol. 2: Naevius and the Later Italic Tradition*. London: Forgotten Books, 2015.

Fortner, Michael, and Sir John Floyer Knight. *The Sibylline Oracles: Revised and Updated*. Revised updated ed. Lawton, OK: CreateSpace, 2011.

Foster, P. et al., eds. *New Studies in the Synoptic Problem: Oxford Conference, April 2008*. Leuven: Peeters, 2011.

France, R. T. *The Gospel of Mark*. Reprint ed. The New Testament Greek Commentary. Grand Rapids: Eerdmans, 2014.

Galinsky, Karl. *Aeneas, Sicily, and Rome*. Princeton: Princeton University Press, 2015.

Gamel, Brian K. "Salvation in a Sentence: Mark 15:39 as Markan Soteriology." *Journal of Theological Interpretation* 6 (2012) 65–77.

Gardner, Jane F. *Being a Roman Citizen*. New York: Routledge, 2010.

Garland, David E. *A Theology of Mark's Gospel: Good News about Jesus the Messiah, the Son of God*. Edited by Andreas J. Kostenberger. Grand Rapids: Zondervan, 2015.

Gathercole, Simon J. *The Preexistent Son: Recovering the Christologies of Matthew, Mark, and Luke*. Grand Rapids: Eerdmans, 2006.

Geddert, Tim. *Mark*. Scottdale, PA: Herald, 2001.

Gentili, Alberico, Benedict Kingsbury, Benjamin Straumann, and David Lupher. *The Wars of the Romans: A Critical Edition and Translation of De Armis Romanis by Alberico Gentili*. Translated by Alberico Gentili. Oxford: Oxford University Press, 1811.

Gibbon, Edward. *The Decline and Fall of the Roman Empire*. London: Everyman's, 2010.

Gilbert, George Holley. "The Hellenization of the Jews between 334 B. C. and 70 A. D." *The American Journal of Theology* 13 (1909) 520–40.

Giorgio, Brugnoli, and Fabio Stok, eds. *Vitae Vergilianae Antiquae*. Rome: Instituto Polygraphico, 1997.

Goldsworthy, Adrian. *Augustus: First Emperor of Rome*. 1st ed. New Haven: Yale University Press, 2014.

Goodman, Martin. *Rome and Jerusalem: The Clash of Ancient Civilizations*. New York: Knopf, 2008.

Grant, Robert M. *Reading Religions in the Ancient World: Essays Presented to Robert McQueen Grant on His 90th Birthday*. Edited by David Edward Aune and Robin Darling Young. Leiden; Boston: Brill, 2007.

Grebe, Sabine. "Augustus' Divine Authority and Vergil's Aeneid." *Vergilius* 50 (2004) 35–62.

Guite, Harold F. "Common Elements in Vergilian and Patristic Philosophies of History." In *Papers Presented to the International Conference on Patristic Studies*. Christ Church, Oxford: Studia Patristica, 1983.

Gundry, Robert Horton. *Mark: A Commentary on His Apology for the Cross*. Grand Rapids: Eerdmans, 1993.

Günther, Hans-Christian. *Brill's Companion to Horace*. Leiden: Brill, 2013.

Gurtner, Daniel M. "The Rending of the Veil and Markan Christology: 'Unveiling' the ΥΙΟΣ ΘΕΟΥ (Mark 15:38-39)." *Biblical Interpretation* 15 (2007) 292–306.

Guthrie, Donald. *New Testament Introduction*. Downers Grove, IL: InterVarsity, 1990.

Guthrie, W. K. C. *A History of Greek Philosophy: Volume 5, The Later Plato and the Academy*. 1st ed. Cambridge: Cambridge University Press, 1986.

Güttgemanns, Ehrhardt, and trans. by William G. Doty. *Candid Questions Concerning Gospel Form Criticism*. Vol. 26. Pittsburgh Theological Monograph. Pittsburgh: Pickwick, 1970.

Gwynn, Aubrey. *Roman Education From Cicero to Quintilian*. London: Forgotten Books, 2017.

Habermas, Gary R. *The Historical Jesus: Ancient Evidence for the Life of Christ*. Joplin, MO: College Press, 1996.

Hadas, Moses. *Caesar: Readings in Latin and English by Professor Moses Hadas*. Washington, DC: Smithsonian Institution: Folkway Recordings, 1956.

———. *Cicero: Commentary & Readings in Latin and English*. Washington, DC: Smithsonian Institution: Folkway Recordings, 2012. Audio CD.

———. *Hellenistic Culture: Fusion and Diffusion*. New York: Norton, 1989.

———. *The Latin Language: Introduction and Reading in Latin (and English) by Professor Moses Hadas of Columbia University*. Washington, DC: Smithsonian Institution: Folkway Recordings, 1955.

———. *Longus-Daphnis and Chloe: Moses Hadas*. Washington, DC: Smithsonian Institution: Folkway Recordings, 2012. Audio CD.

———. *Plato on the Death of Socrates: Introduction with Readings from the Apology and the Phaedo in Greek & in English Trans.* Washington, DC: Smithsonian Institution: Folkway Recordings, 2012.

———. *The Story of Virgil's Aeneid: Introduction and Readings in Latin (and English) by Professor Moses Hadas.* Washington, DC: Smithsonian Institution: Folkway Recordings, 1955.

———. "Vergil, Hebrew Prophecy, and the Roman Ideal: Aeneas as the Roman Moses." *Archive* (blog), *Commentary,* November 1953, https://www.commentarymagazine.com/articles/vergil-hebrew-prophecy-and-the-roman-idealaeneas-as-the-roman-moses/.

Hadas, Rachel. "The Many Lives of Moses Hadas." In *Living Legacies at Columbia,* edited by Wm. Theodore de Bary, 45–56. New York: Columbia University Press, 2006.

Hadas-Lebel, Mireille. *Flavius Josephus: Eyewitness to Rome's First Century Conquest of Judea.* First ed. New York; London: Macmillan, 1993.

Hadrill, Andrew Wallace. *Suetonius.* St. Albans: Bristol Classical, 1998.

Haenchen, Ernst. *Der Weg Jesu.* Berlin: Alfred Tipelmann, 1966.

Hall, Christopher A. "Classical Ear-Training." *Christian History* (blog), *Christianity Today,* accessed March 9, 2017, https://www.christianitytoday.com/history/issues/issue-80/classical-ear-training.html.

Hallo, William W. "The Birth of Rhetoric." In *Rhetoric Before and Beyond the Greeks,* edited by Carol S. Lipson and Roberta A. Binkley, 25–46. New York: State University of New York Press, 2004.

Hamel, Christopher de. *Scribes and Illuminators.* 1st ed. Toronto; Buffalo: University of Toronto Press, Scholarly Publishing Division, 1992.

Hammond, N. G. L., and H. H. Scullard, eds. *The Oxford Classical Dictionary.* 2nd ed. Oxford: Clarendon, 1970.

Hansen, Mogens Herman. *The Athenian Democracy in the Age of Demosthenes.* Hoboken, NJ: Blackwell, 1991.

———. *The Athenian Democracy in the Age of Demosthenes: Structure, Principles, and Ideology.* Revised ed. Norman: University of Oklahoma Press, 1999.

Hardie, C. G. "Virgil." In *The Oxford Classical Dictionary, 2nd Edition,* edited by N. G. L. Hammond and H. H. Scullard, 1124. 2nd ed. Oxford: Clarendon, 1970.

Harrington, Daniel J. *The Maccabean Revolt: Anatomy of a Biblical Revolution.* Eugene, OR: Wipf & Stock, 2009.

Harris, William V. *Dreams and Experience in Classical Antiquity.* Cambridge: Harvard University Press, 2009.

Harrison, E. L. "Cleverness in Virgilian Imitation." *Classical Philology* 65 (October 1970) 241–43.

Hartman, Lars. *Mark for the Nations: A Text- and Reader-Oriented Commentary.* Eugene, OR: Pickwick, 2010.

Haverfield, F. *The Romanization of Roman Britain.* Seattle: CreateSpace, 2016.

Head, Ivan. "Mark as a Roman Document from the Year 69: Testing Martin Hengel's Thesis." *The Journal of Religious History* 28 (October 2004) 240–59.

Heath, Malcolm. *Hermogenes on Issues: Strategies of Argument in Later Greek Rhetoric.* Gloucestershire: Clarendon, 1995.

Heil, John Paul. *The Gospel of Mark as a Model for Action: A Reader-Response Commentary.* New York: Paulist, 1992.

Hengel, Martin. *Acts and the History of Earliest Christianity*. Eugene, OR: Wipf & Stock, 2003.

———. *The Charismatic Leader and His Followers*. Translated by John Bowden. London: SCM, 1985.

———. *The "Hellenization" of Judaea in the First Century after Christ*. London: Hymns Ancient & Modern Ltd, 2012.

Henry, Matthew. *Matthew Henry's Commentary on the Whole Bible: New Modern Edition*. Box Una ed. Peabody, MA: Hendrickson, 2009.

———. *Matthew Henry's Concise Commentary on the Whole Bible*. Nashville: Thomas Nelson, 2003.

———. *Unabridged Matthew Henry's Commentary on the Whole Bible*. 7th ed. St. Petersburg, Russia: OSNOVA, 2010.

Heslin, Peter J. *Propertius, Greek Myth, and Virgil: Rivalry, Allegory, and Polemic*. 1st edition. Oxford: Oxford University Press, 2018. Kindle.

Hidber, T. *Encyclopedia of Ancient Greece*. Edited by N. Wilson. Abingdon-on-Thames: Routledge, 2013.

Hofius, Otfried. *Der Vorhang VOR Dem Thron Gottes: Eine Exegetisch-Religionsgeschichtliche Untersuchung Zu Hebraer 6,19 F. Und 10,19 F.* WUNT. Tübingen: Mohr Siebeck, 1972.

Homer. *The Iliad*. Reissue ed. Translated by Robert Fagles. London: Penguin Classics, 1998.

Homer, and Bernard Knox. *The Odyssey*. Translated by Robert Fagles. Reprint, London: Penguin Classics, 1999.

Homer, and Theodore Alois Buckley. *The Odyssey*. Translated by Alexander Pope. Overland Park, KS: Digireads.com, 2016.

Hooker, Morna D. "Beginnings and Endings." In *The Written Gospel*, edited by Markus Bockmuehl and Donald A. Hagner, 184–202. Cambridge: Cambridge University Press, 2005.

———. *The Gospel According to St. Mark*. Edited by Henry Chadwick. Peabody, MA: Hendrickson, 1991.

———. *The Son of Man in Mark: A Study of the Background of the Term "Son of Man" and Its Use in St. Mark's Gospel*. Montreal: McGill University Press, 1967.

Horace. *The Complete Odes and Epodes*. 1st ed. Translated by David West. Oxford: Oxford University Press, 2008.

———. *Horace: Satires, Epistles and Ars Poetica*. Revised ed. Translated by H. Rushton Fairclough. Cambridge: Harvard University Press, 1929.

———. *The Odes of Horace, English and Latin Edition*. 1st ed. Translated by David Ferry. New York: Farrar, Straus and Giroux, 1997.

Horbury, William. *Hebrew Study from Ezra to Ben-Yehuda*. Edinburgh; London: Black, 1999.

Hornblower, Simon, Antony Spawforth, and Esther Eidinow. *The Oxford Classical Dictionary*. 4th ed. Oxford: Oxford University Press, 2012.

Horsfall, Nicholas. *Poets and Patron: Maecenas, Horace and the Georgics, Once More*. Sydney: Macquarie Ancient History Association, 1981.

Horsley, Richard A. *Hearing the Whole Story: The Politics of Plot in Mark's Gospel*. 1st edition. Louisville: Westminster John Knox, 2001.

Hoskisson, Paul Y., and Grant M. Boswell. "Neo-Assyrian Rhetoric: The Example of the Third Campaign of Sennacherib (704–681 B.C.)." In *Rhetoric Before and Beyond the Greeks*, edited by Carol S. Lipson and Roberta A. Binkley, 65–78. New York: State University of New York Press, 2004.

Hultin, Jeremy F. "Disobeying Jesus: A Puzzling Element in the Messianic Secret Motifs." In *Portraits of Jesus: Studies in Christology, Wissenschaftliche Untersuchungen Zum Neuen Testament 2/321*, edited by Susan E Myers, 7–41. Tübingen: Mohr Siebeck, 2012.

Hurst, L. D. "The Epistle to the Hebrews: Its Background of Thought." *SNTSMS (Society for New Testament Studies Monograph Series)* 65 (1990) 7–41.

———. *The Epistle to the Hebrews: Its Background of Thought*. Cambridge; New York: Cambridge University Press, 2005.

Hurtado, Larry W. "The Women, the Tomb, and the Climax of Mark." In *Wandering Galilean: Essays in Honour of Seán Freyne*, edited by Zuleika Rodgers, Margaret Daly-Denton, and Anne Fitzpatrick McKinley, 427–50. Leiden: Brill, 2009.

Hutto, David. "Ancient Egyptian Rhetoric in the Old and Middle Kingdoms." *Rhetorica, the Official Publication of the International Society for the History of Rhetoric, Berkeley: University of California Press* 20 (2002) 213–33.

Incigneri, Brian. *The Gospel to the Romans: The Setting and Rhetoric of Mark's Gospel*. Leiden; Boston: Brill, 2003.

Irenaeus. *Against Heresies*. Pickering, OH: Beloved, 2014.

Irmscher, Johannes. "Vergil in Der Griechischen Antike." *Klio* 67 (1985) 281–85.

Isle, Mick. *Aristotle: Pioneering Philosopher and Founder of the Lyceum*. New York: Rosen Central, 2005.

Isocrates. "Against the Sophists." In *Isocrates with an English Translation in Three Volumes*, 160–80. Translated by George Norlin. Cambridge: Harvard University Press, 1980.

———. *Isocrates II: On the Peace. Areopagiticus. Against the Sophists. Antidosis. Panathenaicus*. Translated by George Norlin. Cambridge: Harvard University Press, 1929.

———. *Isocrates, Volume I: To Demonicus. To Nicocles. Nicocles or the Cyprians. Panegyricus. To Philip. Archidamus*. Translated by George Norlin. Cambridge: Harvard University Press, 1928.

Italicus, Silius. *Silius Italicus: Punica, Volume I, Books 1-8*. Vol. 1. Loeb Classical Library 277. Translated by J. D. Duff. Cambridge: Harvard University Press, 1934.

———. *Silius Italicus: Punica, Volume II, Books 9-17*. Vol. 2. Loeb Classical Library 278. Translated by J. D. Duff. Cambridge: Harvard University Press, 1934.

Jackson, Howard M. "The Death of Jesus in Mark and the Miracle from the Cross." *New Testament Studies* 33 (January 1987) 16–37.

Jameson, Michael H., David R. Jordan, and Roy David Kotansky. *A "lex Sacra" from Selinous*. Greek, Roman, and Byzantine Monographs 11. Durham, NC: Duke University, 1993.

Jefferis, J. D. *The Theology of the Aeneid; Its Antecedents and Development*. Ann Arbor, MI: Palala, 2015.

Jenkyns, Richard. *Classical Literature: An Epic Journey from Homer to Virgil and Beyond*. 1st ed. New York: Basic, 2016.

Jeremias, Joachim. *The Parables of Jesus*. Revised ed. London: SCM, 1963.

Jerome. *Jerome: Select Letters*. Loeb Classical Library 262. Translated by F. A. Wright. Cambridge: Harvard University Press, 1933.

———. *The Letters of Saint Jerome*. Translated by F. A. Wright. London: Aeterna, 2016.

Jerome, and Gennadius. *Lives of Illustrious Men.* London: Aeterna, 2016.

Johnson, Earl S. Jr. "Is Mark 15:39 the Key to Mark's Christology." *Journal for the Study of the New Testament* 31 (October 1987) 3–22.

Johnson, Michael. "Pax Deorum." In *The Encyclopedia of Ancient History,* edited by Roger S. Bagnall. Hoboken, NJ: John Wiley & Sons, Inc., 2013. http://onlinelibrary.wiley.com/doi/10.1002/9781444338386.wbeah17327/abstract.

Josephus, Flavius. *The Complete Works Of Flavius Josephus.* Translated by William Whiston. London: Andesite, 2015.

———. *Jewish Antiquities.* London: Wordsworth, 2006.

———. "The Jewish Wars." https://archive.org/stream/L487JosephusIIITheJewishWar47/L487-Josephus%20III%20The%20Jewish%20War%204-7#page/n475/mode/2up/search/folly+calamities.

———. *Josephus-Complete Works. Includes Life of Flavius Josephus, Antiquities of the Jews, Wars of the Jews and Others.* Translated by William Whiston. Grand Rapids: Kregel, 1971.

———. *Josephus: The Jewish Wars.* Translated by Thackeray. London: William Heinemann, LTD, 1928.

———. *Josephus: The Jewish War, Books V-VII.* Translated by H. St J. Thackeray. Reprint, Cambridge: Harvard University Press, 1971.

———. *The Works of Josephus: Complete and Unabridged.* Harrington: DelmarvaPublications, 2016.

Juel, Donald H. *A Master of Surprise: Mark Interpreted.* Minneapolis: Augsburg, 1994.

———. *A Master of Surprise: Mark Interpreted.* Minneapolis: Fortress, 2002.

———. "The Origin of Mark's Christology." In *The Messiah: Developments in Earliest Judaism and Christianity: The First Princeton Symposium on Judaism and Christian Origins,* edited by James H. Charlesworth, 449–60. Minneapolis: Fortress, 1992.

Kee, Howard Clark. "Aretalogy and Gospel." *Journal of Biblical Literature* 92 (1973) 114–33.

———. *Christian Origins in Sociological Perspective: Methods and Resources.* 1st ed. Philadelphia: Westminster John Knox, 1980.

———. *Christian Origins in Sociological Perspective: Methods and Resources.* 1st ed. London: SCM, 1980.

Kelber, Werner H. *The Kingdom in Mark: A New Place and a New Time.* Philadelphia: Fortress, 1974.

Kennedy, George Alexander. *A New History of Classical Rhetoric.* Princeton: Princeton University Press, 1994.

———. *Classical Rhetoric and Its Christian and Secular Tradition from Ancient to Modern Times.* 2nd ed. Chapel Hill: The University of North Carolina Press, 1999.

———. *Progymnasmata: Greek Textbooks of Prose Composition and Rhetoric.* London: Brill, 2003.

———. *Progymnasmata: Greek Textbooks of Prose Composition and Rhetoric.* Atlanta: Society of Biblical Literature, 2003.

Kennedy, George Alexander, and Giles Laurén. *Quintilian: A Roman Educator and His Quest for the Perfect Orator.* Revised ed. Berlin: Sophron, 2013.

Kerenyi, Karl, and Carl Kerenyi. *The Gods of the Greeks.* London: Thames & Hudson, 1980.

Kerlin, Robert T. "Virgil's Fourth Eclogue.-An Over-Looked Source." *The American Journal of Philology* 29 (1908) 449–60.

Kilpatrick, G. D. "The Gentile Mission in Mark and Mark 13:9-11." In *Studies in the Gospels: Essays in Memory of R. H. Lightfoot*, edited by Dennis E. Nineham, 152–74. Oxford: Blackwell, 1955.

Kirk, G. S. *Homer and the Oral Tradition*. Reissue ed. Cambridge: Cambridge University Press, 2010.

Klingner, Friedrich. *Romische Geisteswelt : Essays zur lateinischen Literatur*. 3rd ed. Stuttgart: Reclam jun. Philipp, Verlag, 1979.

Knauer, Georg Nicolaus. *Die Aeneis Und Homer: Studien Zur Poetischen Technik Vergils Mit Listen Der Homerzitate in Der Aeneis (Habilitationsschrift.)*. Hypomnemata 7. Göttingen: Vandenhoeck & Ruprecht, 1964.

Knight, Charles. *Biography: Or, Third Division of "The English Encyclopedia."* London: Bradbury, Evans & Company, 1867.

Knight, Kevin, ed. "The Confessions (Book I)." *Fathers of the Church* (blog), *New Advent*, accessed March 11, 2017, http://www.newadvent.org/fathers/110101.htm.

Koester, Craig R. *Hebrews*. New Haven; London: Yale University Press, 2001.

Köstenberger, Andreas J., Michael J. Kruger, and I. Howard Marshall. *The Heresy of Orthodoxy (Foreword by I. Howard Marshall): How Contemporary Culture's Fascination with Diversity Has Reshaped Our Understanding of Early Christianity*. Wheaton, IL: Crossway, 2010.

Kytzler, Bernhard, and Eduard Norden. *Kleine Schriften zum klassischen Altertum*. 2010 ed. Reprint, Berlin; Boston: De Gruyter, 2012.

Lane, Eugene N., ed. *Cybele, Attis and Related Cults: Essays in Memory of M.J. Vermaseren*. Leiden: Brill, 1996.

Lane, William L. *The Gospel According to Mark: The English Text With Introduction, Exposition, and Notes*. 2nd Revised. Grand Rapids: Eerdmans, 1974.

Lee, M. Owen. *Fathers and Sons in Virgil's Aeneid: Tum Genitor Natum*. Albany: SUNY Press, 1979.

Lefkowitz, Mary, and Maureen B. Fant. "233. The Rape of the Sabine Women." In *Women's Life in Greece and Rome: A Source Book in Translation*. 2nd ed. Baltimore: John Hopkins University Press, 1992. http://www.stoa.org/diotima/anthology/wlgr/wlgr-privatelife233.shtml.

Levi, Peter. *Virgil: A Life*. Reprint, New York: Tauris Parke, 2012.

Lewis, C. S. *Fern-Seed and Elephants and Other Essays on Christianity*. Edited by Walter Hooper. London: Fontana, 1975.

———. "Historicism." In *Fern-Seed and Elephant and Other Essays on Christianity*. Glasgow: Collins, 1975.

Lipson, Carol S., and Roberta A. Binkley. "The Birth of Rhetoric." In *Rhetoric before and beyond the Greeks*, 25–46. New York: State University of New York Press, 2004.

———. "Neo-Assyrian Rhetoric: The Example of the Third Campaign of Sennacherib (704–681 BC)." In *Rhetoric before and beyond the Greeks*, 65–78. New York: State University of New York Press, 2004.

———. "Pentateuchal Rhetoric and the Voice of the Aaronides." In *Rhetoric before and beyond the Greeks*, 165–82. New York: State University of New York Press, 2004.

———. "The Use of Eloquence: The Confucian Perspective." In *Rhetoric before and beyond the Greeks*, 115–30. New York: State University of New York Press, 2004.

Livius, Titus. *The History of Rome, Vol. 1 of 2*. Edited by Canon Roberts. London: Forgotten Books, 2016.

Lohmeyer, Ernst. *Das Evangelium Des Markus*. Gottingen: Vandenhoeck & Ruprecht, 1963.

Lucilius. *Remains of Old Latin, Volume III, The Law of the Twelve Tables*. Revised ed. Translated by E. H. Warmington. Cambridge: Harvard University Press, 1938.

MacDonald, William L. *The Architecture of the Roman Empire, Volume 1: An Introductory Study*. Revised ed. Vol. 1. New Haven: Yale University Press, 1982.

Mack, Burton L. *Rhetoric and the New Testament*. Minneapolis: Fortress, 1989.

Mack, Burton L., and Vernon K. Robbins. *Patterns of Persuasion in the Gospels*: Eugene, OR: Wipf & Stock, 2008.

Magness, Jodi Lee. *Marking the End: Sense and Absence in the Gospel of Mark*. Eugene, OR: Wipf & Stock, 2002.

————. *Marking the End: Sense and Absence: Structure and Suspension in the Ending of Mark's Gospel*. Semeia Studies. Atlanta: Scholars, 1986.

Malherbe, Abraham J. *Social Aspects of Early Christianity, Second Edition*: 2nd ed. Eugene, OR: Wipf & Stock, 2003.

Manson, T. W. "Realized Eschatology and the Messianic Secret." In *Studies in the Gospels: Essays in Memory of R. H. Lightfoot*, edited by Dennis E. Nineham, 209–22. Oxford: Oxford University Press, 1995.

Marcus, Joel. *Mark 1-8*. Anchor Bible. New York: Doubleday, 2000.

————. *Mark 1-8*. 1st ed. New Haven: Yale University Press, 2002.

Marmorale, Enzo V., ed. *Naevius Poeta*. Florence: La Nuova Italia, 1950.

Marrou, H. I. *A History Of Education In Antiquity*. Translated by George Lamb. Reprint, Madison: University of Wisconsin Press, 1982.

Martin, Ralph P. *Mark, Evangelist and Theologian*. London: Paternoster, 1972.

Martyr, Justin. *Dialogue with Trypho*. Pickering, OH: Beloved, 2015.

Matera, Frank J. *The Kingship of Jesus: Composition and Theology in Mark 15*. Society of Biblical Literature Dissertation Series 66. Chico, CA: Scholars, 1982.

Matsen, Patricia P., Philip B. Rollinson, and Marion Sousa. *Readings from Classical Rhetoric Front Cover Patricia P. Matsen, Philip B. Rollinson, Marion Sousa SIU Press, 1990*. Carbondale: Southern Illinois University Press, 1990.

Mattingly, D. J. "Being Roman: Expressing Identity in a Provincial Setting." *Journal of Roman Archaeology* 17 (2004) 5–25.

Meeks, Wayne A. *The First Urban Christians: The Social World of the Apostle Paul*. 2nd ed. New Haven: Yale University Press, 2003.

Metzger, Bruce. *A Textual Commentary on the Greek New Testament*. 2nd ed. Peabody, MA: Hendrickson, 2005.

Metzger, David. "Pentateuchal Rhetoric and the Voice of the Aaronides." In *Rhetoric Before and Beyond the Greeks*, by Carol S. Lipson and Roberta A. Binkley, 165–82. New York: State University of New York Press, 1949.

Michel, Otto. *Der Brief an Die Hebräer*. Kritisch-Exegetischer Kommentar Über Das Neue Testament. Begründet von Heinrich August Wilhelm Meyer, Dreizehnte Abteilung. Göttinger: Vandenhoeck & Ruprecht, 1949.

Miller, John F. *Apollo, Augustus, and the Poets*. Cambridge: Cambridge University Press, 2009.

Millet, M. "Romanization: Historical Issues and Archaeological Interpretation." In *The Early Roman Empire in the West*, edited by T. Blagg and M. Millet, 35–44. Oxford: Oxbow, 1990.

Mindel, Nissan, and Kehot Publication Society. "Rabbi Shimon Ben Shetach." *Learning & Values* (blog), *Chabad.org*, accessed December 16, 2017, http://www.chabad. org/library/article_cdo/aid/112342/jewish/Rabbi-Shimon-Ben-Shetach.htm.

Morgan, Robert. *History of the Coptic Orthodox People and the Church of Egypt.* Victoria, BC: Friesen, 2016.

Motz, Lotte. *The Faces of the Goddess.* New York: Oxford University Press, 1997.

Myers, Susan E, ed. *Portraits of Jesus: Studies in Christology.* Tübingen: Mohr Siebeck, 2012.

Naevius. *De Bello Punico Reliquiae.* Charleston, SC: Nabu, 2010.

Nagy, Gregory. *The Best of the Achaeans: Concepts of the Hero in Archaic Greek Poetry.* 1st ed. Baltimore: Johns Hopkins University Press, 1981.

———. *Pindar's Homer: The Lyric Possession of An Epic Past.* Reprint ed. Baltimore: Johns Hopkins University Press, 1994.

Nasrallah, Laura, Charalambos Bakirtzis, and Steven J. Friesen. *From Roman to Early Christian Thessalonike: Studies in Religion and Archaeology.* Cambridge: Harvard University Press, 2010.

Nicolaus of Damascus. *Life of Augustus.* Rochester, NY: Scholar's Choice, 2015.

———. *The Life of Augustus and The Autobiography: Edited with Introduction, Translations and Historical Commentary.* Bilingual ed. Translated by Mark Toher. Cambridge: Cambridge University Press, 2016.

Nineham, D. E. *Studies in the Gospels; Essays in Memory of R.H. Lightfoot.* Oxford: Blackwell, 1955.

Norden, Eduard. *Kleine Schriften zum klassischen Altertum.* Berlin: de Gruyter, 1966.

Ober, Josiah. *Mass and Elite in Democratic Athens: Rhetoric, Ideology, and the Power of the People.* Reprint ed. Princeton: Princeton University Press, 1991.

O'Connor, George. *Athena: Grey-Eyed Goddess.* 1st ed. New York; London: Firstsecondbooks, 2010.

Oorthuys, Jasper, ed. *The Varian Disaster: The Battle of the Teutoburg Forest: 2009 Ancient Warfare Special Edition.* Special ed. Rotterdam, The Netherlands: Karwansaray, 2009.

Orosius, Paulus. *Pauli Orosii Historiarum Adversum Paganos Libri VII.* London: Forgotten Books, 2017.

———. *Seven Books of History against the Pagans.* Translated by A. T. Fear. London: Liverpool University Press, 2010.

Osburn, Carroll D. *The Text of the Apostolos in Epiphanius of Salamis.* Atlanta: Society of Biblical Literature, 2004.

Otis, Brooks. *Virgil: A Study in Civilized Poetry.* New ed. Norman: University of Oklahoma Press, 1995.

Ovid. *Fastorum Libri Sex: The Fasti of Ovid.* Translated by James George Frazer. Cambridge: Cambridge University Press, 2015.

———. *Metamorphoses.* Oxford World Classics. Translated by A. D. Melville. Oxford: Oxford University Press, 2009.

Ovid, Rudolf, and Rudolf Merkel. *P. Ovidius Naso: Amores. Epistulae. de Medic. Fac. Ars Amat. Remedia Amoris - Primary Source Edition.* Charleston, SC: Nabu, 2014.

Paley, William. *Horae Paulinae, or the Truth of the Scripture History of St. Paul: Evinced By a Comparison of the Epistles Which Bear His Name, With the Acts of the Apostles.* London: Forgotten Books, 2012.

Panayotova, S. *Colour: The Art and Science of Illuminated Manuscripts*. Turnhout, Belgium: Brepols, 2016.

Parsons, Jed. "A New Approach to the Saturnian Verse and Its Relation to Latin Prosody." *Transactions of the American Philological Association (1974-2014)* 129 (1999) 117-37.

Pennington, Jonathan T., and Richard Bauckham. *Reading the Gospels Wisely: A Narrative and Theological Introduction*. Grand Rapids: Baker, 2012.

Peppard, Michael. *The Son of God in the Roman World: Divine Sonship in Its Social and Political Context*. Reprint ed. New York: Oxford University Press, 2012.

Perkell, Christine Godfrey. "Christine Godfrey Perkell." *Classic Emory*. Accessed November 28, 2017. http://classics.emory.edu/home/documents/cv/perkell-christine.pdf.

———. *Reading Vergils Aeneid: An Interpretive Guide*. Norman: University of Oklahoma Press, 1999.

Pesch, Rudolf. *Das Markus-Evangelium*. Vol. 1. 2 vols. Herders theologischer Kommentar zum Neuen Testament m. Suppl.-Bdn. Freiburg: Herder, Freiburg, 1989.

———. *Naherwartung: Tradition and Redaktion in Mk 13*. Kommentare Und Beiträge Zum Alten Und Neuen Testament. Düsseldorf: Patmos, 1968.

Peterson, Dwight. *The Origins of Mark: The Markan Community in Current Debate*. Leiden; Boston: Brill, 2000.

Petronius. *The Satyricon*. 1st ed. Translated by P. G. Walsh. Oxford: Oxford University Press, 2009.

Philo. *On the Embassy to Gaius. General Indexes*. Vol. 10. Translated by F. H. Colson. Cambridge: Harvard University Press, 1962.

Plato. *Protagoras*. 1st ed. Oxford World Classics. Translated by C. C. W. Taylor. Oxford: Oxford University Press, 2009.

Plautus. *Plautus: Amphitryon. The Comedy of Asses. The Pot of Gold. The Two Bacchises. The Captives*. 1st ed. Translated by Wolfgang de Melo. Cambridge: Harvard University Press, 2011.

Plevnik, Joseph, ed. *Word and Spirit: Essays in Honor of David M. Stanley, S.J. on His 60th Birthday*. Willowdale, Ontario: Regis College, 1975.

Pobee, John S. "The Cry of the Centurion: A Cry of Defeat." In *The Trial of Jesus: Cambridge Studies in Honour of C F D Moule*, edited by Ernst Bammel, 91-102. London: SCM, 1970.

Poetry Foundation. "Virgil." *Poets* (blog), *Poetry Foundation*, 2019, https://www.poetryfoundation.org/poems-and-poets/poets/detail/virgil.

Pollok, Alex. "Roman Propaganda in the Age of Augustus." Dominican University of California Dominican Scholar Senior Theses and Capstone Projects Theses and Capstone Projects 5-2017, Dominican University of California, 2017.

Polybius, Robin Waterfield, and Brian McGing. *The Histories*. 1st ed. Oxford: Oxford University Press, 2010.

Porter, Stanley E., ed. *Handbook of Classical Rhetoric in the Hellenistic Period, 330 B.C.-A.D. 400*. Boston: Brill, 2001.

Prescott, Henry W. *The Development of Virgil's Art*. Whitefish, MT: Literary Licensing, LLC, 2011.

Price, S. R. F. *Rituals and Power: The Roman Imperial Cult in Asia Minor*. Revised ed. Cambridge: Cambridge University Press, 1985.

Propertius. *Elegies*. Vol. 2. Loeb Classical Library 18. Edited and translated by G. P. Goold. Cambridge: Harvard University Press, 1990.

Purinton, Jeffrey S. "Epicurus on 'Free Volition' and the Atomic Swerve." *Phronesis* 44 (1999) 253–99.

Putnam, Michael C. J. Review of *Vergil at 2000: Commemorative Essays on the Poet and His Influence*, by John D. Bernard. *The American Journal of Philology* 109 (1988) 267–70.

Quinn, Kenneth. *Virgil's Aeneid: A Critical Description*. Ann Arbor: University of Michigan Press, 1969.

Quintilian. "Book I, Chapters 7–12." In *Institutio Oratoria*. Translated by Bill Thayer. Accessed October 13, 2017. http://penelope.uchicago.edu/Thayer/E/Roman/Texts/Quintilian/Institutio_Oratoria/1C*.html#8.

———. *Delphi Complete Works of Quintilian*. 1st ed. Translated by H. E. Butler. East Sussex: Delphi, 2015.

———. *Delphi Complete Works of Quintilian (Illustrated)*. Delphi Ancient Classics 55. Translated by H. E. Butler. East Sussex: Delphi, 2015. Kindle.

———. *Institutes of Oratory: Or, Education of an Orator*. Edited by Curtis Dozier and Lee Honeycutt. Translated by Rev John Selby Watson. Seattle: CreateSpace, 2015.

Rabbis. "Bava Batra 21a." In *The William Davidson Talmud*. Accessed December 16, 2017. https://www.sefaria.org/Bava_Batra.21a.9?lang=bi&with=all&lang2=en.

———. "Pirkei Avot 5:21." https://www.sefaria.org/Pirkei_Avot?lang=bi.

———. "Pirkei Avot: Ethics of Our Fathers." *Talmud* (blog), *My Jewish Learning*, accessed December 16, 2017, https://www.myjewishlearning.com/texts/Rabbinics/Talmud/Mishnah/Seder_Nezikin_Damages_/Pirkei_Avot.shtml.

Reasoner, Mark. "Divine Sons: Aeneas and Jesus in Hebrews." In *Reading Religions in the Ancient World: Essays Presented to Robert Mcqueen Grant on His 90th Birthday*, edited by David Edward Aune and Robin Darling Young, 141–48. Leiden: Brill, 2007.

Regev, Eyal. "Moral Impurity and the Temple in Early Christianity in Light of Ancient Greek Practice and Qumranic Ideology." *Harvard Theological Review* 97 (October 2004) 383–411.

Reid, Patrick V. *Moses' Staff and Aeneas' Shield: The Way of the Torah Versus Classical Heroism*. Lanham, MD: UPA, 2005.

Rhoads, David, Joanna Dewey, and Donald Michie. *Mark As Story: An Introduction to the Narrative of a Gospel*. 3rd ed. Minneapolis: Fortress, 2012.

Rhodius, Apollonius. *The Argonautica*. Translated by R. C. Seaton. Charleston, SC: CreateSpace, 2016.

Richards. "Notices of Books: The 'Latin' Question." *New Englander and Yale Review* 17 (August 1859) 800–1.

Richardson, Herbert. "The Development of the Poetic Epic: Classic, Comic, Cyclic, Romantic, Satanic." Lewiston, NY: Mellen, 2016.

Richer, M. *The Life of Mæcenas: With Critical and Historical Notes*. London: Forgotten Books, 2016.

Ripat, Pauline. "Expelling Misconceptions: Astrologers At Rome." *Classical Philology* 106 (April 2011) 115–54.

Robbins, Vernon K. "Mark as Genre." In *Society of Biblical Literature Seminar*, vol. 19, 371–72. Atlanta: Society of Biblical Literature, 1980.

Roberts, Anna Klosowska. *Queer Love in the Middle Ages*. New York: Macmillan, 2005.

Rodgers, Zuleika, Margaret Daly-Denton, and Anne Fitzpatrick McKinley. *A Wandering Galilean: Essays in Honour of Sedn Freyne*. Supplements to the Journal for the Study of Judaism 132. Leiden: Brill, 2009.

Roller, Lynn E. *In Search of God the Mother: The Cult of Anatolian Cybele*. Berkeley, CA: University of California Press, 1999.

Rushforth, Gordon McNeil. *Latin Historical Inscriptions: Illustrating the History of the Early Empire*. London: Forgotten Books, 2016.

Russell, Donald A. "Plutarch (Ad 50) (of *Chaeronea)." In *The Oxford Classical Dictionary, 4th Ed*. Oxford: Oxford University Press, 2012.

Sage Software. "The Works of Flavius Josephus: Translated by William Whiston." http://www.ccel.org/ccel/josephus/works/files/works.html

Salway, Peter. *Roman Britain: A Very Short Introduction*. 2nd ed. Oxford: Oxford University Press, 2015.

Sanday, William. *Essays in Biblical Criticism and Exegesis*. London: Bloomsbury, 2001.

———. "The Injunctions of Silence in the Gospels." *JTS* 5 (April 1904) 321–29.

Sandbach, F. H. "The Structure of the Aeneid - Theodor W. Stadler: *Vergils Aeneis*. Eine poetische Betrachtung." *The Classical Review* 57 (March 1943) 26–26.

Scaltsas, Theodore, and Andrew S. Mason. *Zeno of Citium and His Legacy: The Philosophy of Zeno*. 1st ed. Lanarca: The Municipality of Larnaca, 2002.

Scarre, Christ. *Chronicle of the Roman Emperors: The Reign-by-Reign Record of the Rulers of Imperial Rome (Chronicles)*. 1st ed. New York: Thames & Hudson, 2012.

Schemann, Ludwig. *De Legionum Per Alterum Bellum Punicum Historia Quae Investigari Posse Videantur*. Charleston, SC: Nabu, 2012.

Schildgen, Brenda Deen. *Divine Providence: A History: The Bible, Virgil, Orosius, Augustine, and Dante*. NIPPOD ed. London: Bloomsbury, 2014.

Seddon, Keith, and C. D. Yonge. *A Summary of Stoic Philosophy: Zeno of Citium in Diogenes Laertius Book Seven*. Revised ed. Morrisville, NC: Keith Seddon, 2008.

Seneca, Lucius Annaeus. *Apocolocyntosis Divi Claudii*: Lawrence, KS: Coronado, 1973.

———. *Apocolocyntosis Divi Claudii: (The Pumpkinification of Claudius)*. Coronado, CA: Coronado, 1993.

———. *Natural Questions (The Complete Works of Lucius Annaeus Seneca)*. Translated by Harry M. Hine. Chicago: University of Chicago Press, 2010.

———. *Seneca: Moral Essays, Volume II*. Revised ed. Translated by John W. Basore. Cambridge; London: Harvard University Press, 1932.

———. *Seneca's Morals: Of a Happy Life, Benefits, Anger and Clemency*. Translated by Sir Roger L'Estrange. Seattle: CreateSpace, 2014.

Shailor, Barbara. *The Medieval Book: Illustrated from the Beinecke Rare Book and Manuscript Library*. 1st ed. Toronto; Buffalo: University of Toronto Press, 1991.

Shim, Ezfa S. B. "A Suggestion about the Genre of Text-Type of Mark." *Scriptura* 50 (1994) 69–89.

Shiner, Whitney. "The Ambiguous Pronouncement of the Centurion and the Shrouding of Meaning in Mark." *Journal for the Study of the New Testament* 78 (June 2000) 3–22.

Sidgwick, A. *The Aeneid of Virgil*. Cambridge: Cambridge University Press, 1960.

Sidwell, Keith. "Purification and Pollution in Aeschylus' Eumenides." *Classical Quarterly* 46 (1996) 44–57.

Siegfried, Carl, and Richard Gottheil. "Hellenism." *H* (blog), *JewishEncyclopedia*, accessed December 18, 2017, http://jewishencyclopedia.com/articles/7535-hellenism.

Singer, Isidore, ed. *The Jewish Encyclopedia*. 12 vols. New York: KTAV Publishing House, 1960.

Smith, Barry D. *Introducing the New Testament: A Workbook*. Moncton, NB, Canada: Crandall University, 2010.

Söding, Thomas, ed. *Der Evangelist Als Theologe: Studien Zum Markusevangelium*. Stuttgart: Katholisches Bibelwerk, 1995.

Spawforth, A. J. S. *Greece and the Augustan Cultural Revolution: Greek Culture in the Roman World*. Reprint ed. Cambridge University Press, 2015.

Spelman, Edward, and of Halicarnassus Dionysius. *The Roman Antiquities of Dionysius of Halicarnassus*. Translated by Earnest Cary. Rochester, NY: Scholar's Choice, 2015.

Spengel, Leonhard von. *Rhetores Graeci*. Vol. 2. Leipzig; Stuttgart; Berlin: Teubner, 1854.

St. Mark Coptic Church. "St. Mark the Apostle, Evangelist." *The Synaxarium* (blog), *Coptic Orthodox Church Network*, 1998–2014, http://www.copticchurch.net/topics/synexarion/mark.html.

Stadler, Theodor W. *Vergils Aeneis. Eine poetische Betrachtung*. Einsiedeln: Benziger, 1942.

Stanton, Graham N. *Jesus and Gospel*. Cambridge; New York: Cambridge University Press, 2004.

Stiewe, Klaus, and Niklas Holzberg, eds. *Polybios*. Darmstadt: Wissenschaftliche Buchgesellschaft; Wege der Forschung, 1982.

Stray, Christopher, ed. *Oxford Classics: Teaching and Learning 1800-2000*. London: Bristol, 2007.

Suetonius. *Lives of the Caesars: The Life of Julius Caesar*. Translated by Catharine Edwards. Oxford: Oxford University Press, 2009.

———. *The Life of Vergil*. Loeb Classical Library. Translated by J. C. Rolfe. Cambridge: Cambridge University Press, 1914.

———. *Lives of the Caesars, Volume II Claudius. Nero. Galba, Otho, and Vitellius. Vespasian. Titus, Domitian. Lives of Illustrious Men: Grammarians and Rhetoricians. Poets (Terence. Virgil. Horace. Tibullus. Persius. Lucan). Lives of Pliny the Elder and Passienus Crispus*. Loeb Classical Library 38. Translated by J. C. Rolfe. Cambridge: Harvard University Press, 1914.

———. *Suetonius: The Life of Vergil*. Loeb Classical Library. Translated by J. C. Rolfe. Cambridge: Harvard University Press, 1914.

Syme, Ronald. *The Roman Revolution*. Revised ed. Oxford: Oxford University Press, 2002.

Tacitus, and W. H. Fyfe. *The Histories*. Edited by D. S. Levene. 1st ed. Oxford: Oxford University Press, 2008.

Talbert, Charles H. *What Is a Gospel? The Genre of the Canonical Gospels*. 1st ed. Philadelphia: Fortress, 1977.

Taylor, Lily Ross. *The Divinity Of the Roman Emperor*. Oxford: Oxford University Press, 1981.

———. *The Divinity Of The Roman Emperor: Philological Monographs, American Philological Association, No. 1*. Edited by Joseph William Hewitt. Whitefish, MT: Literary Licensing, LLC, 2011.

Telford, William R. *The Interpretation of Mark*. Philadelphia: Fortress, 1985.

———. *Mark*. Sheffield: Sheffield Academic, 1995.

———. *The Theology of the Gospel of Mark*. Cambridge: Cambridge University Press, 1999.

Tenney, Frank. *Vergil: A Biography - Primary Source Edition*. 1st ed. Charleston, SC: Nabu, 2014.

Terry, Milton Spenser. *The Sibylline Oracles*. Edited by Roy A. Sites. Seattle: CreateSpace, 2014.

———. *The Sibylline Oracles*. London: Forgotten Books, 2016.

Tertullian. *Against Marcion*. Pickerington, OH: Beloved, 2014.

———. *Prescription Against Heretics*. Pickerington, OH: Beloved, 2015.

Thayer, Bill. "Cassius Dio: Roman History." *LacusCurtius: Into the Roman World* (blog), *LacusCurtius*, accessed December 22, 2016, http://penelope.uchicago.edu/ Thayer/E/Roman/Texts/Cassius_Dio/.

———. "Suetonius: The Life of Vergil." *Suetonius* (blog), *LacusCurtius*, August 29, 2012, http://penelope.uchicago.edu/Thayer/E/Roman/Texts/Suetonius/de_Poetis/ Vergil*.html.

Thomas, Robert L., ed. *Three Views on the Origins of the Synoptic Gospels*. Grand Rapids: Kregel, 2002.

Tidball, Derek. *An Introduction to the Sociology of the New Testament*. Exeter: Paternost, 1983.

Tolbert, Mary Ann. *Sowing the Gospel: Mark's Work in Literary-Historical Perspective*. Minneapolis: Fortress, 1996.

Too, Yun Lee. *A Commentary on Isocrates' Antidosis*. 1st ed. Oxford: Oxford University Press, 2008.

Tregelles, Samuel Prideaux. *Canon Muratorian: The Earliest Catalogue of the Books of the New Testament, Edited With Notes*. London: Forgotten Books, 2017.

Vandiver, Elizabeth. *The Aeneid of Virgil*. Springfield, VA: The Teaching Company, 1999.

Varro. *On the Latin Language*. Vol. 1, Books 5–7. Translated by Roland G. Kent. Cambridge: Harvard University Press, 1938.

Vassileva, Maya. "Further Considerations on the Cult of Kybele." *Anatolian Studies* 51 (December 2001) 51–64.

Vermaseren, Maarten J. *Cybele Andf Attis: The Myth and the Cult*. London: Thames and Hudson, 1977.

Virgil. *The Aeneid*. Vintage Classics. Translated by Robert Fitzgerald. New York: Random House, 1990.

———. *The Aeneid*. Translated by A. S. Kline. London: Poetry in Translation, 2002.

———. *The Aeneid*. Translated by J. W. Mackail. Seattle: CreateSpace, 2016.

———. *The Æneids of Virgil Done Into English Verse*. Translated by William Morris. Seattle: Amazon Digital Services LLC, 2012. Kindle.

———. *Eclogues and Georgics of Virgil*. Translated by David R. Slavitt. Baltimore: Johns Hopkins University Press, 1990.

———. *The Eclogues of Virgil: A Bilingual Edition*. 1st ed., English and Latin. Translated by David Ferry. New York: Farrar, Straus and Giroux, 2000.

———. *The Works of Virgil with a Commentary [3 Volume Set] Vol. I: Eclogues and Georgics; Vol. II: Containing the First 6 Books of the Aeneid; Vol. III: Containing the*

Last 6 Books of the Aeneid. Edited by F. Haverfield. 5th ed. Hildesheim, Germany: Georg Olms Verlag, 1963.

————. *Virgil's Aeneid.* Edited by Charles W. Eliot, LL.D. Vol. 13. The Harvard Classics With Introduction and Notes. Translated by John Dryden. New York: P. F. Collier & Son Corporation, 1937.

Virgil, and Kenneth Quinn. *Virgil's Aeneid: A Critical Description.* Edited by Kenneth Quinn. Second ed. Ann Arbor: University of Michigan Press, 1969.

Walbank, Frank W. *Polybius, Rome, and the Hellenistic World: Essays and Reflections.* Cambridge: Cambridge University Press, 2002.

————. *Polybius, Rome and the Hellenistic World: Essays and Reflections.* Revised ed. Cambridge: Cambridge University Press, 2006.

Walker, Jeffrey. *Rhetoric and Poetics in Antiquity.* 1st ed. Oxford: Oxford University Press, 2000.

Wallace, David R. *The Gospel of God: Romans as Paul's Aeneid.* Eugene, OR.: Wipf & Stock, 2008.

Wallace, J. Warner, and Lee Strobel. *Cold-Case Christianity: A Homicide Detective Investigates the Claims of the Gospels.* Colorado Springs, CO: David C. Cook, 2013. Kindle.

————. *Cold-Case Christianity: A Homicide Detective Investigates the Claims of the Gospels.* Colorado Springs: David C. Cook, 2013.

Wallace-Hadrill, Andrew. *Suetonius.* London: Bristol Classical, 1998.

Walther, Ingo F., and Norbert Wolf. *Codices Illustres: The World's Most Famous Illuminated Manuscripts.* SEW ed. Köln: Taschen, 2014.

Waltke, Bruce K. "The Theological Significance of ᾿Αντί and ῾Υπέρ in the New Testament." PhD diss, Dallas Theological Seminary, 1958.

Wardle, C. *Suetonius: Life of Augustus.* Clarendon Ancient History. Oxford: Oxford University Press, 2015.

Wardman, Alan. *Religion and Statecraft Among the Romans.* 1st ed. London: Humanities, 1985.

Ward-Perkins, J. B. *Roman Imperial Architecture.* Reprint ed. New Haven: Yale University Press, 1992.

Warmington, Lucilius and E. H. *Remains of Old Latin, Volume III, The Law of the Twelve Tables.* Loeb Classical Library 329. Cambridge: Harvard University Press, 1938.

Warren, Christopher Norton. *Literature and the Law of Nations, 1580-1680.* Oxford: Oxford University Press, 2015.

Weigel, Richard D. *Lepidus: The Tarnished Triumvir.* New York: Routledge, 2002.

Wells, Peter S. *The Barbarians Speak: How the Conquered Peoples Shaped Roman Europe.* Princeton: Princeton University Press, 2001.

Wenham, Gordon J., J. Alec Motyer, Donald A. Carson, and R. T. France, eds. *New Bible Commentary.* Downers Grove, IL: InterVarsity, 1994.

Wenham, John William. "Did Peter Go to Rome in AD 42." *Tyndale Bulletin* 23 (1972) 94–102.

White, Peter. *Promised Verse: Poets in the Society of Augustan Rome.* Cambridge: Harvard University Press, 1993.

Wilcox, Max. "On the Ransom-Saying in Mark 10:45c, Matt 20:28c." In *Geschichte— Tradition—Reflexion: Festschriften Für Martin Hengel Zum 70 Geburtstag, Bd 3: Frühes Christentum,* 173–86. Tübingen: Mohr Siebeck, 1996.

Wildfang, Robin Lorsch. *Rome's Vestal Virgins.* 1st ed. New York: Routledge, 2006.

Williams, John, and Daniel Mendelsohn. *Augustus*. Reissue ed. New York: New York Review Books Classics, 2014.

Winn, Adam. *The Purpose of Mark's Gospel: An Early Christian Response to Roman Imperial Propaganda*. Tübingen: Mohr Siebeck, 2008.

Witherington III, Ben. *Conflict and Community in Corinth: Socio-Rhetorical Commentary on 1 and 2 Corinthians*. Grand Rapids: Eerdmans, 1995.

———. *The Gospel of Mark: A Socio-Rhetorical Commentary*. Grand Rapids: Eerdmans, 2001.

———. *New Testament Rhetoric: An Introductory Guide to the Art of Persuasion in and of the New Testament*. Eugene, OR: Wipf & Stock, 2009.

Woolf, Greg. *Becoming Roman: The Origins of Provincial Civilization in Gaul*. Cambridge: Cambridge University Press, 2000.

Wooten III, Cecil W. *Hermogenes' On Types of Style*. Chapel Hill: University of North Carolina Press, 2012.

Worthington, Ian. *Demosthenes of Athens and the Fall of Classical Greece*. Reprint ed. Oxford: Oxford University Press, 2015.

Wrede, William. *The Messianic Secret: Das Messiasgeheimnis in Den Evangelien*. 1st ed. Translated by J. C. G. Greig. Cambridge: James Clarke & Co., 1971.

Wright, N. T. *Jesus and the Victory of God*. Minneapolis: Fortress, 1997.

Xinyue, Bobby. "The Divinity of Augustus in the Poetry of Vergil, Horace, and Propertius." PhD diss, University of Warwick, 2015.

Xu, George Q. "The Use of Eloquence: The Confucian Perspective." In *Rhetoric Before and Beyond the Greeks*, by Carol S. Lipson and Roberta A. Binkley, 115–30. New York: State University of New York Press, 2004.

Zanker, Paul. *The Power of Images in the Age of Augustus*. Translated by Alan Shapiro. Reprint, Ann Arbor: University of Michigan Press, 1990.